ABRAHAM JOSHUA HESCHEL, one of the foremost religious thinkers of our time, was for
many years Professor of Ethics and Mysti-
cism at the Jewish Theological Seminary.
Since his death in 1972, interest in his work
has grown considerably. Among his books
published by Farrar, Straus and Giroux are
The Earth Is the Lord's (1978), *God in
Search of Man* (1976), *Israel: An Echo of
Eternity* (1969), *Man Is Not Alone* (1976), *A
Passion for Truth* (1973), *The Sabbath*
(1975), and *The Wisdom of Heschel* (1975).

by Abraham Joshua Heschel

Maimonides

Abraham Joshua Heschel

MAIMONIDES

A Biography

Translated from the German by
JOACHIM NEUGROSCHEL

Farrar · Straus · Giroux
NEW YORK

Foreword and translation copyright © 1982 by Sylvia Heschel
Originally published in 1935 as *Maimonides, Eine Biographie*
by Erich Reiss Verlag in the series
"Judentum in Geschichte und Gegenwart,"
Copyright 1935 by Erich Reiss Verlag, G.m.b.H.

FIRST PRINTING, 1982

Printed in the United States of America
Published simultaneously in Canada
by McGraw-Hill Ryerson Ltd., Toronto
DESIGNED BY HERBERT H. JOHNSON

Library of Congress Cataloging in Publication Data
Heschel, Abraham Joshua.
Maimonides: a biography.
Translation of: Maimonides.
Includes bibliographical references and index.
1. Maimonides, Moses, 1135–1204. 2. Rabbis—Egypt—Biography.
3. Philosophers, Jewish—Egypt—Biography.
I. Title.
BM755.M6H413   296.8'2'0924   [B]   81-15308
                                              AACR2

Contents

Foreword

IN 1935 the young Abraham Joshua Heschel—he was twenty-eight at the time—went to visit the publisher Erich Reiss at his home in Berlin in order to discuss the manuscript of a friend. Reiss, a cultivated and perceptive person (he later married Lotte Jacobi, the noted photographer), was so impressed by the young scholar that he immediately asked him to write a book. Heschel, surprised and delighted, accepted the offer and in a relatively short time completed this biography of Maimonides.

Reiss's confidence and insight were justified. *Maimonides* was received enthusiastically when it appeared some months later, under the imprint of Erich Reiss Verlag. The following year, a French translation by Germaine Bernard was published in Paris by Payot under the title *Maïmonide*.

The present edition, translated by Joachim Neugroschel, is the first appearance of *Maimonides* in English. Those of Heschel's readers familiar with the unique beauty and rhythmic flow that marked his writing in several languages will inevitably find a different style and quality in these pages. As with all translations of poetic prose, there is an irreproducible tone and essence which is lost. Heschel was unable to find time to translate and re-create the text in English himself, as he often said he wished to do. Earlier translations of only the first and final chapters of the book received his attention; "The Last Days of Maimonides" appeared as an essay as early as June 1955. We are certainly grateful to Mr. Neugroschel for his faithful rendering of Heschel's thoughts and ideas. We are also grateful to him for insisting upon the source of every quotation.

I would like to thank several scholars of the Jewish Theological Seminary for tracing so quickly those citations not listed in the notes of the original edition. For missing Biblical sources, I am grateful to Professors H. L. Ginsberg and Yochanan Muffs; for Talmudic references, to Professors Saul Lieberman and Israel Francus; for Arabic spellings, to Professor Menachem Schmeltzer and Raymond Scheindlin; for the time he gave to the philosophical concepts of certain parts of the translation, to Professor Fritz Rothschild. I am grateful for the help which Daniel Penham, Professor of French and Romance Philology at Columbia University, gave me. I also want to thank Professor Herbert Davidson, Department of Semitic Studies, University of California at Los Angeles, for his suggestions, and Rabbi Wolfe Kelman, executive vice president of the Rabbinical Assembly, who was most helpful in reading the translation. I am grateful to Eva Dobkin, Jack Formen, and Rudigore van Sanden for their careful reading and redaction of the manuscript. Finally, I feel it necessary to mention the warmth and friendship extended to me—as well as their concern about all matters relating to Dr. Heschel's books—by Roger W. Straus and Robert Giroux.

September 1981   Sylvia Heschel
        (*Mrs. Abraham Joshua Heschel*)

Our eyes look forwards, not backwards.

LETTER ON ASTROLOGY

. . . For what has been proved by a correct procedure gains nothing in truth if all scholars agree, and loses nothing if all the people on earth are of an opposite opinion.

THE GUIDE FOR THE PERPLEXED, II, chap. 15

After all, I am a man who—if the subject urges him, if the road is too narrow for him, and if he knows no other way to teach a proven truth except by appealing to one chosen man, even if failing to appeal to ten thousand fools—prefers imparting the truth to this one man. I do not heed the complaints of the greater crowd, and I wish to wrest the one chosen man from his irresoluteness and show him the way out of his perplexity so that he may become perfect and sound.

THE GUIDE FOR THE PERPLEXED, Introduction

I seek no victory, for the honor of my soul and character consists in deviating from the paths of fools, but not in conquering them.

LETTER TO JOSEPH BEN JUDAH

PART ONE

Development and Maturity

I

Life in Exile

BETWEEN the Sahara and the much traveled Mediterranean Sea, between the monumental civilization of ancient Egypt and the emptiness of the Atlantic Ocean, lies a land the Arabs fancifully call Maghreb, the Occident, or Barbary, and which geographers simply refer to as North Africa, the northern appendage of a larger continent. Even in dark antiquity this spot attracted the wanderlust of the Phoenicians, who felt too confined in their homeland on the coast of Syria; and it was here in early times that bitter conflicts between the great powers took place. The natives, however, played no part in the eventful history unfolding on their soil. The Carthaginians, Romans, Vandals, and Byzantines who took possession of the land never succeeded in getting the long-established inhabitants, the crude Berber people, to mature sufficiently to share in their culture. Only the militant missionaries of the Koran could accomplish this. But even though the Berbers adopted a faith in Allah and in his prophet Mohammed, along with Arab mores and manners, they were never fully integrated into Arab cultural circles, nor did they ever fully merge into the vast Arabic world.

The Berbers remained nonconformist. It is because of this resistance that the concept of an Arab world empire, which since the eighth century also included the Occident, nowhere else suffered such a defeat. From time to time through the centuries, the latent resistance of the Hamitic Berbers to the Islamic culture forced upon them, and to the Arab rulers, exploded into furious rebellion. Since they could not throw off their subjugation to Mohammedanism, the reaction against official Islam was transformed into a mania for at least nationalizing the religion imposed upon them. This craze to make the Berber religion victorious was already visible in the tenth century, when we can trace the efforts of the natives to conquer the religion of the conquerors, to transform it according to Berber fashion. North Africa now became the storm center of the Islamic world. Political tempests arose repeatedly out of this land, and three Berber tribes—the Fatimites, the Almoravites, and the Almohades —kept the world in suspense for hundreds of years.

In the southwest of today's Morocco, there lived at that time—the eleventh century—a young man by the name of Ibn Tumart, who even by Berber standards exhibited a most unusual piety.[1]* He was known as the "lover of light" because of the many candles he lit, according to the custom of the country, during his ceaseless worship at the tombs of the saints. He was very fond of learning, and soon the incomplete doctrines taught by African theologians no longer sufficed for him; he traveled to Cordova, then to Mecca, and finally to Baghdad, where the teachings of the renowned Ghazali prevailed. This great thinker, mystic, and indomitable reformer was one of the most inspiring minds of Islamic civilization. He condemned the corruption of the theologians, who, instead of healing the sick with the medicine of truth, poisoned them with rhetorical phrases. After absorbing the theological wisdom of the Levant, he returned to the mountains of his homeland,

---

* For Notes and Sources, see page 249.

where he established a kind of oratorical pulpit and began to proclaim his teachings. He delivered his abstract theories on the interpretation of the Koran to the uneducated Berbers, but they could scarcely understand what he said. The man who interprets the Koran literally, he maintained, must inevitably come to anthropomorphism, to a sensuous notion of God; he must attribute material characteristics to God and believe that God has feet and a face like a human being. But, he went on, whoever believed this was a heretic and deserved expulsion from the religious community of Islam, especially since he was bringing division into the unity of the Divine Being. In those days, anthropomorphic notions of God were indeed widespread among the inhabitants of Spain and North Africa. Since, according to Ibn Tumart, the rulers are responsible for the defects of their nation, he declared a Holy War on the ruling dynasty.

Earlier times had also known theologians who sought to remove anthropomorphism from the concept of God by means of reinterpretations. But the new and extraordinary thing about Ibn Tumart was that he constructed a rationale for his war out of the conflict between prevailing doctrines and his own way of interpreting the Koran. Seeing blasphemy in anthropomorphism, and noting that "religious error" was promoted by the highest government offices, he was left with no choice: for the sake of religion, the leaders of such a state had to be fought and deposed; indeed, a war against them, he felt, was as much a religious duty as the struggle against other infidels.[2]

Ibn Tumart went beyond a theoretical censure of anthropomorphism. He blamed the ruling dynasty for all the vices of public life, for secularization and moral corruption, for the sumptuousness at court and throughout society, for the public sale of wine in the markets (in outright defiance of Koranic prohibition), and for tolerating pigs in streets inhabited only by Mohammedans.

Ibn Tumart became a nuisance to the devout citizens of North Africa, who had always viewed themselves as truly orthodox; they were embarrassed, surprised, and infuriated. They, the pillars of the faith, were suddenly declared to be heretics, even decried as "polytheists" who, like the Christians, claimed a plurality within the Divine Being. They suddenly saw themselves denounced as infidels to the ignorant fanatic mob.

Ibn Tumart developed powerful propaganda. The authorities persecuted him, but the populace venerated him all the more. The Berbers were impressed by the ascetic purity of his life, his pious zeal in emptying every jug of wine and smashing every musical instrument that came before his eyes. Finally, he called his followers to arms, set himself up as a descendant of Mohammed, and told his adherents to pay homage to him as a mahdi, an envoy of the Lord, which meant, he said, that the end of time and the Last Judgment were drawing nigh, and the extermination of infidels and the restoration of the kingdom of God were imminent. He claimed he had come to fill the void with justice, just as it had previously been filled with injustice.

The miracles he performed were, for the throng, a clear confirmation of his mission. The populace obeyed the principles of the mahdi; for example, "commitment to the cause of Allah was better than any consideration of human life and property." For the Berber tribes, it was an established fact that the "command of the mahdi is the commandment of Allah." The idolatrous worship of Ibn Tumart's person, the excellent organization of his supporters, and the unimpaired strength of the mountain tribes enabled his successor, Abd-el-Mumin, to win control of Morocco and Spain after twenty years of bloody rebellion. The theological revolution, permeated with expansionist cravings, had almost unprecedented success in establishing the tremendous empire of the Almohades, or the "Confessors of the Unity of Allah,"* from Syrtis Major to the Atlantic Ocean. The enemies of the conquerors were ruthlessly slaughtered. Many had to pay with their lives when they resisted the "true" Islamic religion. Throughout the empire of the Almohades, from the Atlas Mountains to the borders of Egypt, and then in Spain too, synagogues and churches were destroyed. Jews were forced to embrace Islam or migrate, if they would not accept martyrdom. Many succumbed to fear and pretended to be Moslems.

At first, the rulers were satisfied if their new fellow believers merely pronounced the creed that Mohammed was a prophet. The pseudo-converts could then observe their old religious laws unhindered. Supervision and inspection of the lives of new converts, as practiced later by the Christian Inquisition, did not occur in Islam during that period. In these countries the privacy of the personal sphere and of domestic life was highly respected. Anyone who was and wished to remain a Jew could continue practicing Judaism at home unmolested. But praying in community meant risking death. Any assembly of the new converts even outside a house of worship could draw attention and exposure. The Jews who had recently turned to Islam were regarded as completely bona fide Mohammedans; but holding a Jewish divine service was synonymous with apostasy from the Mohammedan religion. And, according to Islamic law, the apostasy of a Mohammedan is punishable by death.

It was in such circumstances that the Jews lived in this world. They suffered through an existence that could not be endured for long. They had to give up their community life in order to survive as individuals. Their houses of prayer and study lay in ruins. The communities shrank visibly because their members kept emigrating. The community life of these extremely oppressed Jews glimmered

---

* Literally, "those who profess Unity."

in secret meetings for prayer, the discovery of which could result in utter annihilation. Yet, in unwavering devotion to God and His Torah, they exposed themselves over and over to death in order to maintain this final remnant of their religiousness. Their Jewish existence was now an ordeal of courage in a life of peril.

The Jews lived under the shield of a white lie. The more their outer life was exposed to danger, the stronger their inner resistance had to be. The faith of each individual was put to harder and harder tests. Life became a permanent state of peril; Jews awaited each new day as a threat. This condition could seem bearable to them only so long as they realized the indisputable meaning of their situation. The awareness of suffering for their faith as Jews was worn like a nimbus, it was a refuge for the soul. But, meanwhile, their spiritual situation grew more and more dubious.

The doctrine of the absolute oneness of God, which the Almohades propagated with fire and sword, struck the simple people as fully consistent with Jewish doctrine. Were the Berbers now the bearers of the wisdom that Israel had been striving to defend since the days of Abraham? The unprecedented victories won by the Almohadian army might be a confirmation of the favor of Providence. The simple Jews feared that this spelled the end of their having been chosen by God. They asked themselves, has the Lord exchanged the Jews for the Berbers, and has the prophet Mohammed really surpassed our teacher Moses?

A shadow lay across the lives of the Jews. From the gloom of frightened minds rose a distrust of Providence and an intimation of disaster. The fury of the Almohades was aimed not only against Jews but also against Christians and dissident Moslems. The Jew suffered not as a Jew specifically but as a member of a different faith, and was thus not distinguished by anything essential. How else could he interpret this persecution than as a condition in which the Jews were doomed in the same way as the other nations? Their unworthy and disgraceful existence as pseudo-Mohammedans, an existence that was bearable only so long as one was certain of God's loyalty and could expect His help every day, became an unending and increasing torment in a more and more untenable spiritual situation.

Despair lured minds into the most daring and insidious subtleties. The force of circumstances overpowered the suppressed and afflicted pseudo-converts, shattering their last bit of courage. The first symptom of their discouragement was manifested by the sudden feeling that their dangerous worship[3] was questionable. Should they continue risking their lives in order to perform prayers whose sense and purpose were becoming doubtful?

At that time—it was the year 1159—the Jewish community of North Africa received a letter written in the Arabic tongue, aiming to admonish and comfort them. The author, a certain Rabbi Maimon, sought to free the people of their calamitous delusions that the persecutions afflicting them were a sign that God had turned away from Israel and had chosen the Arabs to carry the teaching of God through their prophet Mohammed:

"A king who dismisses one of his officials will instantly appoint another to take over the office and duties of the first official. A man who repudiates his wife will usually bring home another, giving her the jewelry and bed of the first wife. A sign of the exchange is revealed when the successor is granted the rights and honors of the expelled predecessor. But where is there another nation to whom the Eternal One has appeared, given the Torah, and shown signs of favor such as He has granted us? So long as no other nation in the world has experienced such deeds of benevolence and grace, any word of Israel's being exchanged for another people is idle talk. Though we may live uninterruptedly in fear, though we may say in the morning, 'Would God it were even,'⁴ and in the evening, 'Would God it were morning!' we must also be aware, in this state, of the definitive proclamation that 'God will not forget the covenant of thy fathers which He sware unto them.'⁵

"Even in suffering, Israel is different from all other nations. 'For I will make a full end of all heathens whither I have scattered thee; but I will not make a full end of thee; but I will correct thee in measure.' Those are the words of the Lord. His chastisement is mixed with mercy, as in a father rebuking his children. God does not hate us, and He will not cause to pass away from us the name of children, whether we please Him, whether we believe in Him, or whether we turn away from Him. He wishes to purify Israel, not destroy it. We must also regard our present ordeal as a trial and a discipline. How could anyone believe in a hatred by the Eternal One, in an expulsion of Israel? The mission of our teacher Moses, who is distinguished by, and unsurpassed for, his sublimity and his boundless self-sacrifice for our nation, bears witness to the chosenness of Israel. Now for what nation could the Lord have exchanged Israel? The external fortune of a people proves nothing about their value. The merits of Moses and Israel, attested to by divine benevolence, also guarantee the fulfill-ment of divine promises, whose time is incalculable, yet can be brought on by atonement and prayer."

What was the force that preserved the courage and vitality of the Jews amidst continuous persecution? It was loyalty to the Torah. "We should lay hold of the cord of the Law and not loosen our hand from it, for we who are living in captivity are like one who is drowning. We are almost totally immersed, overwhelmed with humiliation and contempt, the seas of captivity surround us, and we are submerged in their depths, and the waters reach our faces ... The waters overwhelm us but the cord of the ordinances of God and His Law is suspended from heaven to earth, and whoever lays hold of it has hope, for in the laying hold of this cord, the heart is strengthened, and is relieved from the fear of sinking into the pit. And he who loosens his hand from the cord has no union with God, and God allows the abundant waters to prevail over him. So none is saved from the toils of captivity except by occupying himself with the Torah, by obeying its precepts, cleaving to it and meditating on it continually, as the Psalmist said: 'Unless thy Law had been my delight, I should have perished in mine affliction.' "

Finally, the author of the epistle to the North African Jews bound together all three lines of thought: the unshakable existence of the Covenant between God and Israel; the incomparable sublimity of Moses; and the immeasurable significance of prayer. He united them skillfully by calling for a daily utterance of the prayer which Moses, on the day of his death, foreseeing the disaster that threatened his people, engraved upon the memory of the nation—the unswerving hope for a return to Israel.

The years passed. The savage proselytizing and the rage of the "Confessors of Unity" did not ebb. There were more and more executions of unconvertible people, who defied the compulsory faith. The sufferings of the forced converts began to turn inward. The second act of the tragedy commenced.

Rabbi Maimon's comforting and admonishing words had provided answers to many an objective doubt; but objectivity was no longer the issue. Skepticism had penetrated their personal depths. Doubt became despair; despondency over God became despondency over oneself. Instead of brooding about the ways of the divine guidance of the world, the Jew tormented himself by scrutinizing his own worth. He pondered on himself, and the spiritual horizon of Jews became utterly dark. They were consumed with self-examination; bitter self-accusations plagued their minds. Was not the very fact that a Jew publicly acknowledged the prophetic mission of Mohammed a sign of apostasy from the faith of the fathers? And what about those who, rather than dying, betrayed God and yielded to force? What else were they but renegades!

There were, evidently, a few Jews who boldly defied peril and force. Convinced that any avowal of Islam and the accompanying public behavior as Mohammedans was an outright desecration of the Holy Name, a betrayal of God, they did everything they could to avoid conversion, and they viewed the converts as apostates, with whom they did not care to pray. The zealots even tried to persuade the forced converts to give up their secret worship because the praying of apostates was a sin. Dark inward despair, outward danger, and pressure from the religious fanatics combined to create the most dismal hardship imaginable. And yet the Jews continued their secret meetings. In dark hiding places, they recited the eternal prayers.

The pressure exerted by the Jewish zealots grew stronger and stronger. They openly declared that the pretense of the pseudo-converts was a far greater peril than total apostasy. They were willing to go to any lengths to expel the "double believers," like lepers, from the sphere of Jewry. To legitimize such a procedure, they sought the approval of renowned teachers of the Law. After all, in doubtful cases, it was customary to turn to well-known Talmudic scholars, usually the geonim, who functioned as the heads of rabbinical assemblies. Their decisions, promulgated in their answering letters (Responsa), were binding on the Jewish communities. Not long after, the following proclamation by an authoritative rabbinical personality was read aloud in all the Jewish communities of Morocco:

"Any Jew who publicly acknowledges Mohammed's calling as a prophet is a heretic and traitor to the faith! Any

Jew who has pronounced the creed of the Almohades, albeit secretly observing all Jewish duties and commandments, is excluded from the Jewish community and put on the level of non-Jews! Any Jew who visits the mosque as a pseudo-Mohammedan, albeit not participating in the prayer, is commiting blasphemy when he says Jewish prayers in his home! His prayer is an abomination in the eyes of the Lord, increasing the burden of his sins. Any Jew who confesses, albeit under coercion, that Mohammed is a prophet is unfit for giving testimony!"

The writer, whose name has not come down to us, entrusted this text to a messenger, who then traveled from town to town. "He has sent out darkness and put a gloom on everything," a contemporary lamented. This verdict was morally tantamount to executing whole communities. Their assaulted courage vanished on the spot. Some, shaken and wounded in their self-assurance, panicked in their bitterness, and plunged from their lost Judaism into the mosques. They abandoned their hideaways, sought refuge in Islam, and earnestly professed belief in Mohammed. Suddenly "proofs" of the genuineness of this prophet appeared, proofs supported by Biblical verses. All at once it was found that his coming was foretold to the patriarch Abraham, and that the salvation of Islam is predicted several times in the Holy Scriptures. Some Jews allowed themselves to violate the Sabbath, hoping that their wretched situation would soon pass and "the Messiah would come to Maghreb and lead them to Jerusalem."

There were others who were of a tenacious faith and did not doubt. But most of the Jewish populace remained indecisive and suffered in silence.

Popular Jewish tradition saw in the Berber tribes descendants of the Philistines, who had to flee to North Africa because of the annihilating defeats inflicted on them by King David and his commander-in-chief Joab. After all, one Moroccan village had an ancient monument known as the "stone of Solomon," bearing the inscription: "Commander-in-chief Joab pursued the Philistines to this point." How else could one explain the "Almohadean Mission" to teach monotheism to the Jews than as the outburst of the ancient resentment of the Philistines, who now wanted to make up for their quondam defeat?

Jews, too, had been dwelling in this land since time immemorial. A legend tells us that they had settled in Morocco as far back as the days of Solomon, that they had come with the Phoenicians. In the town of Boreion a synagogue, which Justian had transformed into a church, supposedly dated from the period of Solomon. When Sargon destroyed the Kingdom of Israel, a portion of the Ten Tribes allegedly migrated to Morocco, achieving new power. They founded a kingdom allegedly first ruled by a king named Abraham of the tribe of Ephraim. Supposedly, they did not follow Ezra's call to return to Israel. Because of this hesitation, their power diminished. In fact, there were Jewish communities in Morocco under the Romans, Vandals, Byzantines, and Arabs. There were houses of study with individual renowned scholars, and these Moroccan Jews gave financial support to the Jewish academies in Babylonia and Palestine.

In 1145 the "Confessors of Unity" conquered the city of Fez. Aside from the Berbers, who formed the majority of the city's population, there was a Jewish community which enjoyed high intellectual prestige in the Jewish world for centuries. The geonim, the heads of the Jewish academies in Babylonia, to whom all Jews turned for religious decisions, received more questions from Fez[6] than from any other city. When the Almohades conquered Fez, the Jews there, like their brethren in the other communities, were given the choice of embracing Islam, emigrating, or being executed. Most of them pretended to accept the Mohammedan creed and waited for better times. Some, refusing to utter the formula, were executed. A few left the country.

Fez was predestined for a life in hiding. The countless narrow and twisting streets intertwined into a labyrinth; the gloomy, sullen, steeply towering walls; the silence of the people, houses, and things; the Berber custom of thick veils on faces, even for men (since "it ill befits noble people to show themselves"); the Moorish architecture of sumptuous interiors but plain, barred and locked exteriors—all these circumstances favored, indeed created a fertile soil for the development of "marrano" life, so that world history virtually had a dress rehearsal in Fez for the Spanish tragedy of the marranos to come.

The terrorism of the new rulers apparently made even the cultivated Moslem uneasy. Skeptically, the normally self-willed Koranic soldiers and Old Believers accepted the new creed. They had to bow to the puritanism of the Almohades, who were hostile to art and lavishness. One of the largest mosques in Fez was adorned with gold and precious ornaments. When the Almohades marched into the city, the inhabitants feared that the conquerors would destroy all this splendor. So they covered the gold and decorations with paper, coated them with plaster, and then whitewashed the entire surface. This concealed the works of art, shielding them from the savagery of the Berber iconoclasts.[7]

Around 1158, Rabbi Maimon, a dayan (judge) and former member of the rabbinical court of Cordova, came to Fez with his family. Rabbi Maimon had been forced to leave his beautiful home city, the "Bride of Andalusia," when it was taken by the Almohades in 1148. The Jewish community of Cordova, which had existed for centuries, was totally destroyed by the Berbers. The synagogues and houses of study were burned, the inhabitants scattered to the four winds. The Maimon family escaped to Almería. In 1157, the Almohades conquered Almería. The Maimon family fled to Fez. North Africa had always been a refuge for Jews fleeing from religious persecutions in Spain.

Rabbi Maimon was probably not unknown in Fez. Between North African and Spanish Jews there had been constant economic, scholarly, and even personal relations. The Jews in Fez knew who Rabbi Maimon was, that he came from a family of scholars and judges, and that the family tree traced their descent from the famous Rabbi Jehuda ha-Nasi, the editor of the Mishnah, and, according to tradition, from King David himself.

Rabbi Maimon had learned the methods of Talmudic scholarship from Ibn Migash, the celebrated teacher at the famous house of study in Lucena, the "city of poetry," and Ibn Migash had been a pupil of the great Alfasi. The venerable Rabbi Maimon, noble and learned, self-assured and deeply pious, the foremost magistrate of Cordova, bearer of an ancient and uninterrupted tradition, in which his teacher, Ibn Migash, was the forty-eighth generation since Simeon the Just, the last survivor of the Great Assembly—Rabbi Maimon continued and cultivated this tradition. He had personally instructed his son Moses, the young Maimonides, transmitting to him both the precious tradition he had received and his own acquired experience.[8]

The revered Rabbi Maimon, offspring of the House of David, had—so the legend went—been told in a dream to marry the daughter of a butcher living near Cordova. He, the heir to the judge's office in proud Cordova, was to wed the daughter of a butcher unversed in the Law. Did not our sages teach that one must sacrifice anything to take a scholar's daughter to wife? Would an ignoramus's daughter, who did not know a life according to the Torah in her father's home, be able to raise her children for study and good works? Rabbi Maimon yielded to the higher directive, led the butcher's daughter to the canopy, and worried about what kind of a son he would be granted. The butcher's daughter became pregnant, and Rabbi Maimon prayed to God. She had a difficult labor. She gave birth to Moses,[9] but her soul departed; she died like noble Rachel at the birth of tender Benjamin. The widower then took another wife.

Rabbi Maimon tried to raise his son in wisdom and erudition. But Moses showed little joy in, or love of, scholarship. The father was deeply pained. Was the blood of the butcher's daughter more powerful than the spiritual strength of all the learned forebears? Tormented by rebukes and censure, by reprimands and punishments, little Moses would run to the synagogue, pouring his heart out to God in the women's section, which was normally deserted on weekdays.

The noble father grew more and more embittered from year to year. In his despair, he hurled some harsh words at the sensitive boy: "You were born for the lowest levels of life." Moses, who had inherited his mother's delicate humility and his father's pride, could not bear to hear these words; he left his father's house and disappeared.

To find solace and to forget, Rabbi Maimon immersed himself in the study of the Torah. He began a commentary of the Pentateuch, he wrote scholia on the Talmud, he conversed with the educated men of his city, he attended the lectures of visiting scholars. And one day the Jews in the great synagogue were listening to an unusual discourse while the audience, the best in Cordova, admired the rare erudition of the unknown lecturer; when the speaker finally removed his prayer shawl from his face after the lecture, they saw that it was a youth: the prodigal son of Rabbi Maimon.

2

In Fez

THE venerable Rabbi Maimon, offspring of a royal line, forty-ninth bearer of a tradition maintained since Simeon, the last survivor of the Great Synod, once pointed out that the Bible tells us the story of the Exodus from Egypt in the present tense, although one would have expected the past: just as the Jews left the land of their bondage with heads held high, so they persisted in this proud stance when the Pharaoh pursued them.[1] Nor could humiliation and persecution crush the spirit of the refugees fleeing the Almohades in Cordova. They moved from one hiding place to the next like princes in exile. They escaped from Cordova, then from place after place throughout Andalusia, which was deserted, plundered, and pillaged, devastated by war, rebellion, and famine, and preyed on by highwaymen; there were almost no Jewish communities left, and refuge was hard to find.[2] They fled; but from their flight young Maimonides learned how to submit to bitter conditions and how to wrest from them whatever they could yield of self-control and a sense of community. Hardship and deprivation are "a school of courage," he later said laconically;[3] and, "Man needs loving people all his life. One needs them in a time of affliction; in a time of physical weakness, one is dependent on their assistance; and in a time of health and fortune, one delights in associating with them."[4]

Rabbi Maimon had a second son, David, who was younger than Moses. He grew up at the side of his older brother, who instructed him in the Holy Writ and the Talmud and taught him the art of Hebrew grammar: "He was my brother and my pupil. My only joy was to see him," the philosopher later disclosed.[5] Young Moses, having no mother, cared all the more tenderly for his little brother, David. He evidently had no other friends. Once, to be sure, he did have a chance for a grand spiritual friendship: he met Averroës in Almería, offering him refuge when the Arabic philosopher had to go into exile for his all-too-liberal exegesis of the Koran. The fact is that Averroës, like Maimonides, came from Cordova, and both men were the sons of judges.

The house of the Maimon family stood in that part of Fez now known as Fas al Bali, the old town, by a flying buttress that arched over the narrow street; no coat-of-arms announced the nobility of the tenants, but a façade that was rare in this city of secrets revealed the nature of these people. The walls were massive and the front wide; between the two floors, a strange frieze attracted notice— a horizontal row of thirteen protruding stone consoles bearing a like number of wide-curving copper bowls. Above these frieze corbels there were narrow, slender windows, whose vertical openings rose like plumb lines over the bowls.[6]

These bowls, it is assumed today, had to do with astronomy and the working out of the calendar, with subtle and difficult astronomical observations and intricate and complicated calendar reckonings. Indian and Ptolemean astronomical tables, revised on the basis of meticulous findings at the observatories in Baghdad and Cairo, celestial globes of copper and silver, armillary spheres, plane and hemispherical astrolabes, mirrors of polished metal, and many other astronomical tools were available to astronomy.[7] Rabbi Maimon, who, it was said, "never studied the secular sciences for even a day, although he by no means turned from this world to the next,"[8] may have made an exception of astronomy. After all, the Talmudic scholars had said: "If a man has the ability to investigate the paths of the sun and the planets and yet fails to do so, of him the Prophet says: 'They do not wish to see the work of God and they do not respect the work of His hands.'" The study of astronomy was deemed a divine commandment. Maimonides himself cultivated astronomy with ever greater passion; he was more interested in the heavens than in the earth.

When the Maimon family came to Fez, they must have aroused the amazement of the old established Jews. Ever since Fez had fallen to the Almohades, Jews had been fleeing the city, yet the Maimon family had fled *to* Fez. Judah Halevi's friend, Judah ibn Abbas, a poet and the rabbi of Fez, had been forced to leave his congregation; and yet the Maimons had moved *to* Fez. It has been claimed that they were led to this dangerous place by the desire to hear the lectures of the Fez scholar, Rabbi Judah ibn Sossan. It is equally possible that Rabbi Maimon wished to have some link with the court of the caliph. Abd-el-Mumin, like his successor, had a taste for intellectual matters, he drew scholars to his court and prohibited the book burnings of his barbaric predecessors.[9] His personal physician was Ibn Tofail, the renowned author of *Hai ben Yakzan*, the Arabian Robinson Crusoe. Ibn Tofail's successor was Averroës. Perhaps Rabbi Maimon hoped for a possible connection with the court in order to enlighten the caliph about the Jewish notions of God and thus move the government to change its Jewish policy.[10]

What could Maimonides learn here? Fez, once the

intellectual and spiritual center of the Jews in Morocco, the city of Isaac Alfasi, the Fezer, was now, under the Almohadean persecution, spiritually impoverished and was turning more and more into a locale of Jewish assimilation of the Arabic cultural heritage; but it still offered possibilities for studying the most diverse sciences. The son of the Fez rabbi, Samuel ibn Abbas, whose later apostasy was to evoke Maimonides's counterthrust, corrected the arrangement of geometric figures in Euclid's textbook. The Jews studied Indian arithmetic, medicine, metrology, and algebra. They read Arabic stories and anecdotes "to find out what had happened in the past, what had occurred in earlier ages"; collections of fairy tales and compendiums, the histories of the viziers and the "scribes"; they conned the speeches of the best rhetoricians to achieve an elegant style.[11]

The educational goal that Maimonides set for himself was to grasp God "so far as this is possible for a human being."[12] Yet he considered it wrong to begin with the study of metaphysics. The man who starts with metaphysics, he felt, will have his faith not only confused but destroyed; he is like a man "who would nourish a baby with wheatbread, meat, and wine; for he would thereby certainly kill it, not because these foods are bad or unsuitable to the nature of man, but because he who receives them is too weak to digest them before he can draw any use from them[13] . . . The subject of metaphysics is very difficult and requires extraordinary acumen and depth." He who can swim can get pearls from the bottom of the sea; but he who cannot swim goes under. Hence only he should dive for pearls who is practiced in swimming.[14] There are countless philosophical concepts that sharpen thinking and eradicate the mistakes to be found in the views of many thinkers. Maimonides believed that for anyone desirous of reaching human perfection, it is indispensable to study logic first and then, in sequence, the mathematical sciences, the natural sciences, and finally metaphysics. This line from the concrete to the abstract is clearly drawn in the order of his scientific writings. At sixteen, he wrote an introduction to logic; at twenty-three, a mathematical-astronomical treatise on the main problems of calculating the Jewish calendar; later, matters of Halakha; and only afterwards, metaphysics.

In his youth, he associated with a son of the astronomer Ibn Aphla of Seville, who had written a famous book on astronomy, and with the students of the outstanding philosopher Abu Bakr, one of whom had instructed young Maimonides in astronomy.[15] He thoroughly studied the *Almagest*, Ptolemy's opus on astronomy, the axioms of algebra, the book on conic sections, geometry, and mechanics, and many similar subjects. His purpose, as he occasionally expressed it, was to sharpen his mind and train his understanding. He wanted to master the skill of distinguishing strictly demonstrative reasoning from other intellectual procedures, and thus attain "the knowledge of the truth of divine existence."[16]

He did not study for the sake of knowledge per se: he strove to arrange all his acts and words in such a manner that they led to his goal. He felt that a man must heed the health of his body and his life style in general, because achieving understanding was dependent on that. Thus "the art of healing performs very great services for acquiring virtues and the knowledge of God as well as attaining true bliss; hence, the study of medicine is one of the preeminent ways of worshipping God." He had already studied medicine in his youth and, even in Fez, had associated with prominent physicians.[17]

He also studied the theological texts of Islam and other religions in depth, and attempted to familiarize himself with the general science of religion in his time. What is more, though he had even read astrological books when young, he declared their contents to be nonsense and foolish superstition. He maintained that there was not a single book on astrology in Arabic literature that he had not carefully read and thoroughly grasped.[18]

Maimonides was not interested in the stories of Mohammed's campaigns, the enumeration of names of the ancient Persian kings, the legends of the old Arabian heroes, the genealogies of the individual Arab tribes and clans—which were the normal reading of the contemporary public.[19] Nor did he care much for the anecdotes and fables proliferating in Arabic historiography at that time: such historical works and descriptions of kings, genealogies and song collections contained neither wisdom nor usefulness; "reading them is a waste of time."[20]

For discipline in study, he lived by the motto, *The greater the pain, the greater the reward.* In wisdom, only what is mastered with effort and torment endures. Reading for pleasure or relaxation is neither useful nor of permanent value.[21] At the behest of a learned friend, he composed an introduction to the terminology of logic; at the request of another, a treatise on the chief rules of the calendar. Then he stopped publishing for years. "Before appearing in public, one must first think over what one wishes to say, once, twice, thrice, four times, and only then should one speak. That holds for an oral delivery; but anything to be spread abroad in writing must be tested a thousand times," he explained during this extended public silence.[22]

"Maimonides had such a perfect memory and such excellent intellectual faculties that he had not even finished his early twenties by the time he had acquired and mastered the sciences. He said with his own lips: 'The forgetfulness that befalls men has never befallen me in my youth.' He needed to study a book only once, and the contents were stamped on his mind."[23] These words are on record, but one should not therefore infer that the strength of his memory was particularly important to him. From the very first, he was something of a polyhistor. He did not organize the wealth of heterogeneous knowledge horizontally; instead, just as he grasped everything intuitively, so too everything in him immediately arranged itself into the order of the greater whole: all knowledge became cognition, all knowing thinking, and the universal fact became personally meaningful. For him, all mental labor was a metaphysical process. Accordingly, he declared the memory to be a function of the imagination and—in contrast to Aristotle—he ranked the imagination as an independent spiritual power.[24]

3

Prophecy

H E studied philosophy with the utmost zeal: the teachings of Alexander of Aphrodisias and Themistius,
Alfarabi and Ghazali, Saadiah and Bahya, Judah Halevi,
Abraham bar Hiyya, Abraham ibn Ezra.[1] But the only
master he recognized was Aristotle: "His knowledge is the
most perfect that a human being can possess, aside from
those who, through divine illumination, have reached the
level of prophecy, the most sublime level that exists."[2] This
remark about Aristotle may likewise point toward
Maimonides's concept of the essence of imagination, the
perfection of which he subsequently declared the prerequisite of prophecy. Even in his youth, Maimonides felt
he knew when prophetic illumination, which had been lost
for centuries, would be possible again.[3] Its time was not far
off, he said; he himself might live to see the era of grace.

This expectation, this inner preparation marked his youth;
and his near silence about it bore witness to his restraint, his
reticence, his singlemindedness. During his long life, the
hidden jewel of this premonition gleamed only a few times.
His family preserved a tradition that was handed down
from father to son since the Destruction of the Temple: as
of the year 1216, the spirit of the illumination would return
to the world. Could Maimonides help being seized with a

yearning to reach the level of prophecy? During his youth, he delved into the arcana of prophecy, and his deep thoughts about it became the nucleus of his entire intellectual and spiritual life.

Only this personal motive offers an explanation for the extraordinary centrality of prophecy in Maimonides's philosophy,[4] for the intellectual passion with which he asked himself these questions, for the uninhibited way in which his prophetological views penetrate the most diverse aspects of his writings. At a very early point, he decided to write a "book on prophecy." Several times, while writing his various treatises between 1158 and 1168, he announced the publication of this book, on which he was simultaneously working.[5] After having written a part of it, he was displeased with the method of his explanations. He feared being misunderstood by the masses; they would "resent his interpretations." Finally, he gave up writing the book altogether and contented himself with allusions in his presentation of the basic teachings of religion and the universal truths, which he was working on at the same time.[6]

To make up for this, he seems to have primed himself all the more intensely for receiving prophetic inspiration. He was convinced that personal qualities are the foundation on which to construct the prophetic man, "that no one receives the gift of prophecy until all intellectual and most of the moral virtues, the most unshakable ones," like wisdom, courage, and moderation, are part of him. Regarding the "opinion of the majority" that the genuine prophet must be able to work wonders, Maimonides held that this is "no axiom of truth."[7]

Maimonides sought prophecy because, from his youth on, he sensed the limits of the intellect: "With all his wisdom, his research and efforts, man has no other choice than to leave his business in the hands of the Creator, to pray to Him and beg Him to grant understanding, lead him to the right road, and reveal the mysteries to him." Prayer is thus a factor in the process of thinking, cognition a gift of God. Hence the esoteric stance of the philosopher Maimonides: "When God reveals something to a man, the man must conceal it."[8]

But all these insights could scarcely dampen his speculative urge, which was always kindled anew by concrete things, by the most obvious things. This urge to understand the meaning of individual existence and the insight that philosophical thinking was unable to answer this question were further motives for his attitude towards prophecy. "Why has Nature provided some species of insects with wings, but not others? Why has she brought forth some worms with many feet and others with few feet, and what is the purpose of *this* worm and *that* insect?"[9] Such naïve inquiry never vanished from his intellectual horizon. Both in his early philosophical speculation and in his mature contemplation, the question of the meaning and purpose of each individual existence defined the frontiers of what was possible for philosophical solution. "The power of the human mind does not suffice for knowing the purpose of each and every thing," only prophecy is capable of unraveling even the most obvious matters. Imagination, which recognizes "nothing but the particular," the concrete individual thing,[10] is, along with the intellect, the organ of prophetic cognition.

The question of purpose dominated him through all phases of his philosophical development. "Each thing necessarily has a purpose for which it exists, nothing exists without purpose," is the apodictic thesis of his youth, "even if knowledge of the particular purpose is often hidden from us." Which purpose? In his youth, Maimonides had an anthropocentric Weltanschauung: "All creatures under the moon were created only for the sake of man . . . If, however, we think that we do not know the use of certain animals and plants for human existence, it merely seems that way to our feeble reason. In reality, there can be no herb, no fruit, no species of animal, from the elephant to the worm, that is not useful to man."

But what is the purpose of man's life? Maimonides's anthropological thinking still dominated his purely theological thinking. "Why was man created, what is the purpose of his existence?" Maimonides found that human beings performed very many different activities. "All animals and plants have only one or two tasks to fulfill. We see, for instance, that the date palms have nothing else to do but bring forth dates, and accordingly so do all other trees. Furthermore, we find animals that only have to spin, like the spider; others, like the swallows, that build their nests in the summer; and animals that tear up other animals, like lions. But man has many different tasks. If we examine all his activities in order to infer the purpose of his existence, we find that he is preordained for only one activity, for the sake of which he was created, and that he does everything else only to maintain his existence, so that he may carry out that one task. This sole task is to contemplate ideas in the soul and to know truth in itself. Obviously, it is absurd to assume that man's purpose is to eat, drink, have sexual satisfaction, build houses, or be a ruler, for none of these things increases his essence; after all, he has these things in common with all other creatures. However, a man achieves the most sublime idea when he contemplates in his soul the oneness of God. The other sciences serve only for practice until one achieves the knowledge of God. Hence, the man who attains and exercises this knowledge is enacting the *purpose of the world.*"

Characteristic of the philosophical naïveté in his youthful thinking is the further conclusion: "If divine wisdom does not create anything in vain, if man is the most sublime of all creatures under the moon and his purpose is to cultivate this higher cognition, why has God brought forth all the people who do not attain such knowledge? After all, we see that most people are without wisdom and strive for pleasure, and that the wise man who retreats from the world is rare among the many, occurring only once in an age." Maimonides supplies his own answer: "All these people live in order to help this one man; for if all people aspired to wisdom and studied philosophy," and no one dealt with material things, "then the world would not go on, and the species of man would perish in a few days."

Maimonides asks: "Why does a fool enjoy rest without working for it, and why does a wise man serve him and do his business for him?" And Maimonides replies: "Even though the fool enjoys resting because of his wealth and riches and can order his slaves about, build a palace and plant a vineyard, it is possible that this palace is being prepared for a sublime man who will someday pass by and take shelter for a day under one of the walls of this palace and thus be saved from death. Or someday someone will take a beaker of wine from this vineyard to prepare treacle, which will preserve the life of a righteous man who has been bitten by an adder."

This philosopher, who was convinced that the wise man is at the center of the world, was full of self-assurance, but for that very reason also full of self-discipline. He held that no one is "by nature capable of all virtues," and especially "in youth, the bodily powers make most virtues impossible."[11] He also knew that the forbearing man whose patience is excessive, so that he can work up no anger, is pious, and that the hot-tempered man is sacrilegious.[12] He was aware of how vehement he himself could be.

He sometimes gave "free rein to his tongue and pen" when his opponents, no matter how wise and learned, disputed a decision or opinion he had expressed. A controversy he had with Rabbi Judah ha-Kohen ben Parhon over two questions concerning the meat laws caused a sensation. And he fought with the judge of Segelmesse and with Abu Joseph, son of Mar-Joseph, over a judicial decision concerning a female prisoner. He had similar disputes with many scholars. He would battle violently, "with his tongue against those present, with his pen against those absent."[13]

He defended his opinions valiantly and resolutely, even when they opposed his father's views. He was certain that his conclusions and decisions were cogent and logical: "Compare what we ourselves have said about it and what others have said about it, and the truth will pave its way to the destination,"[14] he said in a youthful work. Such statements, frequent in his early years, did not issue from youthful exuberance. "Do not look at the jug, but at what it contains; there is a new jug that is full of old wine, and there is an old jug, which does not even have new wine," says Rabbi Judah ha-Nasi. And young Maimonides glossed this pronouncement of his ancestor: "In some young men, we already find secure and reliable teachings like old wine from which the dregs have been removed."[15]

The many bad books and foolish notions with which contemporary literature was bristling aroused his mockery. At sixteen, he ridiculed the profuse hackwork of the Arab moralists.[16] He had a striking style that often came out as biting irony.[17] But this sarcastic manner pleased *him* least of all; and although the numerous disputes he had to take part in gave him frequent opportunities to show sarcasm, his restraint would make it seem that he tried to overcome his satirical bent. Even in his early years, he interpreted the commandment "Honor thy father" as intended to discourage the proclivity to impudence.[18]

But while seeking to suppress and overcome certain

tendencies in his character, he nevertheless affirmed human nature and rejected asceticism. In fact, the virtuous man, "who follows his inclination and spiritual disposition in his deeds and who does good out of pleasure and desire," is better than the abstemious man "who yearns and longs to do evil deeds but struggles against this craze, acts contrary to his strength, lust, and spiritual dispositions, and does good, even though it is difficult for him." When the virtuous feel that their ethical equilibrium is being threatened, they have a tendency to employ self-mortification as a "remedy." "But when fools saw those virtuous men acting in this way but did not know their intention, they regarded these actions as good in and of themselves. They emulated the virtuous, believing they would become like them, tormented their own bodies in every possible way, and thought they had done something virtuous and good and would thereby come nearer to God, as though God were the foe of the body and wanted it destroyed and annihilated; they did not notice that these actions were evil in and of themselves. These people may be compared to a man who, ignorant of medical science, sees experienced physicians prescribing the flesh of bitter gourds, scammonium, aloe, and the like to seriously ill patients, forbidding them their usual nourishment. And when these patients then recover from their maladies, miraculously escaping death, the ignorant man thinks: 'If these things cure sickness, then they must preserve health all the more or even be able to increase it.' Now, if he keeps taking these medicaments and orienting his life in the manner of sick people, he is bound to fall ill himself."[19]

Indeed, any negation of the world was alien to Maimonides. He taught self-control, but rejected self-torment. Still, his rejection of asceticism could never interfere with his openness to the conflict between the body and the soul: "The perfection of the body spells the destruction of the soul, and the destruction of the body spells the perfection of the soul."[20] His frequent disparagement of sensuality would likewise indicate that he sometimes had to overcome a conflict between ethical and metaphysical motives.

4

The Model

Maimonides gained an early access to the vast dimensions of philosophical thinking, the boldness of astronomical constructions, the sublimity of mathematical laws. But he concentrated more on studying the Bible, the Mishnah, and the Talmud than any of the sciences. Although pursuing the general sciences with zeal, he regarded his knowledge and understanding of them as a matter of choice and not vocation, as a "cultural experience" and not an inner necessity. His relationship to the Torah was, for him, a "primal experience." It had, he solemnly confessed, designated him before he even took shape in his mother's womb, it had sanctified him before he even emerged from the womb, and it had selected him to propagate the Torah on earth. For him the Torah was his beloved, the love of his youth. He had, of course, put strange women—the other sciences—at her side as rivals. But the Lord knew, said Maimonides, that he had taken these women only for cooking, serving, and for blending ointments, in order to show the rulers and nations the beauty of his beloved, for she was fair and comely.[1]

The unequal evaluation of the two spheres in his spiritual and intellectual world had to lead to a dichotomy in his thinking. During his youth, he characteristically determined

that, on the Sabbath, one should read only the prophetical
writings and their exegeses, but not works of the profane
sciences.[2] Emulating Alfasi, who was celebrated for com-
piling the judicial parts of the Babylonian Talmud,
Maimonides did the same for the otherwise neglected
Jerusalem Talmud. He undertook the important and difficult task of writing a commentary on the Talmud. More
than half of this labor was done when a different goal
tempted him: a commentary on the Mishnah.

Of the Talmudic writings, no other work was spiritually
so close to him in form, language, and diction as the
Mishnah. He had a deep intellectual affinity for this work,
which excelled in its terseness and purity of style, in its
precision and its arrangement according to certain aspects.
Moreover, he felt a personal kinship with the creator of the
Mishnah, with his forebear Rabbi Judah ha-Nasi. This man,
with the most constructive mind of the Talmudic age, with
a tremendous and unparalleled talent, served as the model
for young Maimonides. His devotion to Rabbi Judah ha-
Nasi had a profound impact on his spiritual development.
This second-century aristocrat and codifier became his
guide in thinking and action, so that it is no coincidence
that Maimonides's inner and outer life showed similarities
to his ancestor's.

"Our teacher was the chosen man of his generation and
the foremost man of his time," Maimonides writes with
emphasis. "In him, the Lord united the most outstanding
human traits. His contemporaries called him the Holy One.
They did not speak his name but simply referred to him
as 'Our Holy Teacher.' He achieved spiritual and ethical
perfection. They also said that not since Moses had learning
and authority been so thoroughly blended in one man. His
ways were utmost humility and devotion to God, and he
left the pleasures of life to others. With his death, modesty
and fear of sin were ended. He was the greatest master of

the Hebrew language among all men. When the scholars of his time were unable to translate a difficult word in the Holy Scriptures, they would ask Rabbi Judah's servants, for the cultivation of the Hebrew language in his home was also transmitted to his domestics. He was very rich. A proverb went: 'The rabbi's equerry is wealthier than King Shapur of Persia.' He supported researchers and scholars. He taught many people in Israel and gathered the legacy, the scholarly opinions of learned Jews who had lived since Moses, and, finally, he composed the Mishnah."[3]

Originally, the Mishnah was an independent codex, comprising all the teachings of the Law. The Talmudic writings, which developed after the redaction of the Mishnah, were detailed discussions, virtually a commentary, referring to, correcting, and interpreting the text of the Mishnah. This evolution caused the Mishnah to forfeit its originally independent position. It was now impossible to use it without reading the Talmud. However, the Talmud had a very different way of dealing with questions. The precise decisions of the Mishnah were replaced by dialectical debate, into which the reader had to immerse himself before he could finally work out a decision that would be binding for practice. Without thorough analytical studies, no one could truly make up his mind about how to interpret the Mishnah.

"In dealing with any Mishnaic passage, the Talmud cites evidence, proofs; it raises questions and answers them, so that the full meaning of the Mishnah can be fathomed only by a keen-witted, experienced student. Furthermore, it is often necessary to study several tractates of the Talmud on one and the same theme." But the Talmud remained the indispensable aid. "For even the greatest scholar, if asked to explain a passage in the Mishnah, can answer only if he knows by heart the Talmudic wording about that particular passage, or else he will admit that he must first look it up.

One cannot have the entire Talmud in one's head, especially since the dialectical discourses of the Talmud, because of the many objections and their rejoinders, often go on for several pages, and the explanation of all the sentences of a Mishnah is often to be found in separate tractates."

Maimonides saw "that the Talmud does something with the Mishnah that one can never grasp with one's reason. It offers precepts and then claims that the Mishnaic passage in question is defective and that its complete wording should have been otherwise; or else the Talmud alleges that the Mishnah expresses the opinion of such and such a teacher, and this opinion is such and such. Sometimes, the Talmud also adds something to the words of the Mishnah or takes something away and offers reasons for what the Mishnah stipulates."[4] Maimonides also realized that the study of the Mishnah was generally neglected, and he did not hesitate to rebuke the great Alfasi for his inadequate knowledge of this work.[5]

Maimonides now came up with the plan of writing a commentary to serve as a direct access to the Mishnah, enabling one to skirt the labyrinth of the Talmud. He wanted to avoid all discussion and to offer, with utter brevity, the most necessary things in the Talmud for understanding the Mishnah. The man who had too little time or ability to find his way through the Talmudic teachings would at last have the possibility of informing himself quickly and easily about all questions of the Law. Because of the tremendous effort required for the study of the Talmud, Maimonides wanted to supplement and restore the Mishnah as an independent compendium.

Going beyond mere commentary, Maimonides aimed at the following: whenever the Mishnah reported conflicting views of the Teachers of the Law, Maimonides hoped to indicate the definitive decisions. His goal was also propaedeutic: to prepare the beginner for the astute dialectics of the Talmud, whereby his laconic and easily retainable rendering of the gigantic mass of material would serve as a mnemonic aid for studying the Talmud. Maimonides began his task in 1158. But, as he said, he did not find time for going on with the commentary on the Talmud.

5

Respect for Israel

WHAT were the conditions in which Maimonides worked on this project? "Since we went into exile, the persecutions have not stopped. I have known affliction since childhood, since the womb." He began his Mishnah commentary while fleeing through Spain. In 1159, at the age of twenty-four, he arrived in Fez. Here, too, the Jews lived under the scourge of the Almohades. They could not comprehend why God seemed to want to make it impossible for His people to remain true to its faith. Maimonides abstained from offering a philosophical justification of the evil. No Jewish scholar, he said, had succeeded in solving this problem. The seemingly dazzling words that circulated about it were "like a silver coating on brittle clay." God ruled the world by the law of justice. "But just as the human intellect is incapable of grasping God's thoughts, so too our thoughts are unable to understand the wisdom and righteousness of His dispensations and operations." Maimonides did not care to imperil his soul with such broodings. "But when the time comes that the Lord wishes to chastise someone, He offers him the possibility of acting contrary to the Torah in order to inflict a just punishment on him. If a man is not ready for punishment, the Lord lets him sin so that he will be ready.

"A thinking man, however, should not be especially

disturbed by adversity. There are many events that at first seem bad, but ultimately turn out good. One should always hold up one's joy and grief and postpone one's emotional reactions." In contrast to his father, who saw the Almohadean ordeal as a test and trial for the Jewish nation, Maimonides believed: "No suffering without sinning."[1]

During this period, Maimonides seems to have retreated into his work. Suddenly, he intervened in a public dispute. He could not help retorting to the anonymous respondent who condemned all pseudo-converts, the "secret Jews," as traitors and expelled them from Judaism. The Law, so Maimonides reflected, dictates that every Jew must sacrifice even his life for the sanctification of the Divine Name when he is faced with the choice of apostasy or death. But did this demand also hold for the new pseudo-converts? The respondent's verdict led the nation astray. What about the Jews in Egypt at the time of Moses? They were corrupt, unclean, nearly all uncircumcised. But when God gave Moses his mission, and Moses uttered doubts as to the piety of the people—"Behold they will not believe me!"—God took him to task: "The Jews are pious children of pious parents, but thou, Moses, shalt fail in thy piety!" Moses had to atone for his distrust and suspicion. His punishment became an example and a statute: "He who casts suspicion upon an innocent man shall himself be struck."

What about the Jews at the time of the prophet Elijah? Nearly all of them bowed freely to the idols and kissed the effigies of Baal. There was hardly a knee that did not bend, hardly a mouth that did not kiss the idols. But when Elijah left the desert, went to Mount Horeb, stood before God, and complained about the Jews, the following dialogue took place:

ELIJAH: I have been zealous for the Lord God of hosts, for the children of Israel have abandoned thy Covenant!

THE LORD: Perhaps thy Covenant?
ELIJAH: Torn down thine altars!
THE LORD: Perhaps thine altars?
ELIJAH: Slain thy prophets with the sword!
THE LORD: Yet thou art alive.
ELIJAH: I alone am left, they are striving to take my life.
THE LORD: Instead of complaining about the Jews, thou ought rather to look upon the nations of the world, who possess untold heathen temples in their cities. Wend thy way back again to the desert!

How about the Jews at the time of the prophet Isaiah? They were sinful and guilt-laden, idolaters, desecrators of the Name, profaners of the Commandments. Their slogan was: Eat and drink, for tomorrow we die. They scorned the Holy Laws and shouted: "Stop bothering us with the sacredness of Israel!" But when the Lord appeared to Isaiah, and Isaiah dared to say: "I live in a nation with unclean lips," an angel had to purge the prophet's lips with a burning coal. It was not, however, the uncleanliness that he had gotten from living among the people whom he described as unclean; his own words had to be atoned for. And he achieved complete atonement only through his martyrdom.

Once, when an angel came before the Lord and complained about the high priest Jeshua the son of Jozadak because his sons had married unworthy women, the Lord banished the angel from the kingdom of Heaven: "I, the Lord, command thee to keep silent! I, who elected Jerusalem, command thee to keep silent."

"If the pillars of the world, Moses, Elijah, Isaiah, and an angel, were punished for daring to utter a word of abuse against Israel, then how much more does a man deserve reproof for making bold to call Jewish congregations blasphemers, heathens, atheists, and to declare them unfit to bear witness! How much greater is the sin of a man who has

committed such words to writing and made them public!"
Did this hasty foreign respondent fail to see that the forced
converts had not played some careless trick, that they had
not deserted in order to gain some advantage? They had
fled from swords, naked swords, from drawn bows, from
the might of war. The Lord would not abandon or reject
them, He has never disdained or despised the misery of the
wretched. "In this forced conversion, the persecutors do
not demand that we perform idolatry. Nor are we compelled to follow the rites of Islam. They merely demand
that we utter, and believe in, what they say, namely, that
Mohammed is a prophet, whereby those who coerce us are
quite aware that we do not believe in these words and
merely utter them in order to deceive the caliph."

The respondent's arrogance was especially reprehensible
because he had made his decision by his own judgment, by
the pleasure of his own heart. After all, traditions and
teachings expressed the opposite of his decision. The famous
tanna, Rabbi Meir, when persecuted, had pretended to be a
heathen in order to escape death. No doubt, in the eyes of
the respondent, who had allegedly grasped the truth of the
Torah, Rabbi Meir was a non-Jew: "Whoever lives as a
non-Jew in public and a Jew at home is equivalent to a non-
Jew." Likewise, the great teacher Rabbi Eliezer had pretended to be a heretic under similar circumstances. The
respondent would probably have considered Rabbi Eliezer
unfit to bear witness. During the Babylonian Exile, when
Jews were forced to worship the image of King Nebuchadnezzar, only the three companions of the prophet Daniel
refused: Shadrach, Meshach, and Abednego. They preferred to be cast into the limekiln rather than to follow
Nebuchadnezzar's order. All the other Jews, however,
bowed to the idolatrous effigy. And never had any scholar
called the Jews of this generation heathen, blasphemous,
or unfit to bear witness. Nor did the Lord regard them as

sinful, because their worship had been extorted from them, and He said: "They did it only for show." The Hellenistic authorities of Antiochus Epiphanes forbade the Jews to close their doors, so that they might not carry out their commandments in stealth. And nevertheless our sages called this generation not blasphemous and heathenish, but perfectly righteous. Ahab, king of Israel, denied God. But, because he once fasted with a pious intention, the Lord did not fail to reward him for this little deed. Eglon, king of the Moabites, afflicted Israel for years and years. But, because he once paid homage to the Lord, God requited it. His descendants mounted the holy throne named after God. For Ruth, the ancestress of the dynasty of David, was Eglon's daughter. Nebuchadnezzar had Jews massacred in great numbers, and he destroyed the divine temple. But, because he once paid tribute to God's Name, his rule lasted forty years, as long as that of King Solomon. Esau, the transgressor, led a life of vice. He observed only one commandment: to honor his father. For this good work, he was recompensed: his descendants would keep their kingdom uninterruptedly until the Messianic Age, for it is a law of history that the Redeemer will not come until Esau has been rewarded for honoring his father. And if the Lord richly repays these evildoers for minor, insignificant works, shall He not credit Israel for secretly keeping the holy commandments, even if it is forced into sham apostasy? And should there be no difference between the man who does not do his duties and the man who does? Between the man who serves God and the man who denies Him?

The responsum did not really merit refutation. But its unsuspecting readers would stop their "sinful" praying if no reward were forthcoming. It could also lead to forming a sect, and a final spiritual collapse of North African Jewry was to be feared. Did not Maimonides have a duty to intervene and attack the fateful document? His father, the venerable Rabbi Maimon, had expressed himself publicly in a similar situation. Now the responsibility fell to the twenty-four-year-old. So far, he had written only for friends; this time he was to step before the forum of the entire Jewish people.

Jews had been forced to convert by the Crusaders in Lorraine, on the Lower Rhine, in Bavaria and Bohemia, in Mainz and Worms; and by the "Confessors of Unity" in Morocco and Andalusia. The persecutions made the alternative between martyrdom and betrayal of faith the existential question of the nation. The phrase about sanctifying God's Name through death was on all lips. By condemning the apostates, the respondent had expressed the heartfelt thoughts of many zealots. Furthermore, the letter of the Law was the anvil on which this fanatic had hammered out his harsh word.

Maimonides, in contrast, had a good sense of the intoxication of martyrdom. He too was ready and able to sacrifice himself. But he let his feeling be shaped and guided by moderation and order, and he reached an epoch-making decision. The theoretical and unconditional demand to give up one's life for the sanctification of the Name could not be applied all that readily to the special situation in Maimonides's time. "In the earlier religious persecutions," he said, "we were forced to transgress certain *shalts* and *shalt nots* through our deeds. In the present-day persecution, no deed is demanded of us, only words. If someone wishes to observe all our 613 laws in private, then no one hinders him. There has never been such a strange persecution, in which we are forced to transgress only verbally. If someone tried to force us to commit a forbidden act, then, of course, we would rather be killed than carry it out." This white lie, this lip service, was no apostasy. Maimonides took into account not only the wording of the Law, but also the very existence of the Jews, which was of paramount importance beyond any other problems. With subtle acumen, he interpreted the Law, not only with sober reason but with heartfelt thinking. The crisis was a misfortune, not a crime; it demanded a physician, not a judge.

The treatise he wrote was to be his first literary publication in Fez. His previous writings had been meant for one person. Their topics were logic and astronomy. Nevertheless, he proved to be familiar with all the stylistic devices of a public pamphlet.

"When I recognized the astonishing facts of the case," he writes, "which is like an illness of the eyes, I resolved to gather herbs and elixirs from the writings of the ancients and to compound an eye ointment that would prevail against this illness. With God's help, I will thereby heal the disease." He delves into traditional wisdom, into the Law, but also into the internal history of Israel, in order to find a solution for the present. "Do not rush in with thy mouth, and let not thy heart be hasty," he writes, for "whosoever answers a question or makes a decision about what is permitted and what is prohibited, he judges in the face of God."

"Here speaks Moses, son of Maimon the Judge, the Spaniard," goes the proud exordium. A few brief sentences, a winning introduction, a terse summary of the adversary's decision and invective—and the refutal begins. Examples are drawn from literature, from history, not concepts, and the abuse uttered by the zealous inquisitor sounds like blasphemy. With mordant sarcasm, Maimonides points out the absurdity of the opinions voiced in the responsum. In closest conformity with the Law, he establishes the guidelines for practice, the meaning and limits of sanctification. The clarity of his thoughts, the simplicity of his diction, the restrained emotional power of a sympathetic soul whose quiet presence is felt, must have had an impact. These were words that brought relief. "One should not shame the Sabbath desecrators when they come to the prayer assemblies: one should not injure the sinners if they secretly wish to steal good works." The sanctification of the Name is transferred from the realm of dogma to ethics. "If someone performs unclean acts, albeit not sins, and ugly rumors therefore circulate among the people, then he has desecrated God's Name."

Maimonides's love for his nation is voiced from a level that is deeper than any atavistic feelings or acquired inclinations, a love filled with awe, a love in the light of the divine countenance.

The years following the missive were devoted to the commentary on the Mishnah. In the form of introductions, Maimonides presented a theory of tradition and a doctrine of the Jewish faith. He felt that a certain amount of knowledge was required for human beings to take part in everlasting life. The universally binding doctrines of Judaism are the minimum that every Jew must learn if he wishes to achieve eternal life. Maimonides, therefore, set up a table of dogmas.

In so doing, he deliberately left out the dogma of the creation of the world. He was filled with a passion to teach ethics, to set up the standards of ethics. When he was working on the missive, he suddenly felt like departing from the theme and writing "about the correct way to behave toward other people, which deeds and words are proper for delighting everyone whom we deal with or speak to." However, "treating these matters would require a separate book." In the course of time, he then also composed a system of ethics.

6

Journey to Palestine

I<small>N</small> his missive, Maimonides rehabilitated the Jews who had converted only for appearance's sake. Nevertheless, if a Jew is faced with the choice of professing Islam or emigrating, then Maimonides advises him to choose his religion rather than his homeland. Jews should leave the countries "about which God has waxed wroth"; they should abandon their homes and property. The teachings that God has given us are more sublime than any externals of life. We should flee coercion and wander day and night, even in danger:[1] "For the world is vast and wide."

The Maimon family wandered from town to town to escape the farce of lip service. In Fez, no one realized they were Jews. But their secrecy could not be maintained. These foreigners stayed true to their religion, which was persecuted by the state. Moreover, in their hidden superiority, they undermined the religious conquests and threatened to wrest victory from the Almohadean mission. Did not the missives of Maimon and Maimonides constitute a conspiracy against the government? The boldness of these actions could only be matched by increased danger.

In 1163, Abd-el-Mumin passed away. Under his successor, Abu Yakub Yussuf, the religious violence knew no limits. A friend of the Maimon family, Judah ibn Sossan, "the great wise and pious man," was "killed amid the most horrible tortures when he refused to convert."[2] Maimonides nearly met with the same fate. But a Moslem theologian and teacher, Ibn Moisha, with whom he probably had scholarly relations, boldly and loyally intervened for him and saved him from danger. There was no further possibility of living in Fez. After a five-year pause in their wandering life, the Maimons again had to seek refuge in flight. Their new hope was the land of the fathers.

The great ease of traveling in the Mohammedan countries inspired a general wanderlust. The fruit of the lively traffic was the great blossoming of trade, with a world market stretching from China and India, Iraq and Egypt, to Morocco and Spain. Pilgrimages and journeys for study were frequent. The Jews followed the precept: "Migrate to a place of study"; the Arabs: "Whosoever journeys toward knowledge, his road to Paradise will be made easier by God."[3] The Maimon family, who had been forced to keep wandering since 1148, were experienced travelers by now. Maimonides had to leave the empire of the Almohades as fast as possible.

Rabbi Maimon and his sons, Moses and David, fled into the night. They kept marching as long as it was dark. During the day, they hid themselves. One night, they arrived in Ceuta.[4] This town lies by the sea, at the northern tip of Morocco, on the narrow neck of the peninsula which runs from west to east. At that time, Ceuta was a center of art, science, and scholarship; it had the first paper factory in the West, and it also showed a remarkable political independence. When Abd-el-Mumin tried to conquer Ceuta in 1140, he was beaten back. Six years later, however, it did recognize his supreme authority and received an Almohadean governor. One year later, Ceuta rose up against the new master, killed the governor, and appointed an adversary of the Almohades in his stead. The rebellion was quelled, and Abd-el-Mumin retook Ceuta, putting one of his best officers in command of the town. But this did not quell the ferment against Almohadean rule. In this town, where Jews also lived, the refugees had the best chance of setting sail unmolested. On a Sunday night, April 18, 1165 (the 4th of Iyar, 4925), Maimonides embarked.

The Arab ships plying the Mediterranean were of a considerable size. "A single vessel," as a contemporary observer admiringly reports, "carries several thousand men. On board, there are wine and food shops as well as looms."[5] To be sure, they avoided the high seas and cautiously hugged the coast.

The descendant of King David and offspring of the patriarch Rabbi Judah ha-Nasi—Maimonides, who described himself as a "Jerusalem exile in Spain"[6]—sailed to the land of his fathers.

Normally, it took thirty-six days to cross the Mediterranean, from the Atlantic Ocean to Seleucia. The passage from Marseilles to Palestine lasted thirty-five days. From Ceuta, where Maimonides embarked, it was a few days less. They could hope to celebrate the Feast of Weeks in the Holy Land.

Maimonides claims: "The forgetfulness that befalls man has never befallen me in my youth." With equal justification, he could have claimed: "The idleness that man is prey to is something I have never known." The project he was working on since his twenty-third year was still unfinished. But, without interruption, he continued his research aboard ship, despite the arduousness of the journey.[7] Persecution and flight did not break his spirit.

The bulk of the work must have been complete by now. This probably included his system of ethics, the main outlines of which must have been done in Fez. Maimonides designates as virtuous those actions that keep to a medium between extremes, of which one is too much and the other too little and both are bad. An example: abstemiousness, a behavior that keeps the medium between craving pleasure and being indifferent to it. Likewise, generosity is a mean between stinginess and squandering, humility between pride and self-abasement, modesty between impudence and excessive timidity.[8] Maimonides obtained the notion of virtue as the middle way from Aristotle. However, the limits that Maimonides puts upon this idea, despite its central position in his ethics, reveal his own character.

His taking the Aristotelian definition of virtue has often made it seem as if his ethical thinking were entirely dependent on Aristotle. But it speaks for "Maimonides's philosophical sensitivity that he makes no ado about his profound departure [from Aristotle] in this point."[9]

For Maimonides emphasizes that the pious do not hold to the just mean but tend toward too much or too little; e.g., from abstemiousness somewhat toward indifference to any pleasure, from humility a bit toward self-abasement, and so forth.[10] This attitude removes the planks from the middle way at points where man wants to break through the intermediate, the line of what is normally right, in order to increase the good. In this way, Maimonides makes a place for those who strive toward fullness and excess of the good. No one, he says, is obligated to reach the extreme of goodness, but the pious man aspires to it. This conception—i.e., demanding the medium from others but spurring oneself toward the extreme of the good—was realized in Maimonides's own life.

A further deviation from the Aristotelian doctrine, and one even more informative about Maimonides's personal stance as a young philosopher, is shown in the following opinion: Even though the middle line should be maintained in the most diverse traits and conduct, humility "should go to an extreme and be practiced to the utmost degree." After all, wherever the Bible discusses greatness, it also mentions God's humility. And as for Moses, who possessed the full measure of intellectual and ethical qualities, who was a master in doctrine, wisdom, and prophecy, God lauded only his humility: "The man Moses was the most humble on earth."[11]

In this period of his spiritual and intellectual development, Maimonides seems to affirm that the extreme humility he demands of all men goes to the extreme of self-abasement. He found the standard for this in a story he enjoyed telling:[12] "A pious Gentile was asked: Tell us on what day you felt the greatest joy of your life. The pious man replied: I was once sailing on a ship. My place was in a shabby corner, where the bundles of clothing were stored. Merchants and well-to-do men were also on board. One of the voyagers, who felt a call of nature, entered this room, where I lay in my spot, with my face looking up. The well-to-do voyager found me so unworthy and despicable that he soiled me. I was amazed at this insolence, but—by God!—I felt neither insulted nor angry. This equanimity of my soul, which I experienced, brought me a feeling of bliss. That was the greatest joy of my life."

This tale of crude humility issuing from the strange medieval sensibility may reflect the ideal that young Maimonides, who was proud by nature, had in mind.

On a Sabbath, April 24 (the 10th of Iyar), when the ship had sailed about one quarter of the route, a tremendous tempest swept up and raged all day long. "I found no one on the sea during this day," Maimonides later noted.

He prayed and swore that if he survived, he would "commemorate this day of the tempest in seclusion until the end of his life, seeing nobody, and praying and reading in solitude the entire day." He swore to fast on every anniversary of the embarkment and of the tempest for the rest of his life; he, the members of his household, his children and descendants until the end of generations would fast and do good works. "Just as I found no one on the sea during this day *except God,*" he wrote explaining his oath subsequently, "so too I will see no one and meet with no one on the anniversaries of this day . . ."[13] This thought also shows that he viewed solitude as a prerequisite for a certain kind of religious experience.

Palestine, "the jewel of the earth," was the lightning rod for Occidental storms in this century. The yearning of Christian zealots, the misery of European peasants, who were crumbling under the oppression of aristocratic lords, the greed for Oriental treasures, the adventurousness of vagabonds, the need for atonement by enthusiastic penitents and frivolous sinners, the dream of world dominion—all these energies concentrated and discharged in the Crusades, which brought crueler and bloodier chaos to the world than any elemental calamity. Holy Jerusalem became a melting pot, blending secular and spiritual passion. The Crusaders managed to conquer the land "on which God's eyes are always resting." A few petty, simpleminded princes sat on David's throne, ruling the state that bore the hallowed name of the Kingdom of Jerusalem.

When Maimonides sailed to Palestine, Amalric was at the head of the kingdom. This king, the historians wrote, always strove "for sensual pleasure, ruthlessly and rapaciously demanding money and valuables." And in his politics he had only one thought, which most of his knights shared; namely, to acquire great riches and live in wealth and splendor. Under this monarch, the kingdom of the "Frankish" knights had no other prospect than more and more imminent collapse. Yet, once, this ruler did succeed in pursuing large-scale politics.

Like his predecessors, he aspired to dominion over Egypt.

The once so glorious and tremendous empire of the Fatimites had been decaying because of its degenerating dynasty. The caliphs were perishing "in harem pleasures and palace revolutions." All power lay in the hands of ambitious generals, who kept violently replacing one another in the viziership, and cared more about gratifying their power lusts than about the welfare of the country. In 1163, Amalric attempted to invade the land of the Nile. The Egyptians saved themselves by smashing holes in the river dams and flooding the entire country. Amalric had to retreat empty-handed.[14]

Meanwhile, a dangerous enemy tied a noose for the Crusader state; a decisive turning point came in the history of the Crusades. Islam, for which the Crusades were much less significant than for Christianity, had so far made only temporary stabs at breaking the power of the "infidels." A few Mohammedan states had even entered into alliances with the "Franks" whenever that seemed advantageous. It was Nureddin, the ruler of a mighty empire between the Tigris and the Syrian coast, who first designated a Moslem war against the Christians a matter of faith and prepared a huge blow against the kingdom of the Crusaders. He began by uniting Egypt with his Syrian land in order to encircle Palestine. Nureddin launched political and military intrigues in Egypt against the ruling dynasty. Now the Fatimites and the Crusaders realized that they shared a powerful enemy in Nureddin, the ambitious Moslem monarch. It was into this country, over which a tempest was brewing, that Maimonides came.

When the coast of the Promised Land emerges from the sea, Christian pilgrims are filled with sheer joy. But sadness and melancholy overcome the Jews when the Holy Land heaves into sight. The ringing bells of the churches of Akko bid the Christian travelers welcome. The Jews fling themselves on the ground, cover the earth of their "homeland" with tears, and rend their clothing.

Rabbi Abba, the Talmud tells us, kissed the rocks of Akko; Rabbi Hanina righted the religious practices of the people of Akko. Now the Crusades had made Akko, the chief station of the pilgrims, an international trading center. Hundreds of ships from the West moored here; huge fleets arrived twice a year from the harbors of Christian Europe, bringing slaves and weapons from Europe and loading spices and costly garments from the East. Above all, the ships annually carried tens of thousands of pilgrims, who arrived in April by the spring passage and in August or September by the summer passage.[15]

A contemporary account portrays the Akko of that time as a wonderful city: "The houses were all of the same height, built of hewn stones, provided with glass windows, and decorated with paintings. They were flat on top, had flower gardens on the roofs, and received fresh water through pipes. Splendid palaces, surrounded by walls and moats like fortresses, erected by kings, princes, and barons, gave their districts a stately appearance. The merchants and the artisans had their homes at the center of town, each trade had its own street, named after it. The merchants from many countries dwelt in comfortable and attractive houses and were able to offer to customers ample stocks of merchandise. Countless churches with domes and spires, and castles of the orders of knights with their turrets and merlons, dominated the city with its enormous multitude of houses. The city was surrounded by double walls so broad that two chariots could pass each other on them. Countless towers, through which the city gates led, rose high above the circular walls. At the times of the yearly pilgrimages and the arrivals of Crusaders, there were pilgrims and other foreigners from all the lands of Christendom, travelers, even from the lands of Islam, clerics and secular princes with glorious retinues, well-armed knights on wonderfully harnessed horses, and the streets rang with all the tongues of East and West. Now one saw princely trains of Syrian barons, now tiltings, tournaments, and other military games were celebrated."[16]

After the long, dangerous voyage, which had been full of privations, Maimonides landed in Akko with his father and brother David. At first, they remained in Akko, which had the largest Jewish community in Palestine, two hundred families. Rabbi Jephet, who was at their head, showed his hospitality to the noble refugees.

There was no Jewish community in Jerusalem. After conquering the Holy City, the Crusaders drove the Jews into the synagogue and set it on fire, so that the Jews perished in the flames. Since then, however, the Franks had come to realize that they needed the Jews and Moslems for their own economic prosperity. Thus, they permitted non-Christians to take part in economic life while maintaining their own national and religious structure. In the second half of the twelfth century, the situation of the Jews improved. They enjoyed almost unlimited civil freedom in the Kingdom of Jerusalem. Dealings between Jews and Christians grew more intimate. There were even family connections now. Several times, the Church found it necessary to warn against marriages between Christian men and Jewish women. There were also protests against summoning Jewish physicians to Christian families. Otherwise, the Jews engaged in crafts, commerce, and merchant shipping. The flourishing manufacture of glass was in their hands, as was dyeing. Indigo was produced in the valley of the Jordan; and along the coast of ancient Phoenicia, the famous purpura was still sought and processed into costly dyes.[17]

Jewish life in Palestine had not stopped altogether after the destruction of the Temple. There are old traditions which, because of their uninterrupted preservation in this country, may be viewed as authentic and reliable. Maimonides, hungry for knowledge, interested in the details of Jewish rites, investigated these customs, and his trust in the old traditions prompted him to make changes in his own practice. For instance, a scholar from Cordova, in a book on the Law, had taught a certain order for the four passages of the Pentateuch contained in the tephillin,* and the Western Jews had taken over that order. But, in Palestine, Maimonides learned the views of the famous geonim and found old Talmudic texts which, deviating from the Western books, yielded a different arrangement. Furthermore, the Jews of Palestine, who observed the commandment of the phylacteries with special zeal, had an oral tradition about the order of the four passages of the Pentateuch, a tradition going back to ancient times. And Maimonides thereupon made a change in his own tephillin.[18] This correction was a not unimportant event for this man, who devoted the best strength of his life to investigating, presenting, and interpreting the Jewish Law.

He studied the local purity rites. The North African Jews, under Arabic influence, so greatly exaggerated their observance of the cleanliness laws that Maimonides was repelled. But here in Palestine he found their conduct more moderate.[19] Nevertheless, for all his esteem, he did criticize the customs of the Palestinian Jews; for example, he saw these Jews avoided writing the Torah scrolls with indelible ink and even declared that a Torah scroll written with such ink was unsuitable. Maimonides called this decision a mistake.[20]

---

* The tephillin, or phylacteries: two small leather boxes used during morning prayers on weekdays, containing two scriptural passages from Deuteronomy and two from Exodus.—*Tr.*

He concentrated not only on the religious life; he attentively studied the flora of the country, just as he had done earlier in Morocco.[21] He was familiar with seven species of cedar. The cedar prescribed for the rites of the Red Heifer was, he felt, identical with the tree that was used for construction purposes in Maghreb. He noticed that this species was not to be found in Palestine. Likewise, he focused on architecture, to which he had always been open, and now, for the first time, he saw Occidental buildings.[22] He had a keen ear for the Jewish dialect of Palestine and, remarkably, he knew the local names for leek, rutabaga, and so forth.[23] Although he was here for only a short time, he took notice of the finest nuances.

We do not know whether Maimonides, during his sojourn in Palestine, his first time in a Christian state, had any personal dealings with Christians, like his relations with Moslems in Fez. His basic attitude toward non-Jews would not have posed any problem, especially since he was convinced "that God demands the heart, that things are to be judged according to the convictions of the heart; that is why the sages of truth, our teachers, say: The pious among the nations of the earth will participate in the world beyond if they know what is fit to be grasped of the knowledge of God, and if they live in accordance with the virtues."[24] It was permissible, he said, to inform Christians, but not Moslems, about the Biblical commandments; because the Moslems "dispute the revelational origin of the Torah." Anything we might teach them, they would reject. They have "confused notions and false assumptions and would misunderstand anything contrary to their point of view." Instruction would not teach them, it would merely contribute to their persecuting us even more; thus, instruction could spell our doom, "since we must live among them because of our sins."

Christians, on the other hand, recognize the authenticity

of the Biblical text in the form that we possess. But they misinterpret it, reading their own ideas into it. If they are suitably taught, perhaps we may convince them of the truth. That would by no means cause us trouble, "since in their doctrine they do not find any conflict with ours."[25] Thus, Maimonides had a clear concept of Christian teachings. However, the Christian reality he encountered in the Kingdom of Jerusalem was far removed from its origins because of the worship of images, the veneration of relics, and the growth of intolerance and superstition. Nevertheless, Maimonides saw the pure source long after his experiences in Palestine.

When the Crusaders conquered Jerusalem, they celebrated their victory with a dreadful slaughter in the square of the Temple. "The torrent of blood swelled up to the knees of the knights, up to the reins of the horses, and the corpses of the victims piled up like mountains." Many years later, Maimonides uttered a thought that obviously alluded to the Crusades. Scripture tells us that our patriarch Abraham chose Mount Moriah, and proclaimed the oneness of God from there. This place consecrated by Abraham was, according to Maimonides, also known to our teacher Moses. For Abraham had ordered that this place become a house of worship: "Here, he cast himself down, prayed, and spoke: Here, the future generations shall pray to the Lord." Now, although Moses knew this place of future holiness, he did not designate it in the Pentateuch, and the reason, Maimonides felt, was one of deep wisdom: the original inhabitants of this land would have conquered the place and defended it to the utmost if they had known that this was the most hallowed place on earth: they would have devastated and destroyed it. Above all, Moses feared that each of the twelve tribes of Israel would strive to make this place part of its legacy and to control it, and that could *lead to much conflict and quarreling* . . . Hence the commandment not to build the Temple until there was a king who alone was fit to order its construction.[26]

Maimonides may have hoped, like Judah Halevi[27] before him, to find refuge in this land, which was ruled by Christians. But there was no field for his abilities in the Palestine of that day. The insignificant and declining Jewish communities and the lack of educated men and educational institutions ultimately made him decide to leave.

The degeneracy of the immigrants, who were mostly driven not by religious enthusiasm but by pleasure and profit, infuriated even the Christian pilgrims, who had journeyed here in truly pious devotion and wanted to turn their backs on the kingdom as soon as possible. "According to Jacques de Vitry, the immigrants, chiefly from the West, consisted mainly of thieves, brigands, murderers, pirates, adulterers, drunkards, and gamblers, monks and nuns who had run away from their orders, wives who had deserted their husbands, and harlots: but in the Holy Land these people give in to their passions all the more licentiously the farther away they are from their homes and from supervision by their own."[28]

The port of Akko had the worst reputation. Maimonides could not remain in this country. "It is in the nature of man to orient himself in his character and actions according to his friends and companions and the practices of his compatriots. Hence, a man must associate with the righteous and always dwell with the wise, in order to learn from their ways of life. He must, however, stay aloof from the wicked, who walk in darkness, so that he will not learn from their actions. For whosoever frequents the wise becomes wise, but whosoever is a companion of the wicked will become wicked himself. If a man lives in a place whose customs are repugnant and whose inhabitants do not walk in the right path, he must migrate to a place whose inhabitants are pious and have good morals."[29]

Perhaps, during his sojourn in Palestine, he believed that conditions would be better in another country. But later on, when he expressed his thoughts about emigration, a dismal sense of resignation could be heard: "If, as in our time, all the lands one knows personally or by reputation are ruled by immorality, or if one cannot move to a land with good morals because of disease or the danger of war, then one must remain all by oneself, as it is written: 'He remains alone and is silent.' But if people are so bad that they want to force a man to be like them and take on their bad ways, then he must go into the wilderness, as it is written: Who giveth me a shelter in the desert, I would then forsake my people."[30]

The Maimon family resolved to go to Egypt, where a large number of Jews were living in prosperity. A few years earlier, it would not have been easy to travel from Palestine to Egypt, for Egypt considered the Christian neighbor an enemy. But, meanwhile, the new political constellation had brought a rapprochement and an alliance between the Islamic and the Christian country. In 1164, when Nureddin had sent an army into Egypt to reinstate an expelled vizier, the Egyptian government had appealed to the king of the Franks, courting his aid with the promise of submission. Amalric then marched into the land of the Nile as a "friend and ally."

This reversal had to be favorable for the new journey of the Maimons. But before leaving Palestine they wanted to visit the Holy Places.

In earlier times, Jews from neighboring countries had come to Jerusalem for the Holy Days. When the Arabs ruled Palestine, they did not prevent the Jews from living in Jerusalem and building a house of prayer and study. But when the Christians took control of the Holy Land, they erected their own place of worship on the site of the Temple, planted the cross, destroyed the Jewish house of prayer, and prohibited the Jews from setting foot in Jerusalem.[31] Now the situation had changed. And by *ca.* 1165 the Jewish globe-trotter Benjamin of Tudela reported that the Jews could again worship at the Western Wall of the Temple.

Maimonides, arriving in Akko on May 16, let the summer months, and even the High Holidays, pass by, without making a pilgrimage to Jerusalem. Perhaps he intended to wait until after the crush of Western pilgrims, who would flood Jerusalem from April through September.[32] In October 1165, on the 4th of Heshvan, Maimonides, together with his father and his brother, made his way to the city of the Temple. They were accompanied by Rabbi Jephet of Akko, who was familiar with conditions in the country. They chose a route through the desert and through the still forested countryside,[33] away from the open highway, probably to avoid being molested; for the roads were very unsafe,[34] especially for non-Christians: "Killing an infidel was regarded, under all circumstances, as a sacrifice to the Lord, and one could be certain that it would be pleasing to God." Christians even believed "that torturing an infidel to death would most surely glorify Christianity."[35] The Maimon family pushed on to Jerusalem in order to pray at the Wailing Wall. According to one tradition, the spirit of God has never left the Western Wall, even after the destruction of the Temple. And the Jews of that time called the area in front of this wall the "Gates of Mercy." The Jewish "community" of Jerusalem consisted of a mere four families. They lived at the end of the town, under the Tower of David. The Talmudic academy, whose renown had once extended as far as the Rhine, had long since been obliged to close its gates and transfer to Damascus.[36]

For three days Maimonides prayed at the "great holy place." He probably focused not only his religious devotion on the place; we can be certain that since the destruction of Jerusalem no man so thoroughly knew the archeology of the Temple as Maimonides.

From Jerusalem, they traveled to Hebron, where they prayed at the Tomb of the Patriarchs. Maimonides swore that he would observe the two days on which he had entered Jerusalem and Hebron as days of prayer and holidays. "God give me strength for everything and help me to fulfill my oaths, and just as I have prayed there on ruins, so may it be granted to me and to all Israel to see the Holy Land soon restored and lifted from its decay." Those are the closing words in Maimonides's account of the journey.[37]

From Jerusalem, one could reach Egypt by way of El Arish, Farania, Tanis, Damietta.[38] But one could also go by sea. In Palestine, Maimonides reports, voyagers used not only the small coastal ships but also larger vessels known as "Alexandrians" because they sailed to Alexandria.[39]

Since their destination, like that of many Jews fleeing from the West, was Alexandria, the Maimon family most likely chose the maritime route.

7

Fight against Assimilation

AFTER the flight from Morocco and the episode in the
Holy Land, Alexandria must have made a friendly
impression on Maimonides. It was a city of international
commerce, no longer the capital of Egypt, no longer the
second-largest city in the world, but still a big, beautiful
city. When Benjamin of Tudela visited Alexandria around
that time, he admired the lovely houses and palaces; the
wise layout of the city; the streets and avenues, which were
so straight "that one could see from one city gate to the
other, a distance of one league"; the wharf and the tower in
the harbor, with a "mirror" at the top of the tower
announcing the arrival of a boat twenty days away; the
lighthouse, which was visible one hundred leagues off to all
boats sailing toward Alexandria, so that they might not go
astray. From Christian Europe and southern Arabia, from
North Africa and India, the merchants came to the "trading
city of all nations," as Benjamin called it, where every
nation had its own storehouse. Here, in a population of
fifty thousand people, there were some three thousand
Jewish families,[1] of whom a Hebrew poet later said:
"Alexandria is the entranceway to the Orient. Here are
men of intelligence and understanding, who do many
charitable acts and love to fill empty hands."[2]

A few months after the Maimon family left Palestine, Maimonides went into mourning. His father had died. Rabbi Maimon's death aroused deep commiseration among the Jews of many lands. Countless letters of sympathy reached Maimonides from the Arabic West and from Christian countries, from places "that were months away from Egypt." Maimonides received these expressions of condolence not without a certain feeling of consolation. Rabbi Maimon, the head of the family, was resting in the "bond of eternal life."

Maimonides was approximately thirty-one years old. So far, he had never had to earn his own living. Now that his father was dead, he was faced with the question of a livelihood. The normal and natural solution would have been the rabbinate. A rabbi's income was certain. According to Maimonides, both individuals and communities were expected to donate specific sums, and attempts were made to convince them that they should maintain scholars, students, and others who studied the Torah and whose trade was the Torah. But it went against Maimonides's grain to use the Torah as a spade.[3] The notion that the communities were obligated to subsidize scholars in their studies was something he regarded as an "error, for neither the Torah nor the books of the later sages have any guiding principle, any indication to support this."

No one could demonstrate that the great teachers of the past "demanded money from people; they did not collect money for respected and distinguished academies, or for the exiles, or for their judges, or for those men who propagated the Torah, or for any important scholar or for anyone else among the people. Had Hillel asked for help, they would have filled his house with gold and precious stones, but he did not wish to take anything, he nourished himself from the proceeds of his work; he scorned donations for the sake of the Torah.

"It is said that a heavenly voice proclaimed about Rabbi Hanina ben Dosa: 'The whole world is fed because of the virtuousness of my son Hanina, and my son Hanina is satisfied with a measure of carob from one Friday to the next, and he never asks anything of anyone.' Karna was a judge in Palestine and a water carrier, and when litigants appeared before him, he said to them: 'Hire someone to carry the water for me or replace what I lose through the trial, then I will decide your case.' The Jews of that time were not so hardhearted as not to practice charity, and we do not find that even one of those poor teachers rebuked his contemporaries for not giving him wealth. But the poor rabbis were pious, they believed in truth, they believed in God and the teachings of Moses, through which man can partake of the afterlife; that is why they did not presume to exact money from people, because they realized that accepting money would desecrate the Name of God, and people might think that the Torah was like any other trade for earning a living. The man who believes this makes the Word of God despicable. Truly, people err when they dare to strike truth in the face and act against the clear and simple statements in the Bible."

In this pamphlet against payment for intellectual accomplishments, Maimonides endeavors to strengthen his argument with numerous quotations from the Talmudic writings. It may be assumed that this revolutionary opinion caused a good deal of protest. His only concession in this respect is that he would allow scholars "to give money to someone else to do business for them at his discretion. This person, if he likes, can return the entire profit to the scholars."[4]

That was how Maimonides attempted to build up his economic existence, and his brother David relieved him of material concerns. With a capital that the two brothers most likely inherited from their father, David began to deal in precious stones. Perhaps the Maimon family had already invested their property in jewels before leaving Spain, in order to protect themselves.

Maimonides saw this easing of his burden and this means of support as a blessing. "He engaged in commerce, and I lived in carefree indolence," he confesses from the perspective of loyal gratitude. Undisturbed, he was able to complete his commentary on the Mishnah, which he had worked on both aboard ship and during his inland travels. He prayed that God "protect me from errors." At the same time, he delved into the worldly sciences.[5]

Just a few years earlier, the great poet Judah Halevi had visited Egypt. In Spain, he had pined away for the land of the fathers and of hope. He left his town and journeyed to Erets Israel. En route, in Egypt, the head of the Jewish community and several other personalities invited him to stay; and then a wondrous change took place in the mind of the poet. Previously, he had regarded his secular songs, especially his love poems, as youthful sins and had resolved never to compose such verses again. But here in sunny Egypt he was overwhelmed by new experiences. "For an instant, the former minstrel of love appeared to be speaking with the voice of the penitent pilgrim. But once again he had an eye for the pleasures of this world, for the charms of the landscape, for the magic of human beauty. The man who had just previously been aglow with Zion, both in waking and in dreaming, now praised the daughters of the land, the power of their gazes, the triumph of their beauty. The white of their arms seemed so sparkling pure, so dazzling, that he could not understand how these arms, which did not let the eye rest upon them without scorching it or endure a gaze without blinding it, could stand the burden of useless trinkets, disfiguring adornment of bracelets. Indeed, these countenances radiated a beauty that demanded sacrifice! Anyone peering into this sun is struck, nay, destroyed!"[6]

How did thirty-year-old Maimonides react to the beauty of the people and the countryside? The philosopher, whose thinking, in its regal superiority, was above the things of this world, had too powerful a reasoning faculty to be intoxicated by the beauty of sensual appearances. He also lacked the "sacred egoism"[7] of the poetic soul. He was concerned with the teachings, with the nation, and he devoted himself to serving the spirit. Maimonides's accounts of his initial impressions in Egypt contain not a trace of any deep sensual emotion. His keen discernment quickly penetrated the fullness of life pulsating in this land; but the power of his mind was shown in his observing and judging, not in a surrender to outward appearance.

The advocate of the forced converts was anything but a hermit or homebody. He wrote and edited his great book and studied the conditions and customs, the peculiarities of the language and the mentality of Egyptian Jews, but also the flora of the Egyptian landscape. To some extent, he integrated his newly acquired knowledge into his commentary.

Alexandria soon had hard times to go through. The country had become a plaything at the mercy of Nureddin of Syria and Amalric, the king of the Crusaders. In 1167, Nureddin sent his troops to Egypt, and the young emir, Saladin, occupied Alexandria. Amalric, whose help was requested by the caliph, joined forces with the Egyptian military. They beleaguered the Syrian-held city for seventy-five days. "The immediate surroundings of the city were horribly devastated; all the trees were chopped down, all the fields burned, while a mighty siege tower and many catapults spread death and destruction in the city . . . Of course, the burgers, like any commercial population, were against the war, they were decimated by famine and pestilence, and the occupation forces themselves were weak; but Saladin kept up the spirits of his people with untiring encouragement and the promise of speedy help."[8] At last, the hostilities came to an end, and both the besiegers and the besieged left Alexandria. The legitimate government took over again and inflicted severe punishments on the compromised citizens of Alexandria, who, disapproving the alliance between the caliph and the infidel Christians, had supported the action of the Syrian Moslems.

Maimonides had little interest in the military conflicts; he merely kept working on his Mishnah commentary. It has not been handed down to us whether he suffered under the siege of Alexandria and the subsequent events in domestic politics. The affliction that lay ahead of him came from elsewhere.

The Jewish communities in Spain and Morocco were going under; in Palestine, only a few ruins were left, crumbling more and more and threatening to vanish altogether. Egypt lay in the ocean of distress like a happy island on which the Jews were permitted to believe and to reside. But here, too, conditions were by no means gratifying. The material prosperity and the prestige were only a shiny façade; the spiritual life of the Jews was utterly menaced. The lax observance of religious laws and the general ignorance had recently made a deep impact on a Jewish scholar from Byzantium: the Jews disdained the scholars and were horribly unlike the other communities in Israel. This observer blamed the deplorable state of affairs on the lack of educated rabbis and saw the cause as ignorance, not malice.[9]

Maimonides, who had gained a marvelously quick insight into the conditions of Egyptian Jewry, was dismayed to note the signs of religious decay. He detected the source of danger in the Karaites.

This Jewish sect, originating in the eighth century, was an independent branch, leading a completely separate existence from the trunk. Of the Jewish religion, they retained only the letters of the Torah; and theirs became a domain that was utterly alien to Judaism. But, while this sect was already declining in other countries, it kept gaining ground in Egypt and finally threatened to crush Jewish life. In dealing with the Arab government, the Karaites would present their secession from Judaism as a parallel to the position of the Shiites vis-à-vis the Sunnites, the orthodox in Islam. The Karaites thus evidently won the special goodwill of the Shiite Fatimites, who had been ruling Egypt since the tenth century. The Mohammedans also assumed that the Karaites were closer to Islam than to Talmudic rabbinical Judaism. Egypt had large, influential Karaite communities, and they made highly offensive attempts at wooing followers for their doctrines among the Jewish traditionalists. The propaganda had considerable success. Many Jews joined the politically favored Karaites. But even those who did not definitively convert fell prey to the influence of the Karaite teachings and began to neglect the Talmudic prescriptions.

The rabbis seemed powerless in the face of this assimilation. They could not even prevent mixed marriages between Jews and Karaites.[10] Only Maimonides tried to bring help against this breach. The first task was to determine the boundaries between Jews and Karaites. Around 1167, in Alexandria, a "God-fearing and learned man, who reverently honored the word and commandment of God," asked Maimonides how the Jews who were loyal to their tradition ought to behave toward the Karaites. Could they receive and return their visits, could they circumcise Karaite children and enjoy Karaite wine? Anyone knowing Maimonides's tendency toward isolating the Jews from the Karaites would expect a negative answer. But his recommendation, "according to what we have learned from Heaven," is that Jews should show the Karaites the honor due every human being, and act justly, peacefully, truthfully, and humbly towards them. This attitude is proper so long as the Karaites deal sincerely with the traditional Jews, "without twisting their mouths or using a vicious tongue," and so long as they refrain from denigrating contemporary Jewish authorities, "not to mention our holy teachers of the past, whose words we live by." We should then circumcise their children even on the Sabbath, bury their dead, and comfort their mourners. Since we must practice the commandment of brotherly love toward non-Jews, then how much more so toward the Karaites. We are allowed to enjoy their wine, for they are not idolaters. But if they desecrate the Holy Days and celebrate our festivals at other times which they have devised, a Jew faithful to his tradition should not visit them on those days.[11]

From the very start, Maimonides seems to have advocated a separation from the Karaites. And perhaps it was during his Alexandrian period that he gave his decision in response to a question: he said that the Karaites were not fit to take part in a minyan, the required quorum of ten for prayers in a congregation; nor could they be one of the three necessary for saying prayers at a meal. The philosopher explained his judgment by pointing out that the Karaites themselves do not recognize the Talmudic rule about this number, and thus they cannot fulfill that obligation.[12] The very fact that this problem was so important shows how far the social dealings between the two religious groups had gone in cultic matters, the true area of division. Maimonides disqualified the Karaites. Their expulsion from Jewish life had begun.

In his commentary on one of the most popularly read portions of the Mishnah, Maimonides made a statement that could only be intended as a defense against Karaite assimilation: "The tanna [Talmudic teacher] Antigonos once said: 'Do not be like the servants who serve the Lord for the sake of a reward, but be like the servants who serve the Lord out of love.' Antigonos had two disciples, Zadok and Boethos. When they heard what he said, they left him, saying one to the other: 'Lo, our teacher expressly says that for man there is neither a reward nor a punishment nor a hope for a coming life.' They abandoned Judaism, forsaking the doctrines, and each of them founded a sect. They claimed they did believe in the Torah and contested the oral tradition. That was how *corruptive sects like the Karaites in Egypt* were born. They began to take issue with the teachings and interpret Biblical verses as they liked, without relying on any authority, and they acted against the Word of God."[13]

This sharp offensive by a newly arrived young scholar against the old established and powerful Karaites aroused the anger of those he had attacked. The objectivity of his stance in dictating a radical segregation in religious matters but no break in social life could not protect him against the enmity of the Karaites. Maimonides was unable to remain in Alexandria.[14]

8

In Fostat

Fostat, today's old Cairo, was where Maimonides settled.[1] Because of the justice and peacefulness for which the inhabitants were renowned, he may have hoped to find the safety and quiet that he needed for finishing his commentary.

Decisive for the position of this city in Jewish life was that the nagid, recognized by the government as the official representative of the Jewish community, made his home in the neighboring residence of Cairo. The nagid, "the supreme head of the Jews," whose office topped a national self-administration, had a leading political position, like the patriarch in Palestine in former times or, in Maimonides's day, the exilarch in Baghdad. The nagid was in the service of the ruler, and he had leadership over all the Jewish communities in the empire of the Fatimites, which, before the invasion of the Crusaders, had also included Palestine. He appointed rabbis and cantors; he set up courts of law in all cities, and authorized these courts to pass verdicts and draw up documents by his authority. He also had jurisdiction as a judge, issued religious regulations and excommunications, and directed a Talmudic academy. The man who held this office was usually also court physician to the caliph. He was normally chosen from the rabbinical community, though he also had legal jurisdiction over Karaites and Samaritans.

The office of nagid, which had existed since the conquest of Egypt by the Fatimites, was created probably to counteract the influence of the exilarch residing in the hostile empire of Baghdad, whose authority was acknowledged by the Jews of all countries. Legend describes the origin of the nagid's office as follows: The caliph had married a princess from Baghdad. Upon coming to Egypt, she asked about the conditions of the Jews in her new homeland. She was very surprised to learn that the Jews here were not under the leadership of a man from the house of David. The caliph therefore summoned a man descended from David; this man came to Egypt, and the caliph granted him the rank of nagid as corresponding to that of the Babylonian exilarch. The subsequent holders of this position of honor were likewise chosen from the descendants of this house. If no worthy representative of such descent could be found, the office was given to a scholar who excelled in his personal qualities and his learning.

When Maimonides settled in Fostat, the nagidate was going through a crisis. In 1140, in Cairo, Judah Halevi still admired the noble Samuel, who was nagid at that time. It seemed to the poet as though "a reflection of Israel's past sovereignty were virtually shining at the threshold of the Holy Land."[2] In songs of praise and laudatory epistles, Halevi paid homage to the just and noble man and proclaimed in Biblical diction that he "furthered the welfare of his people and sought the peace of his brethren." But the rule of the Fatimites was decaying, the administration of the empire became corrupt, and the power lusts of ambitious generals caused frequent changes in the viziership. All these things endangered the nagid's position, and the political chaos naturally disrupted the life of the Jewish community.

With a bribe of one thousand drachmas, a man named Sutta obtained the position of nagid; and by means of denunciation, he forced the removal of Samuel, who was generally popular and highly esteemed.[3] This usurpation would have sufficed to make the people rebel against the interloper; moreover, his rule was altogether arbitrary. He called himself the Prince of Peace, but his actions proved the contrary. He began a reign of terror in the Jewish community, illegally acquiring a mass of property, and his judicial rulings shook the activities of the courts. He showed himself to be venal in the very first weeks of his administration; "the entire community suffered greatly from his mischief." The complaints of the people could no longer be overlooked, "their calls for help reached the ears of the caliph and were heard." Sutta was dismissed, and Samuel took office again. "His head hanging in shame, Sutta sadly went home, and he was the laughingstock of the city for many years. His wife and children lived in want and poverty and dressed in rags. For the Lord did not allow him to enjoy the wealth he had unjustly acquired; easy come, easy go."

Samuel died around 1160. The people lamented, and the poets composed lengthy elegies on the demise of their prince and Maecenas, who had suffered so much toward the end of his life. Sutta, however, felt that his time had come again. "To whom should the caliph pass on the dignity if not me? Now he will call me to the position!" He applied to see the sovereign; and, to ensure his favor, charged that the deceased nagid had left behind ten thousand pieces of gold. The caliph, whose treasury had shrunken, was delighted at the news, which, however, turned out to be slander, for investigations disproved this claim. The caliph lost his temper and said to Sutta: "You are never to look upon my face again. You will never again be permitted to come before me! A liar has no status in my eyes!" And Sutta's hopes were dashed. This episode discredited the nagid's office for a long time, and the Jews greatly regretted this circumstance.

In 1168, Maimonides completed his opus. To accompany its publication, he added a strange and—if you like—ironic note to the critics: "The burden I assumed was by no means light. Anyone who has a fair sense of judgment and a proper intelligence will realize that the goal I set myself was not one that could be completed soon. My heart was afflicted by the miseries of the time, by the fate of exile that God has brought upon us, by the constant expulsions and wanderings from one end of the world to the other. But perhaps this lot is a grace, for exile atones for sin.

"God knows that I composed the explanation for my treatise during my journeys, that I did many a scholarly compilation on shipboard during my ocean voyages.

"Furthermore, I also delved into other sciences throughout these years.

"I am discussing my circumstances rather prolixly only to justify my critics, in case anyone resents their criticisms. For criticizing is not an act of injustice, it is rewarded by Heaven. It is dear to me, for it is a divine craft.

"The situation I found myself in during these years also forced me to spend such a long time on the composition of this work."[4]

In another conclusion, he exhorted the reader: "Read my book over and over and reflect on it carefully. If your vanity should mislead you to believe that you understand the contents after one reading or even ten, then, by God, you have been misled to foolishness. You must not advance hastily in the perusal of this book. For I have not just written it down haphazardly, but only after long research and reflection."[5]

With a verse from Isaiah (40:29), he thankfully finished

his work: "He giveth power to the faint; and to them that
have no might He increased strength."

The author wanted his commentary to bring about a
renewal and improvement of study. The Talmud had sup-
planted the study of the Mishnah; Maimonides rebuked
even great Talmudic specialists for not being grounded in
the Mishnah. It was necessary to restore the Mishnah to its
lost position; that was why Maimonides had written his
commentary. But he seems to have had little success. Aside
from the introduction and the explication of *Ethics of the
Fathers*, the commentary was paid scant heed until com-
paratively recent times. Such a response was not in keeping
with its merits or the gap it fills. The publication of this
book should have stirred up the basic question of the
Mishnah's place in Jewish education; but this did not
happen. The publication neither caused offense nor aroused
admiration. It garnered respect for the author in a small
circle, but it did not even manage to make him a local
celebrity. Benjamin of Tudela was staying in Cairo at this
time, and when he listed the renowned men of that city,
he did not mention Maimonides.

The philosopher lacked the normal conditions for attaining public prestige. Authority could be achieved by way of
the house of study, mainly through a teaching position as a
gaon, or at least through the recommendation of a representative academy. However, Maimonides, who certainly
took the rank and the rulings of the academy directors
seriously,[6] did not follow this path. He did not let himself
be carried away by status or by any position of honor.
Pompous and pretentious titles, all in keeping with the style
of the period, were awarded even to men devoid of quality,
and Maimonides's good taste and dislike of such titles probably affected his attitude. But the true reason for not want-

ing to teach must have been more profound and fundamental.

Maimonides seems to have had no passion for immediate public instruction. His need to teach was fulfilled in written form, not in oral lecturing. He loved direct instruction, but apparently only to a single person, not to a group of listeners. He saw his special mission not in founding an academy but in writing books. Apparently his soul, given the thoughtful length of its inspirations, found expression in the silence of the written word, avoiding the haste, frailty, and sketchiness of speech.

He could not relate to free discourse, especially since a short, terse presentation was the most important thing to him. His goal was not to spin out a thought and let it swell to rhetorical breadth; he wanted to structure terse paragraphs. "If I were able to sum up the whole Talmud in one section, I would not use two sections."[7] Nor did he have to give up his propensity. His brother David ensured his independence from the authorities and the community, thus keeping him immune to slander and suspicion. Like Moses, Maimonides could have said in regard to his abstinence from pay and wages: "I have not even taken a donkey from any of them . . ."

A fortunate event ordained that the commentary be published by 1168, for in September of that year Fostat met with an unusual fate. The Fatimite empire stopped paying obligatory tributes to the king of the Crusaders, and Amalric, the former ally and comrade in arms, invaded Egypt in late October 1168. In his mind's eye, he saw himself as lord of the realm, carrying out the old plan of the Crusader policies, and in his confident mood of victory he distributed towns, terrains, and incomes of the still-to-be-conquered country to his loyal followers. He occupied Lower Egypt, struck down the inhabitants, plundered their houses, and marched on toward Fostat, threatening disaster and arousing horror throughout the land.

Cairo had fortifications and bulwarks, but Fostat was an open city. There was no possibility of defending it, yet capitulating would have meant sacrificing the entire country, since Fostat was a strategic point, dominating the access to Upper Egypt. The vizier ordered the inhabitants to quit Fostat immediately and go to Cairo after setting their houses on fire. "The people surged and thronged," writes an Arabic author, "as though they were hurrying from their graves to the place of resurrection; the father was heedless of his children, one brother ignored the other. Many saved only their bare lives, for renting a horse to travel from Fostat to Cairo cost over ten dinars, and a camel as much as twenty dinars."[8] On November 22, 1168, the slaves, at the vizier's bidding, set fire to the city. Twenty thousand bottles of petroleum were distributed throughout Fostat, ten thousand fuses were lit. The conflagration lasted fifty-four days.

But not even a burning Fostat could induce Amalric to retreat. He set up camp outside Cairo. Meanwhile, the caliph had sent the hair of his wives to Nureddin of Syria, telling him: "This is the hair of the wives in my castle, they beg you to free them from the enemy!" Thereupon, Nureddin dispatched a well-equipped unit led by a courageous and experienced commander. When Amalric learned this, he began to retreat.

The rescuers were exuberantly welcomed. Nureddin's commander and man of confidence was made vizier, but he died a short time later. Saladin, his nephew, took over the office in March 1169, and his vizierate launched a new era in the history of Egypt.

Fostat quickly recovered. The fire had left a few streets unscathed, and shortly after Amalric's retreat, the government allowed the inhabitants to go back to the charred city.

"In the year 1169, pestilence and soaring prices destroyed the incipient prosperity"; but then came another period of economic flourishing. "Of course, the city is mournful, the city gates and many houses have decayed, the streets are narrow and filthy, the mosque is untended and serves as a passageway." But the well-traveled man who recorded this impression had never laid eyes on such a wealth of ships and goods as in this port on the Nile.[9] As before, commerce and industry still had their headquarters in Fostat, and all wares had to go through Fostat before reaching the capital, Cairo.

Saladin, who ruled officially on behalf of the powerless Fatimite caliph, was actually Nureddin's governor in Egypt. His was a delicate position as vizier to the Shiite caliph and also as implementer of the policies of Syria's orthodox Sunnite king. At first, the names of both sovereigns were included in the Friday prayers at the mosques. But Saladin, who had himself studied theology with an orthodox orientation, strove to destroy the Shiite caliphate. His ambitious plan of establishing an independent monarchy could best be carried out through a religious revolution.

Ever since Mohammed's death, the choice of successor to lead the faithful had always aroused the keen interest of the Islamic community. The Shiites, who recognized the descendants of Ali and Fatima (Mohammed's daughter) as having the rights of succession, saw the regime of any other dynasty as a hindrance to the "realization of an empire pleasing to God." They opposed the caliph who was appointed by the adversary party of the Sunnites, and they regarded his rule as usurpation. "Instead of a caliph placed on the throne by human beings, they recognize, as the only legitimate secular and spiritual leader of Islam the Imam, who is given this right solely by divine command and determination; this name, more suitable to the religious dignity of the office, is what they prefer to call their recognized leader, who descends directly from the Prophet . . . Seldom do they manage to unfurl the banner of the Imam pretender; and even then their struggle, hopeless from the very outset, is inevitably defeated. They have to resign themselves, hoping that God will bring about a just change in public conditions. Submitting outwardly, they inwardly render homage to the Imam pretender, preparing for his victory with secret propaganda."[10] In underground organizations they carried on "a propaganda of agitation rather than of combat."

The empire of the Fatimites was established in 909 on the basis of such secret intrigues; it was one of the few successful attempts by the Shiites at organizing themselves as a state religion. Egypt did have a powerful Shiite movement, but the majority of the population was orthodox. They were upset when the Fatimites brought in Shiism as the only valid religious form and remained loyal to their orthodoxy. When the orthodox caliph was publicly cursed, the masses were indignant.

During the administration of the Fatimites, the masses privately yearned for the orthodox creed.[11] When Saladin, who managed to gain the confidence of the people very quickly, restored the Sunnite rites to the country at the very start of his rule, this ecclesiastical revolution met with little resistance. In 1171, the last Fatimite died; and Saladin, as sultan and founder of the Ayyubite dynasty, was now officially the absolute monarch of Egypt. He had no difficulty taking possession of the caliph's palace. By generously handing out the treasures, which supposedly included a library of two million volumes, he bound his followers and comrades in arms even closer to himself.[12]

While this political and religious upheaval took place in Cairo, Maimonides was living in nearby Fostat. A marriage document issued in 1171 ends with the following formula:

"With the permission of our Lord Moses, the great Rabbi in Israel." Presumably, at this time, Maimonides held the honorary office of rabbi in Fostat.[18]

After trying to halt the danger from outside (the influence of the sect of Karaites), he began to reform from within. His first task, so far as we know, was to unify and improve the prayer practices. The resistance Maimonides aroused by this undertaking was to be disastrous for him. First of all, he wanted to eliminate the split among the Jews of Cairo. The capital had a Jewish community of seven thousand families, most of whom probably lived in Fostat, the oldest part, and were divided into two groups, known as the Babylonians and the Palestinians. While the Babylonians apportioned the Sabbath readings of the Torah in such a way that it took a year to go through the entire text, the Palestinians had a three-year cycle. Each group had its own synagogues, and aside from Simchat Torah and the Feast of Weeks, there was no ritual sharing between them. The well-known Babylonian/Palestinian antagonism was not restricted to synagogal matters.

The contrasts of practices within the Jewish community struck Maimonides as unseemly. Only one of the two kinds of ritual could be suitable. He was guided not only by logical but also by aesthetic reasons; as a Spanish Jew accustomed to a unified liturgy on the basis of Amram's order of prayers, he evidently regarded the discrepancy between ritual procedures as inconstant and inconsistent. The idiosyncrasies of the members of a congregation might be based on the power of habit. Nor was devotion to traditional customs for the sake of local or familial sentiments alien to Maimonides, but the logic of the Law and his liberal thinking had to exclude the indolence of habit.

With his peculiar blend of conservative humility and revolutionary daring, he tried to improve other aspects of synagogal life. It was customary in the synagogue to have the silent prayer of the congregation followed by the cantor's repetition aloud. Maimonides observed that during the repetition, instead of listening in respectful devotion, they stood around as though compelled or else chatted with one another, on the assumption that they had done their duty with the silent prayer. Maimonides was offended by this laxity, and he felt that the indifference of the congregation during the cantor's delivery showed disdain for the honor of the Lord. He therefore decreed that the service should commence with the cantor's recitation. The silent prayer could take place simultaneously, but not, as was normal, beforehand.

The reform that he dared to introduce by eliminating the voiced repetition, despite the Talmudic order of prayers, was recognized by contemporary scholars and accepted throughout Egypt. "No one in the land resisted the ordinance, which deviated from the Talmudic regulations. No one accused [Maimonides] of betraying tradition, even though this ordinance struck down a deep-rooted custom. There was neither envy nor argument, there was no basic rejection either because of ignorance or because of fanaticism," goes a later account.[14] But when Maimonides first set about unifying the rites, he naturally faced stiff opposition from the nagid.

The political upheaval that led to a change of dynasty gave the former nagid, Sutta, another opportunity to fish in troubled waters. Saladin needed money for his numerous military campaigns; and finally, against a yearly payment of two hundred dinars, the new ruler restored Sutta to the position of nagid. Sutta once more oppressed the Jews and tormented his opponents with his resentment, which he had been nourishing during seven years of impotence and humiliation.

Was it possible to resist the new nagid? After taking power, Saladin had thoroughly altered many institutions because of the change in political and religious life. Any opposition to change could be misconstrued as disloyalty toward the new ruler. One can readily see that in such a situation of political hypersensitivity, even the most insignificant measures could be misinterpreted as fundamental actions of state. Opposition to a nagid installed by the vizier could be interpreted as high treason.

9

Educational Reform

MAIMONIDES's *Commentary on the Mishnah* has the following structure: the selected introductions, loosely written, contrast sharply with the terse *explications des textes* of the Mishnah. One perceives in the contents several divergent tendencies, as if the author were trying to attain conflicting goals. The strictly explanatory parts contain his conclusions about relevant interpretations, as well as some independent observations, but the author often introduces digressions whose connection with the Mishnah is extremely slight, so that they appear in the work almost as foreign matter.

This twofold character reveals a divergence between the author's way of thinking and the nature of his task, yet the force of his own original thinking cannot always be restrained and, on occasion, breaks through. These conflicting aspects reveal the author's uneasiness about the book's form; the appendices attached to the text sometimes go beyond its framework. Maimonides, with his scrupulous concern for form, had to cope here with a disturbing and complicated problem: how to find a satisfactory style of presentation.

He indicates in the work itself several literary projects which he intended to develop, but he could not proceed with them until the Mishnah commentary was finished. In considering the special results he achieved in the work, the group of systematic introductions is the most surprising. These reveal the author's originality and intellectual strength far more intensely than the explanatory parts dealing with the Mishnah text. It could be assumed that Maimonides would now finally conclude his summary on the Talmud, which he had put aside half-done for the sake of the Mishnah. It was utterly necessary and even urgent at that time to have a commentary on the Talmud; only the knowledgeable hand of an interpreter could guide the reader amid its obscurities and unintelligibilities.[1] Very few Jews could find their bearings in this fundamental work of the Jewish teachings, on which the inner and outer life of Judaism was based. A commentary on the Talmud would also have been a natural continuation of the commentary on the Mishnah. The skill and experience that Maimonides had acquired from his first great work could be developed and expanded. He was now faced with the alternative of beginning a systematization or a commentary. In this dilemma, he decided on the former; it had become clear to him that he was a codifier, not a commentator.

The evolution of Jewish literature always circled rather peculiarly around a central work that remained the focus of intellectual labor for whole eras. In the post-Biblical period, the Scriptures were the object of study and research. For centuries, nearly all intellectual activity concentrated on the Biblical word. At the beginning of the third century, the results of investigation and exegesis were selectively summed up in the Mishnah. Rabbi Judah ha-Nasi, the redactor of the Mishnah, shaped the gigantic mass of traditional teachings into a unified and self-sufficient whole. The contents of these teachings had mostly been handed down as explanations for individual Biblical verses; Rabbi

Judah detached them from their link to the Biblical text and let them crystallize as standards and decisions. Commentary was replaced by compendium. For the practice of study and life, an authoritative book of laws had been created.

The course of further development was mapped out by this compendium. The Talmud, both the Palestinian and the Babylonian, had been developing for centuries as a commentary on the Mishnah. The wealth of new opinions and insights was viewed and arranged as a continuation of the Mishnah. In the fifth century, the development of the Talmud came to a close. Even in its definitive redaction, it kept the form of an appendix to the Mishnah. Its peculiar character was that of a protocol on the controversies and discussions that took place at the academies but seldom led to any decisions. This form deviated more and more conspicuously from the structure of a systematic compendium. The Talmud records an entire and varied culture, as well as the teachings of several thousand personalities. It is grand in its dimensions, wide-ranging in its contents, and intoxicating in its dynamic presentation. It quickly became obvious, however, that the common people were not up to this lofty school. Without living contact with learned scholars, a study of the Talmud was impossible. But this sort of teaching and learning was tiresome. In order to follow the many intellectual directions of the individual teachers, one had to have a correspondingly flexible faculty of thought. Hence, very few people delved into the Talmud.

To make this work useful for practical life, the teachers of the post-Talmudic age incessantly focused on interpreting the individual parts. An enormous number of inquiries reached the geonim, the scholars of Babylon, from all countries of the Diaspora. And all these questions required explanations and elucidations for individual passages in the Talmud. Only rarely would Jews have the ability to study the work on their own and to reach decisions on the basis of their own reading. The decisions of the geonim, as recorded in their answers, were of cardinal importance for practice. Collections of such opinions served judges, rabbis, and teachers virtually as a textbook for instruction and practical decision-making. However, the inadequacy of this method became more and more apparent in the course of time. The randomness of their origins, the improvisational nature of their formulations, and the unreliability of their copyists made these opinions highly imperfect. Through the centuries, countless treatises and compendiums had emerged from these, one of the most outstanding being the magnificent Talmudic anthology by Rabbi Isaac Alfasi of Fez. But they were all experiments that were to prepare for a huge achievement.

"Since sufferings now dominate, the times are gloomy and anguished, the wisdom of the wise is lost, and the intelligence of the intelligent is gone, the explanations, treatises, and opinions that the geonim composed and considered universally understandable are intelligible to very few people these days—not to mention the texts themselves, the Babylonian and the Palestinian Talmud, *Sifra*, *Sifre*, and *Tosefta*. For the comprehension of this work presumes a vast intellectual capacity, a wise soul, and a great deal of time. Only when these conditions are met, can one find the right way through the questions of what is forbidden and permitted, and the other subjects of the teachings."[2] Maimonides sadly notes "that the people are without a book of Law in which they could find established tenets that are not mixed in with controversies and errors." He therefore makes up his mind, as he says, "to be zealous in God's service."[3]

With sublime pathos, Maimonides reports how he carried out the plans maturing within him. "I have shaken the dust from my cloak, and with the help of God, praised be He,

I have perused all works in order to compile the conclusions of what is permitted and not permitted, what is clean and unclean, and the other laws of the Torah, in a clear language and terse brevity, so that the oral law may be familiar: on the lips of all, without any questions and answers, without any difference of opinion, in lucidly unequivocal words, according to the standard derived from the works and commentaries that have appeared since the time of Rabbi Judah the Holy."[4]

Maimonides reflects: "If a man writes a book about the Torah or about some science, then, whether he is one of the ancient pagans who were masters of the sciences, or a physician, he will choose one of two forms of presentation: a systematic summing-up or an appended elucidation; the former is carried out as an independent work, a codex, the latter as a commentary. An independent work offers solid tenets, with no objections or justifications and no demonstrations, such as Rabbi Judah the Holy did in the Mishnah. A commentary, on the other hand, along with fixed tenets, also cites the possible arguments against them and the refutations, as well as the objection to each thesis and the proof that this is true and that false, this evident and that not evident. Such is the procedure of the Talmud, for the Talmud is a commentary on the Mishnah." Maimonides's goal was the form of an independent presentation. He decided on the "method of the Mishnah."[5]

For the sake of overall unity, the introductions in his Mishnah commentary ignore a practice common to Jewish literature: they omit the sources from which the individual tenets were drawn, as well as the names of the Talmudic teachers whose opinions he repeated. Alluding to this practice when he began to tackle his great plan, Maimonides wrote:

"As is my habit, I intend not to mention the controversial and refuted opinions in this work and to record only the

decisions that have been made laws, so that this collection
will contain all the religious rules coming from our teacher
Moses as well as those that we need in the time of exile and
those that we do not need. It therefore struck me as
appropriate to leave out the sources and demonstrations
that mention the carriers of the traditions; thus I will not
add to each individual utterance that these are the words of
so and so, or so and so says such and such. Instead, I want
my collection first to list all the teachings of the Mishnah
and the Talmud in full by pointing out that all the precepts
of the Torah that form the oral doctrine are handed down
by so and so, who has them from so and so, all the way back
to Ezra and our teacher Moses. Together with every person
who has handed down the teachings, however, I want to
name the renowned people who worked with him and
taught traditions like his; all this, in order to be as brief as
possible . . ."[6]

"After concentrating my thoughts on this goal, I reflected
on what form and fashion this collection of laws should
have, whether I should follow the Mishnah and divide
accordingly, or undertake a different kind of division and
bring some things up earlier or later, depending on whether
I feel that this or that is appropriate and most readily facili-
tates instruction. Consequently, I found that the division
would be most practical if the treatises of the Mishnah were
replaced by sections, so that there would be a section on the
tabernacle, a section on prayer thongs, a section on the
mezuzah, a section on the fringes, and so forth; I will then
subdivide each section into chapters and paragraphs, as the
Mishnah does; thus, for instance, the section on the prayer
thongs will contain chapter 1, chapter 2, chapters 3 and 4,
each of which will then be subdivided into individual paragraphs, so that every reader will retain it in his memory
without difficulty."

He decided "that the treatment of a regulation, com-

mandment, or prohibition will not be spread out over two
sections; instead, every necessary separation will be made
by means of a division within the chapter. Furthermore, a
section will cover several regulations in case they have some
common relationship, or in case several precepts have the
same purpose."

For the sake of clarity and completeness, he assembled
all the *shalts* and *shalt nots* in order to place them at the
beginning of his work. It is significant to note what difficulties he complains of in this enterprise: he cannot rely on
previous works. "God, who is, after all, a credible witness,
knows that our misfortune lies heavy on my heart whenever
I reflect that they [i.e., previous works] include things
which, as one can see at first sight, should not be included,
and that one follows the other without examination; and
we convince ourselves of the inevitable fulfillment of
God's threat upon us: You will see each thing like the
words of a sealed book that one gives someone who under-
stands a book, with the words: 'Read this!' He, however,
says: 'I cannot, for it is sealed.' And whenever I hear the
countless *Asharot*[7] [hear ye] that have been penned in our
land of Andalusia, I am overcome with grief at seeing how
well known and widespread these poems are. Of course, one
cannot fault the authors, who were poets, after all, and not
scholars; for what they had to achieve in art, namely in-
gratiating felicity of expression and beauty of versification,
—this they achieved utterly. But in the verses they have thus
constructed," they are like the inadequate scholarly stereo-
types. "This is the wisdom of the most educated people in
our times, that they judge the truth of a statement not by
its content but by whether it accords with the statement of
a predecessor, without, however, any proof of the earlier
statement. This may shed light on how things stand with
the great masses."

Maimonides sets up fourteen rules as principles for counting the laws; and he presents the 613 commandments and prohibitions thus derived from the Torah in an overview that is as exact as it is concise. This *Book of Commandments* was completed shortly after 1170.

If we compare his systematic overview of the arrangement of the Codex with the completed work, we may speculate about his compositional procedure. In formal terms, he took new routes. His precursors, who had tried to systematize the contents of the laws, generally followed a traditional form in their arrangement: the sequence in the Bible or in the Talmud. But, given his original sense of form, Maimonides could not go along with a stereotype. He could not even take over the structure of the Mishnah, in which, for instance, the pertinent and nonpertinent laws are often treated side by side.

Maimonides set up 613 compartments, which he arranged into eighty-three sections and fourteen books. The material he had to cope with was enormous and tremendously complicated as well. He had to gather all the rules, regulations, laws, special decisions, local institutions, customs, establishments, and standards and fit them into the "compartments" of the system. In absolute loyalty to the Jewish tradition, Maimonides followed the Talmud strictly and consistently: he regarded each of its decisions as a law. If, as was usually the case, the questions were undecided, he made the decision himself. That, and not the activity of collecting, was his main accomplishment.

The principles and methods he employed with meticulous consistency in his decisions were so lofty in their thinking that they make the heads of scholars whirl in subsequent centuries down to our own day. Maimonides distinguished between binding Halakhic and nonbinding Haggadic elements in the Talmud. He therefore took a very liberal position on any views the Talmudic teachers had developed outside the religion even if he could not approve of them in scholarly terms. But he did take in any unequivocally sanctioned regulations that derived from such views. A tactful remark hints at the relativity of the premises for these regulations. The nobility of his conservative mind and the purity of his critical attitude are expressed equally in such cases. The resulting balance of independence and fidelity, of originality and authority, is a work of intellectual art. He strives "to bring all or most laws" closer to understanding,[8] by also presenting, as far as possible, their ethical or religious motives; so that the result is not a dry collection of paragraphs, but virtually an organism whose meaning pulsates through all its parts.

Philology was not the forte of this masterful stylist.[9] But he did make thorough textual studies; and before making any decision, he compared numerous manuscripts of the Talmud, which frequently diverged in essential points. He thereby ascertained over and over again that errors, creeping into certain copies, had misled major legal scholars, including the geonim.[10] In Egypt, he succeeded in obtaining a seventh-century Talmud written on parchment, and the readings of this manuscript were apparently authoritative for him.[11]

Out of scholarly objectivity, for which every area of the Halakha is equally important no matter what its relevance, Maimonides also treats laws that had been inapplicable since the destruction of the Temple. As early as in his Mishnah commentary, he complains: "No one asks or investigates, no one is interested in these laws, so that in this area the great scholar is on the same footing as an ignoramus."[12] He thereby follows Rabbi Judah ha-Nasi, who paid as much heed to these materials as to the applicable laws; the later scholars, in contrast, overlooked these disciplines. Perhaps one reason why Maimonides respects the totality of the Law is the Messianic hope that it will soon be possible to apply that totality.

He extended the borders even further. The Talmudic writings treat botany next to ethics, medicine next to sacrificial laws. No distinction is made between religious and profane thinking. This unity vanishes from subsequent literature. The chasm between the secular and the spiritual grows deeper and deeper. In a work on ritual precepts, it becomes unthinkable to treat secular science. But Maimonides sees that many questions about religious life can be answered only with the aid of the general sciences. Thus, the investigation of the calendar, for instance, requires astronomical reckonings. So that one need not "do research in alien books for questions of the Jewish Law,"[13] he adds a presentation of the auxiliary sciences: "No path in the paths of teachings must be left out." The religious character is what unifies the work; metaphysics, ethics, dietetics, and physics are absorbed into the rhythm of worship, and the universality of knowledge permeates the totality of the Law.

At the same time that Gothic architects in the North were capturing their mystical passion in the stone shapes of the cathedrals, a man in Fostat was driven by a titanic passion into the architecture of the spiritual. From the chaos of rules and standards, he took the material, sentence by sentence, for the gigantic structure of doctrines under whose roof the world of Judaism was to find its place. In northern France and western Germany, the Tosaphists were constructing their intricate discussions of the Talmud with arches, artful figures, flourishes, and adornments. But the man erecting his colossal structure in Fostat worked without flourishes and without arabesques, he created a self-contained whole with the simplicity and precise order of straight lines, with the lucidity and transparency of the southern sky. What normally took a score of architects to do, he did alone. The equilibrium of his soul permeates the style of this work, which was written in the confines of a small house in old Cairo, a cave. Through the tens of thousands of sentences, each line shows harmony, every phrase is concordant with every other part of the work—in form and content. Every part fits organically into the whole and has its own distinct, complete shape. The harmony of composition is preserved in the utmost economy of words and ideas.

Maimonides was aware that he was writing a *definitive* book. The omission of the customary footnotes found in scholarly literature is correlative with this awareness. Maimonides did not want to convince, he wanted to be conclusive.

He had a reformative goal in mind: "that no one will need any other aid for getting to know the Jewish Law, since this work will be a complete collection of all institutions, customs, and rules from Moses down to the termination of the Talmud, including the later explanations by the geonim." He therefore gave the Codex the proud Biblical title *Mishneh Torah*—i.e., "repetition of the Law (Deuteronomy)"—"for if someone studies first the Scriptures and then the Codex, he will know all the teachings of oral tradition and will not have to consult any other work."[14]

Like Rabbi Judah ha-Nasi, his aim was decision, and he skipped discussion. In contrast to the analytical investigation almost exclusively practiced in Talmudic scholarship, he devoted himself utterly to synthesis. He did not care for closely reasoned debates, he disliked controversy and hairsplitting. He wanted his Codex "to smooth the way for students and to remove the obstacles so that their understanding will not be fatigued by excessive discussion."[15]

In the Talmudic academies, "theory for theory's sake" was the pedagogical policy. Study did not focus on decision, which was important for practice; the students were oriented to theory instead. The ideas and thoughts of the Talmud exerted a powerful suggestiveness on the students, arousing an unprecedented devotion of the intellect. They studied not only with the mind but also with all the resources of the imagination. They absorbed the motifs of Talmudic thinking with all their twists and turns, and all this left the students in a state of excitement. Intricate constructions were the result of their thought processes; it was a matter of "thought and imagination," a consequence of spiritual arousal.

Maimonides wanted to reform education and methods of thought, but in this one respect only, for in practice he showed great respect for the authority of Talmudic decisions which, in his opinion, were accepted by all Jewish communities and were therefore binding. This educational reform—an aim that emerged clearly in the introduction to this work he wrote in 1177—was a return to the style and thinking of the Mishnah. The difference between the Mishnah and the Talmud was obvious to him by the time he began working on the Mishnah commentary. His guiding principle was to go back to the Mishnah in scholarly terms. He explicitly states that he composed his Codex according to the "method and language of the Mishnah," and he presents a detailed characterization of his method.[16] Even the title he selects makes clear what his model is, as does his refusal to justify individual decisions, his wish to examine nonrelevant laws, and many other elements.

A change in the style of Jewish thinking, a breakthrough to a new way of thinking were actualized in Maimonides. In studying the Talmud, he shut out his inventive imagination. He wanted to clarify, not expand; sum up, not continue; offer an overview, not a conjecture.

Maimonides rejected the elaborate thinking that loses itself in the uncontrollable and endless effects of speculative intoxication; he rejected the tendency toward intricacy, complexity, and complication. The slender trunk of his thought grew like a palm tree, straight and taut; the branches and twigs were symmetrical and articulated. The tree withstood the tempests of dialectics. It regarded the rank underbrush and entanglement as deadly, and it rejected the acumen and dialectics of Arab philosophers, such as the Mu'tazilites. Maimonides always took the shortest path of thought, he avoided breakneck leaps, the dizzying rapture of hairsplitting conjectures; his work was guided by plain, simple reasoning, by the pride of fundamental thinking. His mode of thinking would have managed to find acceptance, had he created an original work. But was it possible to tame the surging and mightily heaving ocean of the Talmud? What skills and methods were necessary to accomplish this?

Maimonides was ruled by a passion for discrimination and clarification. He saddled himself with jurisdiction over all the writings, over the intellectual history of many centuries. In order to steer the manifold and divergent movements of more than a millennium into a single road, it required the highest degree of control over ideas and concepts, the utmost faculty for evaluation, for putting order into confusion, and for the sharpest simultaneity of thought. It was a unique case in history of one man daring to capture the entirety of Jewish knowledge in a single creation. In the thousand years since Rabbi Judah ha-Nasi, the variety of intellectual forms and themes had widened their dimensions and enriched their contents, but this accomplishment consisted of analytical work, individual research and interpretation. All efforts at synthesis got stuck in one fragment, one sector of the whole. Attempts to capture the totality always failed: Rabbi Judah ha-Nasi's achievement remained out of reach. The rhythm of Jewish intellectual history, which seems to follow a law of alternating synthesis and analysis, had come to a halt. Systematic thinking reemerged only in Maimonides.

The nation's home was the Talmud. Anyone reading it had intercourse with the generations, with the academies, with the people. It contained and preserved the breadth of growth, the movement of tradition. Maimonides, for whom the Talmudic teachers were "the holy leaders," took in the theoretical opinions, but left out the concrete circumstances, the promptings and processes of forming judgments, and the names of the disputants and the pronouncers of decisions. Here lies the inherent defect of his codification: instead of the process, the concept; instead of the case, the law; instead of the people, the matter; instead of history, theory; instead of the living atmosphere, the anonymous authority; instead of the situation, the abstraction.

For ten long years, day and night, Maimonides labored, gathering the scattered material which, as he said, "lay confused and concealed among hills and mountains." The work that his decade of effort saved future generations can be measured only in astronomical figures. And the dignity of this labor is shown in that it takes its stand for all time as a much-admired edifice next to the Talmud, the fortress of Jewish literature.

"The night after he finished his work, he dreamed that he saw his father Maimon cross the threshold of the room; another man was with him. Rabbi Maimon pointed to the stranger and said: 'This is our teacher Moses, the son of Amram.' Maimonides took fright, but Moses spoke: 'I am come to see what thou hast done.' After looking at the work, he said: 'May thy strength increase!'" Thus goes the legend.

The Codex was multiplied book by book by professional copyists. And it was purchased and carried to all parts of the world by Jews who visited Egypt from many countries selling wood and metal and buying spices and gems. The Codex soon made triumphant progress throughout the Jewish Diaspora. It reached Palestine, Syria, Arabia, and

Babylonia; it came to North Africa, Spain, the South of France, and Italy. And it conquered the hearts of the scholars, the students, the rabbis, and the judges. It soon gained admission to the academies and courts of law, to private cabinets and public houses of study. It became a textbook for students, a compendium for judges, and a reference work for all Jews who were thirsty for knowledge. Many communities made it their book of Laws. The work also spread abroad the name of Moses ben Maimon, the regal sound of which echoed to the farthest hamlets in distant countries, inspiring awe. The good tidings entered North Africa and Yemen as a new impetus to increase the admiration already there; and, like the legend of the inconceivable treasures of the faraway East, his reputation penetrated Christian lands, which as yet scarcely knew of Maimonides's existence: "The light of Exile" lived in Fostat!

"Truly we have not heard, nor have our forebears reported, that such a work as this has been written since the completion of the Talmud! From one end of the inhabited earth to the other, there is no man who could accomplish a work with such form and perfection," said Aaron ben Meshullam of Lunel. And the scholar Benveniste writes: "Before the work reached Spain, the study of Alfasi, and even more so of the Talmud, was so difficult for the Jewish inhabitants that they were dependent on the rabbi's pronouncements; for they could not find their bearings in trying to determine the outcome of the rambling discussion. But when they laid hands on the Codex of Maimonides, which was accessible to them because of its intelligible language, and when they admired its luminous order, and particularly when they perceived its truth and profound ethics, their eyes were opened to its vast significance. Each Jew made his own copy, their minds were absorbed in it: young and old gathered to take in the contents. Now there are many who know the Law and, in case of litigation, they are able to form their own verdicts and check the judge's decision."[17]

The incomparable success did not astonish Maimonides. He was quite aware of the paramount importance of his epoch-making achievement, and he had anticipated its impact; the triumph was a confirmation and not a surprise. The admiration expressed by his contemporaries was a reflection of the unparalleled effort of composing the work.

Maimonides gave his *Mishneh Torah* to the public like a monarch who proclaims a constitution for his people in accord with the sources of tradition. Not since time immemorial had the word of an individual attained such power among Jews.

10

Messianic Yearning

IN Egypt, the Jews lived in peace and calm. Nevertheless, Maimonides felt the full bitterness of the persecutions in the rest of the Mohammedan world.[1] He knew—indeed, from personal experience—that the Arabs were sorely oppressing Israel, who lived scattered among them, that they tried to demean and abuse his people. And Maimonides thought: There has never been a nation that acted more hateful toward us, that strove so hard to insult and humiliate us. "Like a deaf man who does not hear, like a mute who does not open his lips," the Jews bore the yoke and the slanders, whose weight exceeded the limits of human forbearance. "We endure all suffering and disgrace in accordance with the Biblical verse: 'To the smiters did I give my neck, to the ruffians both my cheeks, nor did I conceal my countenance from insult and injury.' And yet we cannot save ourselves from their rancor and wantonness. We wish peace and friendship with them, and they wish our shame and destruction. If we speak of peace, they prime themselves for war."

Maimonides delved into the meaning and basis of the suppressions, he tried to fathom the chief historical motives. His outline of an interpretation of history stems from that time. The reason why other nations have fought against

Judaism is, so he feels, the desire to make Israel abandon its faith. This has been a religious war, from Amalek down to the recent leaders of the Shiite sect.

"God," said Maimonides, "has chosen us among all nations not because *we* are better but because *He* is good, not because we surpass other nations in number—we are the smallest of the nations—but because he loves us and wishes to keep the covenant that he swore to the patriarchs. His gift to us of the perfect tenets and teachings has aroused the envy of the pagans in all times. The kings who wanted to wage war against the Lord and could not do so have striven to vent their hatred upon us. They hated us not for our sake but for the divine that dwells in our midst. Since the Torah was awarded to us, hardly a period has gone by without an attempt by a heathen king to compel us, by force of arms, to destroy our teachings. Amalek and Sisera, Sennacherib and Nebuchadnezzar, and many others form the line of those who sought to break the divine structure by violence. A different method was used by the more cunning and civilized of the heathens; for instance, the Romans, Persians, and Greeks, who pursued the same end with different means. They hoped to undermine our faith by questioning and challenging it. What the earlier ones had tried with force of arms in warfare, these heathens strove to attain through persuasion, through books. Both forms of attack will always bounce off and leave no effect, for the Lord guaranteed us: 'Every weapon forged against thee will be of no avail, and to every tongue that attacks thee thou shalt give the lie.' The heathens braced their strength to the utmost, even though they realized that this edifice is indestructible. They mustered all their might, they did everything in their power, but He who sits on the Heavenly throne laughs at them and mocks them. We were persecuted by both these enemy groups when we had our own land, and also in the time of our dispersion.

"Finally, there came a movement that made our lives bitter with all the methods it took over from both groups. It proclaimed a new prophetic teaching and alleged that both our old and their new doctrine were given by God. This created a dismal confusion in our people: two conflicting doctrines and both from God? Then came the founder of Islam, who followed the road paved by Christianity and merely reintroduced the political note. Both wanted to make their religion similar to the divine teaching."

Maimonides found the emergence of the founder of Islam announced by the prophet Daniel: "And he shall speak words against the most High, and shall wear out the saints of the most High, and think to change times and laws" (7:25). But the destruction of this dominion is also foreseen: "The judgment shall sit, and they shall take away his dominion . . . And the kingdom and dominion, and the greatness of the kingdom under the whole heaven, shall be given to the people of the saints of the most High." (7:26–27).

Evil tidings reached Maimonides. It looked as if the disaster would be overwhelming the Jews with greater and greater violence. One Jewish settlement after another was catastrophically wiped out. Was this meant as a test, a temptation at a time when faith was collapsing under the weight of the ordeal? These events bore the marks of doom, they seemed like final decisions about the fate of the world.

Maimonides also regarded the present as the end of time and began to view the terrible afflictions as death throes preceding imminent redemption. Since the time of Daniel, the period preceding the Messianic era has been described as an age of tribulation; rebellion, warfare, pestilence and famine, apostasy from God and His teachings will all be foretokens of the Messianic era, Messianic pangs announcing the arrival of the Redeemer. And Maimonides felt: Our

sages prayed that they would not have to experience these
pangs in the time of the crusades and the Almohades, and
the prophets were seized with horror when they saw these
sufferings in their visions. "Woe, who shall remain alive if
God inflicts such a doom."

Maimonides found the key to the enigmas of the period
in the Book of the prophet Daniel. Here he found illumi-
nating utterances that anticipated the events of the present
in detail. The indecision of the shortsighted and the confidence of the men of understanding are foretold by Daniel:
"Many shall be sifted, purged, and purified, the wicked do
not understand and they shall do wickedly; but the wise
shall understand" (12:10). And in this anxious hour,
Maimonides had a foreboding that even those men of
understanding, whose faith still appeared immune, would
suffer a far greater ordeal, until they too would give in to
qualms and go astray; for even some of the wise do sink.
Only very few will remain indomitable. There would be
much unhappiness until God keeps His word and has the
Redeemer come. "But who shall endure it on the day that
he cometh?" This day will come, says Maimonides, "when
the power of Edom [the Christians] and of Ishmael [the
Mohammedans] shall be at their peak and their dominion
shall extend throughout the world as it is today . . . There
is no doubt," Maimonides says openly, "that these are the
birth pangs announcing the Messiah."

Maimonides yearns for the Messianic era "not so that
Israel may rule the world and subjugate other nations or
that it may be called to high honors by other nations or that
it may give itself over to excessive pleasure and immoderate
joy; but so that it may be free of any constraint and devote
itself undisturbed to studying the doctrine of God and
knowledge and partake of everlasting bliss. For, in that
time of salvation, no one shall feel hunger, there shall be
neither war nor envy nor fighting, goodness will flow

toward everyone, sensual delights will appear worthless, all people will strive only toward the true, pure knowledge of God. Israel as bearer of the teaching of God shall become perfect in wisdom and knowledge. So far as possible for men, it shall grasp and carry out the will of the highest being, as is written, the earth shall be full of the knowledge of God, as the sea is full of water."[2]

It was an apocalyptic time. The decay of the Almoravites, who ruled Spain before the Almohades, and the decay of the Fatimites in Egypt had a terrible effect on contemporaries. The struggle between Christianity and Islam, which was to be fought out on the symbolic soil of the Holy Land, kept those who were full of forebodings in suspense. People were overwhelmed by an eschatological mood, which readied them for an unprecedented upheaval in history. For Jews, the Messianic yearning grew into their thoughts, their everyday life, into every last corner of their souls. Was not the Christian–Islamic struggle over Palestine paving the way for the advent of the Messiah? To determine when this great hour would come, Jews studied the Book of Daniel. They wanted to solve its apocalyptical enigmas, which contained the date of the Messiah's arrival. In the predictions of the prophet Daniel, Jews saw the Arabic empire as the fourth and last kingdom, which would be followed by the Messianic dominion.

The attempts at fixing the "end of years," the time of the Messianic Redemption, are very old. They began during the Second Temple and were continued in the Talmudic period. Now the Talmud warns: "Whosoever reckons the end, he shall have no share of the coming world." And there is the curse: "May the bones of those who reckon the end be blasted away." But Jews did not stop trying to calculate the year of the Salvation. The founder of philosophical rationalism in Jewish thought, Saadiah Gaon,

figured out the end of days, and many communities preserved his results as a comfort and a precious secret. The
conquest of Jerusalem in the first crusade was received by
Jews as an apocalyptic event. Rashi announced the time of
the great fulfillment, his contemporary Abraham bar Hiyya
composed *The Scroll of the Revealer* in order to strengthen
his brethren in their faith by deciphering the signs of the
Messiah. Although not convinced that he would succeed in
his reckonings, he legitimized them with Daniel's words:
"Many shall investigate it so that knowledge shall be increased."[3] Gabirol, the subtle poet and metaphysician of
the eleventh century, was the first to apply the astrological
method in attempting to explain the Messianic mystery.
And Abraham bar Hiyya also used astrology to interpret
the entire course of history from the Creation till the end
of time, to uncover the true plan of history and divide it
into a series of periods terminating in the Messianic
eschaton.

Egypt, too, was astir with Messianic hopes. Sutta, an old
man now, claimed he had dreamed that he was the bearer
of the highest honors of Judaism, and that the Messiah
would receive them from his hands. In some circles, this
dream strengthened Sutta's position. In any case, no one
dared to confront the nagid—except Maimonides.

Maimonides now attacked assimilation; above all, the
women under the influence of the sect of Karaites, who
tended more and more to disregard the Talmudic rites of
cleanliness. This time, however, Maimonides was no longer
an individual as in Alexandria. He was now the spokesman
of a sizable group of prestigious scholars, who had immigrated from many countries. It was he who called these
scholars together and organized them for joint action.[4]

His action was also aimed against the particularism of the
"Palestinians." He was especially offended by the deviation
in the cycle for reading the Torah. The partition of the

Jewish year according to sections of the Torah integrated the passing of time into the spiritual arrangement of the Holy Scriptures—not just into the natural course of the moon; and this partition wove the words of the Bible into the rhythm of the year. Perhaps it was already playing a decisive role at that time for the spiritual life of Jews. The action to gain uniform acceptance for this internal calendar was applauded by the scholars around Maimonides. The Palestinian community might not have let themselves be talked into it anyway; in any case, the reform effort made Sutta, the ruling nagid, intervene and this "worst of all men" obstructed the enterprise.[5]

Sutta resisted this action either because he viewed Maimonides as his personal adversary or for his own objective reasons. As an outsider and alien, Maimonides showed no reverence for the rooted local customs and, in his objective attitude, did not relate to the institutions which were legitimized only by their age. In this respect, the nagid's behavior is understandable, for he was protecting centuries-old traditions.[6]

Maimonides yielded in this conflict, not because he felt he was wrong, but for tactical reasons. He still had a decisive battle ahead of him, against Sutta himself. "During these dismal years, Maimonides probably worshipped in neither of the two synagogues, but rather in the house of study, where the like-minded rallied about him."[7]

II

Epistle to Yemen

THE wave of persecutions that dashed across the empire
of the Almohades, southern Spain, and all North Africa
broke off in Egypt, only to hurtle along the southwestern
corner of the Arabian peninsula, in Yemen. Humiliated and
despised by the Arabs, these Jews led a wretched existence.
The scourge of Islam lay heavy upon them, and they
yearned for the Messiah, for miraculous deliverance. The
Mohammedans mocked them and claimed self-assuredly
that the Torah had been superseded by the Koran. But the
Jews remained loyal to their heritage. Among them, there
were always a considerable number who knew the Torah
and studied the Law all day long, zealously observing the
commandments. "Their hands were held out to every way-
farer, their doors stood wide open for strangers, every
weary man found rest in their homes," says Maimonides.
But they themselves found little rest. And now an insurrec-
tion among the Arabs once again made the existence of the
Jews questionable. Egypt's abolition of, and struggle
against, the Shiite creed triggered a reaction in Yemen, the
homeland of the Shiites. Around 1172, two leaders of this
sect seized power in Yemen, and the Jews here found themselves in difficulties similar to those of their brethren in the
empire of the Almohades.[1] The Shiites had always been

more intolerant of other faiths than the Sunnites; they considered every non-Mohammedan an unclean being whose touch sullied the faithful. Victorious in Yemen, they resolved to wipe out the Jews if they did not convert to the Shiite form of Islam.

Many Jews accepted the Mohammedan religion, and voluntary apostasy was no rarity in this period: the historical successes of Islam had made a deep impact, particularly on those who had no Jewish education. The decline of spiritual development, as caused by the persecutions, was followed by apostasy. Judah Halevi had tried to use a historical basis for the faith in the truth of the Jewish religion. But in the conditions that prevailed during the epoch, this attitude was highly perilous. It is thus understandable that Maimonides chose a different route and sought to put the Jewish teachings on a different foundation.[2]

At approximately this time, when Maimonides was boldly and uprightly defending the position of the forced converts, warding off the sneak attacks of fearful conscience and trying to restore the validity of the pseudo-converts beyond all doubt, a peculiar adversary was starting to display effectiveness. Samuel, the son of Rabbi Judah ibn Abbas of Fez, a poet and physician whose scientific aspirations, as we have seen, brought about no improvements in Euclidean geometry. But he did denigrate Jewish teachings and shake up the religious condition of the Jews. In a book entitled *Silencing the Jews*, he tells about two dreams he allegedly had. In the first dream, the prophet Samuel shows him several Biblical verses that refer to the coming of Mohammed; and in the second dream, he actually has a conversation with Mohammed himself. The dreams then prompted him to go to a Moslem friend the next morning and inform him that he was converting to Islam. The friend, absolutely delighted, had him solemnly escorted to the mosque, where the cleric on the pulpit called out his praises, since he was now being led to the right path by Allah. The following night, he began to set down his book, which was quickly circulated. He then added many chapters until, so he thought, it was an outstanding book such as had never been written in Islam against the Jews.[3]

The action of the Shiites found support in Ibn Abbas, who now began to act as a missionary among the Jews of Yemen. He, too, practiced the usual method of proselytizing the Jews; i.e., picking out evidence from Scriptures in order to beat the Jews with their own weapons. Thus, violent conversion was now joined by the struggle of persuasion. The verse in Genesis 17:20 ("And as for Ishmael, I have heard thee: Behold, I have blessed him, and will make him fruitful, and will multiply him exceedingly") was applied to the founder of Islam, the descendant of Ishmael, since the numerological value of the Hebrew word for "exceedingly" was equal to that of the name of Mohammed. Evidence of this kind was offered to prove the authenticity of the Mohammedan mission. Ibn Abbas proclaimed to the Yemenite Jews that Mohammed had appeared as a second prophet in order to replace the Law of Moses and found a new creed in Mecca.

The insidious strategy of disaster drove the Jews into desperate straits. Not one of them could strike back at either thrust—the head-on assault by the Shiites, or the rear attack by the renegade.

Furthermore, one day a man from the people came forth and proclaimed that the time of salvation was nigh. The good tiding spread rapidly, the people thronged around the man, and he announced: "The King Messiah will reveal himself first in Yemen!" And many people gathered about him, Jews and Arabs. He said he had come as the harbinger of the Messiah to pave the way for the Redeemer. He traveled from mountain to mountain, calling: "Come and meet the King Messiah!" He worked great miracles, he even brought dead people back to life. He introduced new prayers and practices and told the people to distribute their property among the poor, and they did as he bade them.

In his proclamation, the "harbinger of the Messiah" cited the authority of Saadiah Gaon, who was greatly esteemed in Yemen, and who had computed the year of salvation. Hope and faith in the Messiah were the other side of despair. The Jews withstood the present by conjuring up the end of the world. This irritated the ruling Shiites, who proclaimed the Imam as the Redeemer; the Messianic delirium became a major political danger.

Those Yemenite Jews who were not dominated by fatalistic notions felt an even deeper despair. They saw the "conjunction of the earthly triplicity," which determined their fate, as an astrological sign of their ineluctable doom. Moreover, an astrologer had calculated the next conjunction, finding that all seven planets would soon unite in a constellation and cause an inundation of air and earth.

Merchants from Egypt, arriving in Yemen, told about the erudition of Maimonides, who lived in Fostat. Solomon ha-Kohen of Egypt, temporarily staying in Yemen, lauded his great mentor to the skies. On the other hand, there was Jacob al Fayyumi, who was probably the son of the author of the philosophical work *Garden of the Intellects.*[4] Having succeeded the latter as head of the Jewish community in Sana, he was a leading personality in Yemen. Al Fayyumi was undecided. He did not regard the "harbinger of the Messiah," who quoted Saadiah, as a deceiver; nor did he doubt the astrological predictions. He could challenge neither the proofs of the mission nor the demands of the Shiites. In this predicament, he resolved to ask Maimonides for advice and guidance; and he wrote him an extensive letter describing the complications.

Maimonides was shaken to the core. The "Confessors of

Unity" were raging in the West, the Shiites were storming in the East; and the Jews, afflicted on both sides, were virtually between two fires. From the letter, Maimonides saw that a portion of the people was steadfastly resisting the danger, while another portion was yielding to grief and skepticism. Maimonides was crushed under the burden of the sufferings he himself had experienced. He prayed with the prophet Amos (7:5): "O Lord God, forgive! . . . By whom shall Jacob arise? He is too small." The renegade's attack challenged the apologist in Maimonides; the Shiite persecution, the comforter; the pseudo-Messianic fanaticism and the astrological confusion, the enlightener. In this multiple ordeal, he spoke his mind; he stepped forward as a courageous defender on all four fronts.

Maimonides said: The evidence offered by the renegade had been refuted long ago, it could impress only the masses of the ignorant. If one banked on words taken out of context as this missionary did, one could also "infer" precepts from the Bible such as *Worship idols*; or, *Follow false prophets*. Even the Mohammedans did not take such alleged confirmations of their faith seriously, for they had long since realized their absurdity. Precisely because they found no confirmation, they took refuge in the claim that the present text of the Bible had been adulterated by the Jews, who had removed the predictions of the coming of Mohammed. Yet the nonsense of this claim, Maimonides felt, was obvious. Centuries before the advent of Mohammed, the Bible had been translated into Aramaic, Persian, Greek, and Latin, and diffused from East to West; and not the slightest deviation could be found in a single copy. How, then, could anyone speak of a falsified text!

Maimonides had his own opinions of the theological theories of the renegade interpreter of the Bible, and the stargazing fatalists. Maimonides had thorough knowledge of the ramified literature of the Arabs, and he detected the source of astrology in heathen worship of the stars. He rejected astrology both as an astronomer and as a philosopher. The science of astronomy, so he felt, refuted the two basic assumptions of astrological belief; i.e., that there are lucky and unlucky stars, and that the position of such a star at one point is "favorable" and at another "unfavorable." Both assertions were false, he said, because the spheres were the same everywhere.[5]

He spoke of the absurd arguments "that the astrologers dig up when they allege that a specific time of birth will endow an individual with a virtue or a failing and irresistibly force him to act the way he does. A precept which is taught in concordance by both our religion and Greek philosophy and whose certitude is substantiated by the most conclusive evidence is that a man's actions are up to him, that he is not subject to any outer constraint or influence. There is only a temperamental disposition which makes something easy or difficult for a human being; but it is not true that he must do it or cannot do it. If a man were fated to perform his actions, then all the commandments and prohibitions of the divine Law would be useless and purposeless, they would all be sheer trumpery, since, after all, a man would have no free will. It would likewise follow that teaching and education, as well as mastering any practical skills, would be futile, and all such things would be mere trifles, since, according to the theory of the astrologers, a man would be unavoidably compelled by an outer force to do such and such, attain such and such knowledge, acquire such and such a characteristic. Moreover, every reward or punishment would be crassly unjust, and not permissible for us toward one another or for God toward us. It would also be useless to construct houses, procure food, flee danger, because, after all, what has been fated would have to come irrevocably. But all this is utterly unthinkable and contradicts all intellectual understanding and sensory perception, it tears down the wall of the Law and attributes injustice to God."[6]

Maimonides, himself ruled by Messianic moods, nevertheless was not carried away by forebodings. He remained cognizant of the principle that no one can determine the end, "for hidden and sealed are the words until the time of the end." Many contemporaries made the attempt and imagined they had found a solution. But the most passionate investigator resigned himself,[7] declaring that this secret was irrevocably unknowable. The prophets, he said, had foreseen that human beings would try to calculate the end of time, and that their reckonings would not come true. But no one must have qualms or waver because of such blunders. "Revelation still has its term, and it is hastening toward the end and will not deceive us. If it hesitates, wait for it, for it shall come and shall not fail to appear." The Psalmist, he said, had thought of the long absence of the Messiah with fear and anxiety: "Wilt thou everlastingly wax wroth against us, lengthening thy wrath from generation to generation?" And Isaiah had said about this end of time: "And they shall be gathered together as prisoners are gathered in the dungeon, and shall be shut up in prison, and after many days shall be punished."

Nor, says Maimonides, is the advent of the Messiah in any way dependent on the constellation of the stars. "One of our scholars in Andalusia wrote a book about calculating the end of time on the basis of constellations and he announced the year of Salvation. There was no one among us who did not scorn him for this prediction. But reality did even more than we, it made him ridiculous. For the time that he foresaw for the arrival of the Messiah brought the rebel and agitator Ibn Tumart."

Maimonides decided to warn the Yemenite Jews to blot astrology out of their thinking. "Purge your thoughts

of astrology, the way one cleanses a sullied garment of filth!
. . . Pay no heed when someone speaks of a superior or
inferior conjunction!" he called to them. The Yemenite
Jews thought that the decay of education was due to the
prevailing conjunction, the earthly triplicity. Maimonides
declared that the cause was neither the earthly nor the fiery
nor any other triplicity. "For all astrological statements
are senseless and untrue, anyone making them is a fool or a
madman, or intentionally contradicting the Torah—as
though the Deluge and the destruction of Sodom had been
caused by the stars and not by the sins of men and the will
of God!"

Upon reading the reports on the behavior of the alleged
Messianic harbinger, his ritual innovations, his sermons and
supposed miracles, Maimonides became convinced that this
man was pious, simple-minded, and utterly uneducated.
Anything said about his miracles and anything that people
claimed to have perceived as the work of his hands was a
pack of lies. Maimonides then penned three treatises "for
the benefit" of the Yemenite Jews: on the King Messiah,
on his true features, and on the unmistakable signs of the
Messianic era. He enjoined the Yemenites to warn the
alleged wonder-worker in time so that he would not perish
and would not bring harm upon the communities.
Maimonides wrote his enlightening works in the Arabic
language spoken by Yemenite Jews, so that every reader—
man, woman, or child—might understand. He had reason
enough to fear that his epistle would fall into the hands of
the Moslems and be misconstrued. But he did tell himself
that "whosoever wishes to work for the collective good
must not cringe before any danger." He placed his trust in
the Talmudic saying: "The envoys of a good work shall
never suffer harm."

It was no easy tactic that Maimonides had to employ. If

he totally rejected the notions and behavior of the Yemenite Jews, his intervention would be ineffective because of its harshness. To be sure, the solace he offered was benevolent and heartening; but it was not sufficiently helpful or tangible for the concrete mentality of the people. In Maimonides's heart, the love for Israel won out over loyalty to a secret. This public epistle to the men, women, and children of southern Arabia revealed the important tradition that had been handed down in his family from father to son ever since the destruction of the Temple: Maimonides indicated the exact point in time when the spirit of prophecy would once again rest upon Israel. The Messianic age would commence as it is written: "I shall pour out my spirit upon all men; your sons and daughters shall prophesize, your old men shall have dreams, and your youths shall see visions."

"We must," writes Maimonides "be satisfied to endure all this suffering, persecution, exile, damage to property, and insult; for all these horrid things are an honor that God shows us." All suffering is a sacrifice to be offered up on the altar. God promised us that no oppression would go on for long, that He would never let us be wiped out, that we will never stop living as a nation. "Just as it is unthinkable that God's existence should end, so too it is impossible that we shall cease and vanish." God Himself assured us that He will never spurn us, even though we anger Him and do not satisfy His precepts. The present-day afflictions are not sufferings, but preliminary pains announcing the Messianic kingdom.

What did Maimonides do in Fostat? He was presumably a rabbi; and in any case, during 1173, he performed a great task for the public welfare. The Egyptian Jews were accustomed to paying huge ransoms to pirates for Jewish prisoners.[8] When the slave trade grew rampant, the

Alexandrian Jews could no longer afford the vast sums. They therefore appealed to the community of Fostat. In the summer of 1173, the number of Jewish slaves was so high that not even all the Egyptian Jews together were able to raise the money for their release. Maimonides, the judges, the elders, and the scholars of the town "admonished day and night and exhorted the people in the synagogues and prayer houses and at the doors of their homes. Some funds came forth for this important matter," but the donations did not suffice; and so Maimonides composed an epistle to the Jewish communities of North Africa, "asking the rabbis and heads of communities to launch a collection for the purpose of ransoming the captives." He handed his appeal over to the scribe Aaron ha-Levi, who was to read it in public everywhere. "And when he has presented the distress of our brethren to you," Maimonides added, "you should think about the matter and apply yourselves to this great merit. You should do unto them according to your generosity, since your sense of charity and your zeal in acquiring merits are well known. And whatever contributions you gather for them, you should note them and make sure to receive them and send them to us through Rabbi Aaron ha-Levi. And God, praised be He, shall not let you be struck by misfortune and He shall guide you in your great mercy, and your salvation shall grow until the end of days."[9]

In Fostat, Maimonides married (presumably for a second time) a sister of Abu'l-Ma'ali, who was "privy scribe" to a wife of Sultan Saladin, the mother of Al Afdal, successor to the throne. Abu'l-Ma'ali, who had in turn married Maimonides's sister, most likely got the philosopher his court connection, which must have been important in the struggle against Sutta.

There is a Biblical commandment obliging every Jew to

make a copy of the Torah, in order to bear personal witness to its everlasting validity. But this rule is seldom carried out. And even the rare observing Jews normally hire a professional scribe to do the work. Maimonides, however, did find time for this lengthy task.

Egypt had the famous manuscript of the Bible which the Masorete Ben-Asher had corrected in years of work. The manuscript, comprising all twenty-four books of the Scriptures, was preserved for a good long time in Jerusalem. All new Biblical manuscripts were compared with, and corrected according to, this generally acknowledged model text. While the Crusaders were annihilating the Jewish settlement in Jerusalem, this copy was brought to safety in Egypt. Maimonides used this prominent manuscript for his copy of the Torah. He wrote in such a way that each column was four fingers wide, the Song of the Red Sea and the Song of Moses six fingers wide; every column contained fifty-one lines, every scroll 226 columns. The entire scroll, Maimonides reports, was approximately 1,366 fingers wide.[10]

While in Fostat, Maimonides took the opportunity to read the works of the Mu'tazilites, which he knew only by hearsay.[11] He studied as much of them as "he could get hold of," although not as intensively as the writings of the Peripatetic philosophers.[12] Egypt had closer relations to the Eastern centers of Arabic culture than Spain or Morocco. None of the Mu'tazilite books, in which the Mohammedan religious philosophers proclaimed reason as the source of religious cognition, had, as Averroës reports, reached Spain. The same must be true of North Africa.[13] The Andalusian Jews, so Maimonides notes, had therefore remained free of the Mu'tazilite influence. In contrast, the leading Jewish philosophers of the Orient, especially the heads of the Babylonian academies, adopted their doctrines.

The Mu'tazilites relentlessly criticized many elements in popular faith that Islamic orthodoxy viewed as indispensable components of the creed. They tried to purge the notion of God of all concepts detracting from belief in the justice and purity of the Divine Being. Maimonides, although sharing some of their orientations, rejected individual tenets.

The Mu'tazilites rejected the idea of causality and taught: What seems like a law to us is merely a "habit of nature . . . It is not a law but merely a custom that God has placed in nature that certain phenomena follow others. This sequence, however, is not necessary. It is not necessary that the lack of food and drink entail hunger and thirst, but it is usually so. The Nile rises and falls out of habit, but not as a result of causal natural processes. Every event is a special creative effect of God, who normally determines the habitual course of nature. The persistence of habit corresponds to new acts all the time." We are used to ascribing shade to the absence of the sun. But shade is not the consequence of the nonpresence of the sun. It is created.[14] "They call this the true faith in God as the Creator, and whosoever does not believe that this is so denies—according to them—that God is the Creator. I, however, believe, and every rational man believes along with me," says Maimonides, "that one would have to say about such opinions about faith: 'Do you want to laugh at God the way one laughs at a man!' "[15]

The Mu'tazilites followed the principle that no heed is to be taken of reality, since it also rests on a habit whose opposite is equally conceivable. But Maimonides writes: "Reality is not contingent on opinions, opinions are contingent on reality."[16] The Mu'tazilites, he goes on, set up their propositions to prove that the world was created. As soon as we establish that the world was created, it is obvious beyond all doubt that the world has a Creator. Maimonides rejected this procedure, which makes the knowledge of God's existence dependent on the question of the creation of the world. To his mind, it would be the highest possible achievement of a truth-loving believer to invalidate the philosophers' evidence of the noncreation of the world. "What an honor it would be for him who could do this!" He realized, however, that the philosophers had been of divided opinions on this issue "for three thousand years," and that this question could not be solved; one could therefore use it as a premise for the existence of God.

The Mu'tazilites also taught that anything imaginable is also conceivable even though it may not agree with the forms of reality, which, after all, rest only on convention. Maimonides, however, viewed reason as a verifying authority which tells us "what is necessary, conceivable, and impossible."[17] How can one rely on the imagination, which can never detach itself from matter, and which can know God only as a body or as a power inherent in a body?

The Mu'tazilites contested the notion that stasis is the cessation of movement, blindness the cessation of vision, death the cessation of life. They claimed that these qualities had a positive existence. God created stasis in every part of a static body as a quality that is re-created as long as the body remains static. They thought of death in the same way. "But I would like to know," Maimonides asks ironically, "how long God re-creates the quality of death in a dead man . . . Since we find the teeth of people who have been dead for thousands of years, God must have been re-creating the quality of death throughout these millennia."

Maimonides had to reject the conception of the negative as a form of existence. For him, the "no" is the neutral zone between the borderline of the knowable and the unknowable. This zone, which exists for him only as a form of thinking, but whose conceptual tangibility is very close to him, is the area where he meditates about God and the theodicy.

Maimonides performed his immense labor of codification between 1170 and 1180. Questions about the Law were addressed to him from many Egyptian towns and also from other countries. His opinions gained extraordinary prestige, and his renown grew. Because his joint appeal with other rabbis against the Karaite customs of cleanliness had little effect, he announced a new decree in 1176:[18] Any unobservant wife is threatened with the loss of all claims to her husband's property in case of divorce or widowhood. The new decree was apparently formulated by Maimonides, signed by the same group of scholars, and read aloud in all Egyptian congregations. In the Codex, he likewise continues to reject the Karaite influence. Aside from a few exceptions, the geonim had not been active in this respect. Karaite influences had even penetrated the gaonic teaching of the Law.[19] Maimonides once and for all eradicated these elements from Jewish thought.

Ever since his first few years in Egypt, judges in various Egyptian communities, especially Alexandria, had been consulting Maimonides in difficult cases.[20] And early on, he actually, if not nominally, seems to have been acknowledged as the supreme judge. Even a former dignitary, living in Egypt and boastfully styling himself "Judah, prince of the entire Exile, descendant of God-anointed David," confirmed that Maimonides's verdicts were "convincing, cogent, and irrefutable." But Maimonides wrote at this time: "I am the least of the sages of Spain, whose brilliance has darkened in exile. I always stand at my post, but I have not attained the wisdom of my forebears, for evil and difficult days were my lot, I was granted hardship but no rest. From town to town and from kingdom to kingdom was I driven. But behind the reaper, I gleaned on all roads and gathered the ears, the sound and full ones, nor did I scorn the thin, parched ones. Only recently have I found a home. Were it not for the assistance of God and the instruction of my mentors, I would not have garnered the scant pickings on which I feed today."[21]

12

Sutta

IN 1174, Nureddin passed away, to be followed a short time later by Amalric, King of the Franks. Saladin, glad that he no longer need fear his burdensome protector or the most unpleasant adversary, saw a clear road to conquering their legacy, Palestine and Syria. After this political turn of events, the Jews also managed to achieve what had seemed impossible to them before. They were freed from Sutta, the "evil of all evils." A Hebrew poet later wrote a rhyming chronicle, *The Scroll of Sutta the Villain,* which speaks of this memorable occurrence: "The Lord took pity on us, dethroned the arrogant man, and wiped the tears from every face. He sent the loyal messenger, the sign of heaven, the wonder of the age, Rabbi Moses [Maimonides], the light of the East and the West, the clear radiance, the glowing star, the most outstanding man of his time, and its miracle from the Orient to the Occident. He set the Law upright, restored order, and removed the idols from the sanctuary. Thus, the first help for Israel came through him." At the same time that Maimonides was subduing Ibn Abbas and the pseudo-Messianic forerunner in Yemen, he was also being celebrated as a savior in Egypt.

However, the joy at this success was short-lived. The

Sutta affair had not yet reached its end. The worst still lay ahead.

"A twig sprouted from the stump. An adder came from the seed of the serpent. Sutta had a son, who sucked in an excess of dragon venom. Like his father, he turned out violent and brutal. He followed the ways of his father, soon outstripping him in villainy. The son said to the father: 'I will assist you and support you.'" And they pondered how to win back the power. They knew, however, that Saladin was a just ruler, "an uprooter of thorns, who wipes out terrors and spurns corruption." Sutta appeared before the sultan and accused the Jews of complicity with Egypt's enemies, of concealing messengers of hostile powers in their homes and providing them with meat and drink. And because, Sutta declared, we remain faithful to the state, they have rebelled against us. These accusations made sense to the ruler, and in order to quell the subversive activities, he put Sutta, who was loyal to the government, back into the saddle, so that he might watch over what the Jews were doing. Once again, the triumphant Sutta was supreme head of the Jewish community. "A trembling filled their hips, and this lasted two years."

Actually, it is not quite clear what motives Sutta was driven by in his regime. Villainy and ambition could hardly have filled out his program, his aims and goals, making his power possible. Sutta's high opinion of himself and his office is proved by the fact that he dreamed of being a forerunner of the Messiah, and by the use he made of this dream. Allegedly, he was also a great scholar. For all that, it is likely that he also had some support and approval among the people.

Maimonides had organized the recently immigrated scholars to do something about the low intellectual level of Egyptian Jews. This action was aimed chiefly at the Karaites, who probably utilized their high social standing and their close relations with the court to repel the attack. They may have protected Sutta as their exponent with the government, so that he became the minion of the authorities. The changes introduced by Maimonides in the synagogal institutions were cause enough to stoke the resentment against him "with consideration of piety." The sympathy of the upright, conservative members of the Palestinian community may have turned to the man who protected the old and venerable rite against the "unseemly and unauthorized" reforms of the foreign scholar. Perhaps, as so often in Jewish history, a governmental agency was made aware of these "revolutionary" machinations.

Two years after Sutta's restoration, a campaign against the Christians took his patron to Palestine, and the Jews felt the time had come to make a new thrust. But since they procrastinated and could not keep their goals secret enough, Sutta's son arrested three Jewish immigrants, brought them before the governor, and said: "These are the conspirators that the Jews concealed. They came to Egypt from a faraway country to agitate against the sultan, and they have been supported by the local Jews." The governor had the three Jews beaten and clapped in chains.

This affair put Maimonides in a precarious situation. Sutta's fury would have to be discharged against the man who had recently ousted him. Furthermore, Maimonides had migrated to Egypt from the kingdom of the Crusaders shortly before the Franks had again become the foes of Egypt. At this point, anyone from a Christian country had everything to lose. Maimonides had to reckon with being suspected of espionage and with persecution by the distrustful masses.[1] Thus, Sutta could assume that a denunciation of Maimonides would be heeded. So he denounced him, probably as one of the foreigners involved in subversive activities; he also pointed out that Maimonides's resistance to the nagid installed by the sultan would have to be viewed as an action against the government. Another Jew had been punished for conspiracy on a different occasion.[2] The crucial thing was that, under Saladin's rule, there were repeated conspiracies, and the plotters were in communication with the sultan's fiercest opponents, the Crusaders. In April 1174, Saladin had to quell a dangerous revolt in his land; the rebels "wanted to restore the rule of the Alites with the help of Christians." The Shiites, who still had not lost all influence, rejected Saladin, a Sunnite, and demanded a ruler descended from Ali. "Upon recovering from their initial surprise, the followers of the Fatimites began forming secret societies," and they elected a Shiite from Yemen as successor to the deceased caliph.[3]

History has spread a veil over what now happened to Maimonides. All that he himself wanted to make known to posterity is contained in a letter to a friend, which says that "publicly known misfortunes" and losses had befallen him, and slanderers wanted to take his life.[4]

His situation was extremely dangerous. Two of the denounced Jews died in prison as a result of beatings; and several popular legends agree[5] that Maimonides had to hide in a cave because his adversaries had slandered him to the authorities. These sources also report that he continued working on the Codex in his hiding place. An eyewitness account glows softly with the mood of those years: An admirer from Toledo, who had sworn "not to rest until he had seen Maimonides," started out and traveled for nine months, until he arrived in Egypt. But Maimonides was not to be found in his home; and at first no one wanted to reveal the persecuted man's place of refuge to the zealous pilgrim. "It took fifteen days," he later told in his memoirs, "until I managed to get secret information on his whereabouts. At last, I found him concealed in a cave. He recognized me and was happy to see me. I said to him: 'My lord, I am here to serve you until God takes pity on you . . .' " He learned that Maimonides had to conceal himself because "the king's servants had calumniated him" and wanted to harm him; and that he had written "seven books during his sojourn in the cave," which probably means seven of the fourteen books that constitute the Codex.[6]

13

The Transformation

SCARCELY anywhere else on earth has the mystery of death so moved and fascinated people as in the valley of the Nile. The entire mentality of the ancient Egyptians focused on the depth of this enigma. The shattering passion of Osiris, who perishes every year with the drought of the fields and the death of the plants, seized hold of Egyptian minds like no other myth.

The series of misfortunes for Maimonides was not yet ended with his gloomy life in the cave or with his losses. One day he received word that his brother David, who had been sailing in the faraway Indian Ocean, had met death at sea. The wise man of Fostat, who had resisted all the tricks of life with equanimity and whose inner strength could not be broken by any human affliction, collapsed before the power of this death.

His love for David, whom he "had raised on his lap," had been unusually strong. In the years of increasing troubles after the loss of their father, the mutual devotion of the brothers had become closer and deeper. When Rabbi Maimon passed away, David was not only "the brother and pupil" but also the breadwinner. Maimonides could carry out his grandiose plans only because of his brother's support and assistance. In his abandonment, during almost incessant ordeals, his brother always offered comfort and refreshment. "My only joy was to see him."

But no avowal of love and devotion can explain a grief such as overwhelmed Maimonides. The pain crushed him utterly; a protracted and critical heart disease resulted, followed by a high fever and a nervous skin ailment. He sank into abysmal melancholy. "I was at death's door," he commented later. He lay in his sickbed for a year; and for many more years he was overcome with depression and melancholy.

"Years have waned, but I still mourn and find no solace. And what could bring me solace anyway? He grew up in my lap. He was my brother and pupil. He had a business and earned a livelihood, but I could live without cares. He was conversant with the Talmud and knew the grammar of the Hebrew language. My only joy was to see him. All my joy is gone. He has passed on to eternal life, leaving me shattered in a strange land. Whenever I see his handwriting or one of his books, my heart turns over in me, and my grief comes awake again. 'For I will go down into the grave unto my son mourning.' If it were not for the Torah, which is my pleasure, and the other sciences, which make me forget my sorrow, I would perish in my wretchedness."[1]

Later he writes: "Weeping and arousing grief until physical strength no longer suffices to bear the suffering of the soul—this soothes mourners, just as the cheerful let themselves go in jests."[2] And another time, as a medical man, he describes the bodily changes wrought by the affect of grief: "When a man with a powerful frame, a sonorous voice, and a radiant complexion hears sudden news that greatly afflicts him, one can see his face turning pale, the glow dimming, the body hunching, the voice faltering, and when he tries with all his might to raise his voice, he is unable to do so, his strength is weakened. Indeed, he often trembles with feebleness, his pulse slows down, his eyes move back in their sockets. His eyelids grow so heavy that he cannot move them, his body becomes cold, and his appetite vanishes."[3]

His teacher Judah ibn Sossan, who had summoned him to Fez, had been murdered by the Almohades; his father and mentor, Rabbi Maimon, had passed away shortly after their arrival in Egypt; and now his brother, the friend of his youth, had died an unnatural death. All these events occurred within a short span of time. He himself had been in the same danger as his brother when sailing to the Holy Land. Perhaps in his imagination he experienced, in ineffable horror and down to the last detail, all the terrors that his beloved brother had suffered until his final breath.

The dizzying depth of his grief is no more fathomable than the infinite vastness of his thinking. He had disapproved of allowing emotions to get the upper hand, and he had realized the particular harmfulness of grief. He also knew that the gift of prophecy disappears during a time of mourning, "prophecy does not exist in affliction and dejection"; he knew that Jacob, throughout the time of his grief, was not found worthy of any inspiration because his mind was preoccupied with the person he was mourning.[4] The perfection Maimonides strove for, the total alertness of the entire soul, of reason and imagination, for inspirations of the "active intellect," were diminished by this depression. Virtue, he had taught, is that disposition of the soul which holds the middle between two extremes. As a physician of the soul, he wrote about the method of curing spiritual ailments, which he diagnosed as any turning to an extreme. In the extant writings, we find no hint of his having weighed whether there is a realm of the soul in which reason does not prevail. The doctrine of virtue, which he presented in his Codex during this critical period, also dwells on this point of view, even though he himself could not master his own feelings. But death and sorrow apparently triggered a spiritual crisis that was rich in decisions; and if we may follow the subjective correlative of objective thinking, this crisis was the sole cause of the subsequent radical reversal of his thinking and the transformation of his picture of the world.

In the Mishnah commentary, he had been dominated by the view that everything in this world exists only for the sake of man. And the purpose of man is knowledge. Most people, who are without knowledge, exist in order to serve the wise.[5] This view had been the fundamental feature of his image of the world and the basis of his conduct in life. It justified the structure of his economic existence. He could permit his livelihood to be assured by his brother's strenuous and dangerous work, so that Maimonides could devote himself to realizing his plans in peace and quiet. This view also had a place in his self-confidence and probably aroused a certain awareness of the relationship of providence to his own life. But now events seemed to be thwarting and foiling his plans. The exile from Spain was followed by the escape from Morocco, the afflictions by the Karaites gave way to the persecution by Sutta, the loss of his property, and the death of David. Poverty and illness, disquiet, melancholy, and mortal danger passed like doom through his life. Did these experiences not have to weaken and refute his view that the life of the wise is the ultimate purpose of all occurrence? The bulwark of his self-confidence seems to have collapsed at this point, and his anthropocentric view of the world also crumbled. Man, even the sage, was now inconceivable as the center of the world, the final goal of its development. Amid the bitter pangs of despairing melancholy, in which Maimonides felt death palpably at hand, his image of the world disintegrated.

During his youth, he had made an effort to avoid the question of the meaning of evil. It struck him that no Jewish thinker had managed to cope with this problem.

With light optimism, he had waved the question away. A thinking man, he had felt, should not excite himself about the disagreeable parts of life. There were, he said, many things that at first seemed bad yet ultimately turned out good. One should always wait with one's joy or grief and delay the emotional reaction.[6] But, in a tragic moment, this credulous trust proved to be a shoal, almost wrecking Maimonides's mind and spirit.

"*All* thinking men," Maimonides now claimed, "are rendered perplexed and helpless by experiences like those of Job, so that in regard to God's knowledge and providence one may say that sometimes the blameless, perfect man, whose dealings are upright and who eschews all sin, may be struck by heavy, unexpected, and uninterrupted evils—to wit, concerning his property, his children, and his body—and this may happen through no fault of his own."[7] Maimonides himself was scarcely in the mood of a Job. He once claimed that Job had spoken his rebellious words "only so long as he possessed no wisdom and knew God only through tradition, like the great mass of those who profess a religion. But as soon as he truly knew God, he had to admit that true happiness, which is the knowledge of God, is doubtless reserved for all men, and that no afflictions can destroy this happiness."[8]

Maimonides, who since his youth had aspired to know God not merely through "reports and descriptions" but out of his "own thinking," knew "that the things one looks upon as the goods of happiness, such as health or riches," are not the purpose of life. "All people—namely, the masses —praise God with their words and depict Him as just and good at a time of happiness and when they are carefree, or at a time of grief if they can endure it. But when the afflictions mentioned in Job come upon them, then some will deny God at the very loss of their property, and they will believe that the universe lacks a rational order; others, even despite their grief at the loss of their goods, will maintain their faith in justice and in the order of the universe, but will be unable to maintain it if they are afflicted with the loss of their children; still others will endure even this and not lose their faith even if they lose their children; but when it comes to physical suffering, not a single one of them will endure it, they will grumble and lament about injustice either aloud or quietly."[9] Maimonides never lost his faith in the just and meaningful working of the universe. His experience did not turn him against God but, to all appearances, against himself.

David had run a business and traveled, as though to demonstrate the precept about the position of the wise in this world. Did this not pose a question, did David's death not arouse the most tormenting qualms in Maimonides's philosophical conscience? A discreet confirmation of this surmise can be found in a line he wrote about grief during this critical period: "The man who does not grieve for someone who has passed away . . . is cruel and brutal. One should be more anxious, test one's own conduct and do penance."[10] These words, unsupported by any Talmudic sources, written in his Codex out of personal experience and attitude, betray his stance. The sorrow, which first bored through the stratum of his feelings, was obviously beginning to torture his conscience. The self-testing he demanded of other mourners was something he now applied with heightened rigor to himself.

Several years after David's death, Maimonides described the ills "that come to every single human being as a result of his own actions . . . All people complain about this kind of disaster, for there are few men who have not sinned against themselves. Such ills are the consequence of all vices . . . and the cause of all physical and spiritual ailments. These ailments occur when the soul becomes accustomed to unnecessary things and the desire for things that are not needed, for the survival of the individual or the species becomes second nature to the soul. Such desire knows no bounds. The necessary things are actually few in number, the superfluous things are unlimited. If, for instance, you wish that your utensils were of silver, then would it not be lovelier if they were of gold? Others make them of sapphire, some even of carbuncle stone or ruby, or anything one might devise. A fool with such a poor way of thinking never stops being sad and sighing that he cannot afford superfluous things that this man or that man can afford. Often he puts himself in great danger; for instance, by sea voyages."[11] Do these words not contain a sense of guilt and a veiled but relentless confession?

"We lament and are dissatisfied because of our defectiveness. We feel pain from the ills that we inflict upon ourselves, and we attribute them to God."[12] Here lies the pivot of pessimism for him.

Alfasi, who was still popular, had written in the tenth century that evil was more frequent than good, and life a punishment. In contrast, Maimonides polemicized with the most unequivocal formulations of his new standpoint: "The cause of the entire error lies in the fact that this fool and those of a similar opinion among the masses contemplate existence only in a single human individual. Yet every fool imagines that the whole universe exists only for his sake, as though no other being existed outside of him. But if he meets with the opposite of what he wanted, he decides that all Being is bad. However, if he were to contemplate and understand all Being and recognize the insignificance of his share in it, then the truth would become obvious to him. It would also be shown that all human opinions about the many 'ills' of the world have arisen not with respect to the angels, spheres, and stars, the elements and their compounds, primeval rocks, plants, and animal species, but solely with respect to this or that individual of the human race. The right way of looking at things consists in seeing the totality of existing mankind—and how much more the remaining species of animals—as of no importance in regard to the interdependence of all Being." Man must know his relationship to the universe and must not fall prey to the error that the universe exists for his sake. For the human species is the lowest in relationship to the sublime, to the spheres and stars.[13]

Maimonides feels that there is no way to investigate the purpose of the universe, that it would be absurd to believe the world existed for the sake of man, the monkey to entertain man. The assumption that the goods of the world exist for the sake of man is thus the same as when, say, a burger believes that the king exists to protect his, the burger's, house against nocturnal thieves, "even though this is true in a certain sense."[14]

An anthropocentric view of the world was dispelled once and for all by this conclusion. And it also exposed pessimism for what it is. Maimonides was not content with proving that pessimism was based on false reasoning. In his opinion, all beings that exist in this world are made up of matter and form. Matter is sheer possibility, an indefinite stuff that is fundamental to everything. Form, however, is the essence of things, growth in plants, reason in men. "Nature, the true essence of matter, consists in her never being able to escape combining with non-Being, hence no form can remain permanent in her; instead, she discards one form and then always dons another form. She may be likened to an adulterous strumpet. For simply no material exists without a form. Hence, she is always married. She is inconceivable without her husband and simply never exists unwed. But even though she is always one man's wife, she constantly seeks another man to replace her spouse, she seduces this man and draws him to herself in every way until he gets from her what her husband has gotten. And that is the condition of matter. It consists in her moving incessantly in order to discard every form she has and take on another, and she proceeds in the same manner after the new form has gone into her.

"It is thus clear that all decay, all destruction, and all defects are actually the consequence of matter. Every living creature dies or grows ill only because of its matter and not because of its form. And all the delinquency and sinning of a man are caused only by his matter and not by his form, whereas, on the other hand, all his merits are determined only by his form. As an example: man's knowledge of God, the conception of all thoughts, the control of his passions and his wrath, and the weighing of what he must choose or abhor—all these things are the effect of his form; whereas his eating and drinking, his sexual activity, his frequent desire for these things, likewise his wrath and any vice existing in him, are caused by his matter."[15]

Evil is nothing real, and nothing positive; it is a lack. It consists in the privation—i.e., nonpresence—of good. "Thus, for instance, dying is an ill for man, but it consists in non-Being. And likewise, disease, poverty, and ignorance are ills that concern him; however, they all consist in the nonpresence of certain qualities"; for death is, in regard to all living things, the non-Being of form, and likewise the passing of all other existing things is the non-Being of their form. "One simply cannot say that God himself creates an ill. That is inconceivable. On the contrary: all His works are perfectly good, for he creates only Being, and all Being is good. The ills, however, are all privations to which creation does not refer. Thus, the essence of God's work is consistently good, since it is Being; and that is why the

Book, which illuminates the darknesses of this world, describes Being with the words: 'God saw everything He had made, and behold, it was very good.' So that even the existence of this lower matter, such as it is, is likewise good, despite its connection with the privation causing death and all ill . . . That is why Rabbi Meir interprets the verse 'And behold, it was very good' as follows: 'And behold, dying is a good.' "[16]

Maimonides seems to have found comfort and consolation in this hymnal philosophy. Metaphysical knowledge produced what the doctrines of virtue and spiritual therapy were unable to do. The crisis invaded Maimonides's existence like a thunderstorm; but then the impetuosity of his youth and the volatility of his passion subsided. He became more balanced, more circumspect, and his mind achieved an early transfiguration, blending the lucidity of old age and the colorfulness of maturity, stillness and warmth, the remoteness of ideas and the proximity of objects, renunciation and desire, shaping self-control and quiet resistance into unique human wealth. He overcame suffering. The hardships and adversities that later entered his life could never again shatter the equilibrium of his character. In his youth, bitter sighs kept struggling out of his breast, they even found utterance in his works. As for the period following his spiritual transformation, all that reaches us is a mere echo of the internal bliss that filled his soul.

He was only in his early forties, a master in the art of forbearing and forgiving. "My character traits are now very different from yours," he wrote to a disciple, who was irate about a hostility directed at the master. "The years and my experiences have, God be praised, greatly pacified me. The same effect has been wrought by understanding, which was attained through contemplation and through study of the true sciences. I forgo honor and overlook insults. Of course, you, my son, because of the heatedness of your temper and the passion of your youth, are unable to defend yourself against bitter anger and to endure all the contumely."[17]

And in another letter: "Know that I have set myself the goal of behaving humbly in every action, even though it damages me in the eyes of the crowd. If someone wishes to flaunt his own excellence by demonstrating my failings, then I forgive him, even though he may be one of the most insignificant students. Our leaders along the paths of the good have said: If one has to help both friend and an enemy, then one is required to help the enemy first in order to subdue and to tame passion. Anyone who wishes to be a human being should work toward perfecting his character and acquiring knowledge, he should not occupy his mind with stupidities. As for your pain and your powerful excitement, they are determined by your age. In my youth, I was even more vehement than you. As you have heard, I would obtain satisfaction for myself with my tongue and my quill, even against great men and wise men, when they polemicized against me. You have doubtless heard about the controversies I have had, against those present with my tongue, against those absent with my pen."[18]

The early coming of the fine qualities of old age delighted him. The echo of this feeling is found in his exegesis on the antithetical verses in Ecclesiastes 10:16–17: "Woe to thee, O land, whose king is a boy . . . Blessed art thou, O land, whose king is free." As a contrast to "boy" we find the word "free," although we would expect the word "man." The reason for using the word "free" as the opposite of "boy," according to Maimonides, was that the youth is the slave of desires. A rule by men who are prey to their desires would have to be a curse, just as a rule by men who are free of enslavement by their desires is a boon.[19]

The inner transformation of Maimonides was reflected

in the deliberate way he changed the nature of his ethical conviction. He had, as we know, deviated from the Aristotelian principle of moderation in one point: the demand for utmost humility. In the new presentation of his ethical teachings, which he offered at this time, he now spoke of two "qualities in which man should not be moderate but, even more, should hold back from the extreme way." Along with pride, "anger is a very ugly quality. One must therefore keep away from it altogether. One should train oneself not to lose one's temper about a thing at which one could rightfully get angry. One should not even get wrought up at things that normally arouse justified annoyance."

Maimonides won his victory over evil by annihilating it philosophically. "No ill exists!" he established unequivocally. This exposé robbed disaster of its strength. The lacunae in Being, which appear delusively as areas of reality, as the power and existence of evil, are merely the tiny interstices of good and solely real Being. Any other conception of evil is sheer fantasy. This victory was won in the sphere of actual reality, seeing evil as it really was and thereby freeing the soul from anxiety, from the feeling of being haunted by the ghost of evil.

The consequences of this decisive change were not only on the level of mere thought. The death of his brother David confronted him with the problem of earning a livelihood. He had no sense of business. He would not be able to use his reason to cope with the zeal of merchants. He had to make an effort to understand the existential meaning of this class of men, and he finally told himself: "Without madness, the world would be bleak." This stamp of men, he went on, would sacrifice body and soul in order to accumulate a mass of dinars. Then they begin to distribute the money among architects so that the latter might lay a solid foundation of lime and rock on the level of the land in order to erect a building that is to last for many centuries, although the merchants know that the years of their lives will not even suffice to use up a structure made of reeds. "Is there a greater folly than this?"[20]

The Egyptian Jews were prosperous, and Maimonides could easily have obtained a salaried office as rabbi. But his convictions were "useless for life," preventing him from becoming a merchant or rabbi. In the catastrophe, the family's entire wealth, as well as other people's property that David was transporting, had sunk beneath the waves. This left Maimonides unpropertied. Having to support his brother's widow and young daughter, he made up his mind to become a physician. From now on, he devoted his time and activity increasingly and then exclusively to this calling.

The fact that he was subject to intense grief for many years seemed to arouse distrust in him, and that undermined one root of his knowledge. His youthful work on logic had listed merit—along with sensory perception, reason, and tradition—as one of the four roots or sources of knowledge. In his old age, when touching upon this theme in a letter to Marseilles, he taught only the first three sources of knowledge; apparently, he no longer cared to bank on merit.[21]

So far, Maimonides had penned all his writings and letters in the Arabic which the Jews in Spain, North Africa, Egypt, Syria, and Persia were using at that time. However, like nearly all Jewish–Arabic authors, he employed the Hebrew alphabet. The introduction to the Codex, the *Book of Laws*, was likewise in Arabic. One can rather safely assume, therefore, that he originally intended to write the entire Codex in Arabic, since it is unthinkable that he would have wanted to compose the introduction and the work in two different languages. However, a change occurred in this respect, too. He even regretted having written the

Mishnah commentary and the *Book of Laws* in Arabic, and he decided to translate both works into Hebrew. The result was that he composed the Codex in the Hebrew tongue. "On no account do I wish to translate this work into Arabic," he wrote to a follower. Characteristically, his Arabic style is permeated with vulgarisms, but his Hebrew diction is elegant and polished.

The self-control of passion, the reshaping of his image of the world, the elimination of the sense of merit, the change of language, the effect of his profession on the structure of his life, all hint at the depth of this crisis.

Meanwhile, Sutta had gone too far. His outrageous deeds aroused a tempest among the people. By taking decisive steps, Rabbi Isaac succeeded in getting the monarch to depose the tyrant. Egypt was finally liberated from Sutta. Yemen was likewise rescued from its Messianic enthusiast. The movement, as Maimonides then learned, had ended when " 'the Messiah's messenger' was captured while all his followers scattered. One of the Arab kings, who had ordered the false prophet's arrest, said to him: 'Just what have you accomplished?'

"And the man replied: 'My Lord and Ruler, I have done all this at God's command.'

" 'And how will you prove this?' the king asked.

"To which the prophet replied: 'Have me decapitated and I will promptly reappear in my former shape.'

" 'That is truly a great miracle,' the king exclaimed, 'and if you can indeed perform this action, then I and the entire world with me shall no longer doubt that your words are true and that our forebears have left us nothing but useless and idle chitchat.'

"Thereupon, the king ordered his servant to bring a sword, the unhappy man's head was chopped off, and thus he met his end. May his death be an expiatory sacrifice for him and for all Israel."

That was how Maimonides ended his description. Twenty years later, there were still people who believed that the false prophet would soon rise from the grave.[22]

14

Maimonides and Aristotle

JUST as Maimonides was troubled by the lack of a unified system for teaching the Jewish Law, so too he was saddened by the fact that the Jews had no relationship to philosophy. Over and over again, he reaffirmed the intellectual thoughtlessness and irresoluteness, the lack of judgment and reason among his contemporaries. Most of them felt a gap between belief and knowledge, between the contents of revelation and the theories of philosophy. Maimonides, however, wrote: "Our nation is a nation of perfect wisdom. God himself said through the Master who led us to perfection: 'Surely, this great nation is a wise and understanding people.' But when wicked people, who belonged to ignorant nations, put an end to our happy situation, destroying our sciences and our brethren and killing our sages, so that we once again became ignorant (a misfortune that God had already announced to us earlier, because of our sins, with the words: 'The wisdom of its wise men will be lost, and the understanding of its understanding men')—when all this happened, we became mingled with these nations, and their opinions, customs, and behavior were transplanted in us . . . Because we have grown up in these ignorant opinions, the views of philosophers have become as alien to us as if they opposed our Law as they do the opinions of the ignorant . . .[1]

"The concealed thoughts of the Bible are like a precious stone that has dropped from a man's hand in his home, indeed in a dark house, in which there are many objects. The gem now rests in the dark house, but the man does not see it and does not notice it . . ."[2] The people, however, were satisfied with literal meaning, and did not delve into concealed and subtle thought.

For Maimonides, the Haggadah* too was a wellspring of philosophical wisdom: whatever it offered by way of allegory overlapped with the knowledge expressly taught in abstract philosophical thinking. Maimonides's contemplations and investigations focused largely on showing the congruence between Biblical–Talmudic and philosophical thinking. The image of the world that he drew could be valid only if its reflection in the mirror of philosophy resembled its reflection in the mirror of Jewish literature. Now the doctrines of philosophy were clear; however, the texts of Jewish literature were partly clear and partly— because of their allegorical form—ambiguous. Hence he had to analyze and interpret these writings.

"If you wish to make the king of a country known to an inhabitant who does not know him, there are many ways of doing so. You can tell him, for instance: 'The king is that tall, gray-haired man dressed in white.' Thus you describe him in terms of secondary qualities. But you can also tell the questioner: 'The king is that man you see surrounded by a throng of people, by riders and men on foot carrying drawn swords, with flags waving over his head and trumpets blowing before him.' Or: 'He lives in a palace in such and such a city of his kingdom.' Or: 'It is he who has had this wall or

---

* The Haggadah or Aggadah is explanatory matter in rabbinical literature, often taking the form of a story, anecdote, legend, or parable. Large portions of the Talmud are aggadic.

this bridge built.' Or similar things about his deeds or his relations to other people.

"However, you might also prove his existence by things that are less explicit. If the questioner, for instance, asks you: 'Does this land have a king?" you will say to him: 'Yes, without a doubt, it has a king.' Now if he should ask what proof there is, you will reply: 'This money-changer here is, as you see, a man with a homely and feeble body; in front of him lies this great heap of gold pieces. This other man, standing before him, with a squat and bony physique, is a pauper. The latter asks the money-changer for a very small alms. But the money-changer refuses to give him anything, he threatens him and sends him away with vehement words. If the pauper were not afraid of the king, he would try to kill the money-changer or push him aside and take his money. That is proof that this land has a king.' You have thus proven the existence of the king through the orderly conditions of the country, which are based on fear of the king or of his punishments. But none of this gives us any information about the personality of the king, or of his true nature insofar as he is the king.

"The same thing happens in all books of the prophets and even in the Pentateuch, when the masses are to be taught the knowledge of God. Since it was necessary to lead the entire people to believe in God's existence and teach them in faith that He possesses every perfection—i.e., that He not only exists as earth and Heaven exist, but also as a living, all-wise, all-powerful, and creative being—people were led to think that He exists in the same way as a body. Likewise, it was made believable that He lives by presenting Him as animated. The crowd, you see, will not regard any object as existing beyond doubt if it is not physical."[3] Many people believed that God had a figure and a shape, and they thought they would be denying Scriptures if they disavowed this belief. They attributed to God everything they considered perfection, even though, in respect to God, most things that people hold to be perfect are highly defective.

"The Holy Writ speaks in the language of human beings so as to be comprehensible even to beginners, and teachable to women and children, indeed to the entire nation, which is not capable of understanding the words in their true sense."[4] And Maimonides launched into a thorough discussion of the anthropomorphic expressions in the Bible. This discussion was to "create the key to help reach those places whose gates are locked."[5]

All statements that humanize God, says Maimonides, are circumlocutions. According to the Biblical view, one knows God through a spiritual grasp, not by sensory seeing. Even the slightest hint of sensory conception is eliminated from the notion of God, as well as from concepts like soul, angel, reward, and punishment in the afterlife. Maimonides accepts no excuse for anthropomorphism based on ignorance.[6]

Thinking is something that Maimonides sees not as a random activity but as existence itself.

All beings consist of matter and form. Man has several capacities of the soul. His special form, the soul, constituting his essence, is reason. This "soul" is not something that one is born with as a substance. It is given to man purely as a faculty, as a sheer possibility. At birth, man receives only the disposition toward reason, *potential* reason. It is left up to him to form his self, to acquire his soul. But how does this shaping of the soul occur? Thinking actualizes the faculty, and the acquisition of knowledge turns the soul from a possibility into a reality. *Acquired* reason, which is nothing else but the entirety of the knowledge one has taken in, is the true essence of man. The contents of knowledge are thus not externalities that one has assimilated but, to a certain degree, the constitutive components of the self, the true reality of man. The contents of knowledge are the essences of the things that one thinks. The spiritual self of man, his essence, is thus identical with the totality of the essences he has taken in. When man thinks of God, his essence is identical with the idea of God.

Maimonides saw thinking per se not as an internal human activity: potential reason, like everything that exists only potentially, requires a power outside itself, a power that lets it pass from the condition of possibility to that of reality. All possibility is passive, and can never awaken from its rigidity without a motive factor. A higher power, the "active intellect," performs the actualization of human reason and brings our thinking from mere capacity for thought to reality. This doctrine of thinking resulted from Maimonides's contemporary (i.e., medieval) view of the world, which he constructed out of the elements of the Aristotelian/Neo-Platonic philosophemes.

Man is called a microcosm, a "small world." But no one has ever heard of a donkey or a horse being referred to as a "small world." Hence, it is not the organic structure of man but his inherent reason that constitutes his similarity to the universal whole. For just as man is guided by reason, so too is the cosmos guided by God. Maimonides regards the universe as an organic whole whose parts are coherent, as in a human organism. The earth is the center of the universe surrounded by countless celestial spheres that are in constant motion. Every movement, every event taking place in the world, originates in the motion of the spheres. "And just as man instantly dies when his heart stops, so that all his movements cease, so too, if the spheres stood still, the entire world would have to die and everything in it would have to cease."[7] But what is the cause of the movement of the spheres?

Maimonides felt that the views which Aristotle advocated about the motion of the spheres, and from which he drew the belief in the existence of nonmaterial rational beings,

came closest to the truth, even though they were only assertions for which no valid evidence as yet existed. Maimonides
considered those views more methodical and less open to
challenge than any other statements of opinion. Furthermore, they were in agreement with the Scriptures and the
Midrashim.[8]

His thoughts in this respect were the following: It is clear
that each of the spheres is truly possessed of a soul. But
anyone hearing this for the first time will either think it
difficult to comprehend, or simply reject it. Why? Because
when he hears the word "soul," he will picture the sphere
as having a soul like a man or a donkey or a bull. In fact,
however, it means this: The orbiting of the sphere implies
that it has a principle in consequence of which it moves—
and this principle is, beyond any doubt, a soul. True, the
circular motion takes place because of a condition requiring
it to move in that manner. Yet this condition could not be
present in the sphere if no reason dwelled within it. However, not everything having reason, by means of which it
conceives something, and having a soul, by means of which
it is moved, actually moves when it conceives something;
for conception alone does not cause motion. If someone
conceives many things and can move toward them, he will
nevertheless not move toward them if a compelling desire
for the conceived things does not arise in him. He will
move only in order to reach what he has conceived. The
sphere has a desire for the object of its love, and that is
God. God, the unmoved mover, moves the sphere in that
the sphere aspires to become similar to what it has come to
know; namely, the conceived being that is completely nonmaterial and in which there is absolutely no change and no
arising of a condition, and from which the good always
emanates.

The fact that the stars differ from one another in speed
or slowness of motion as well as direction is proof that there

are many spheres. There are probably as many nonmaterial rational beings as there are spheres. Every sphere yearns for the rational being that is its cause and determines its motion. There are nine spheres; namely, the starless sphere surrounding the cosmos, the sphere of fixed stars, and the spheres of the seven planets. Every sphere has its sphere spirit, a rational being, from which it emanates, which it desires and strives toward, which presides over it and moves it.

The tenth rational being is the "active intellect." Its relationship to our world is the same as the relationship of every nonmaterial rational being to its sphere. Its existence is proved by the fact that our thinking passes from mere capacity and possibility for thought to reality, and by the fact that the forms that are merely possible in the matter of this world can also become real. For everything that passes from possibility to reality must have something outside itself that brings it to reality, and this must necessarily be of the same kind as what is brought to reality. For the carpenter does not make the cabinet because he is a craftsman but because the form of the cabinet was present in his reason. The relationship of the real reason present within us (coming from the emanation of the active intellect) to the active intellect is the same as the relationship of the reason present in every sphere (and emanating from the sphere spirit that rules it, and by means of which reason the sphere thinks of and conceives of the sphere spirit, aspires to become like it, and moves) to the sphere spirit.[9]

The control of all events "is passed on through God's effect on rational beings according to their order; from rational beings, some of their properties and that of light flow to the sphere bodies," and from them to our growing and decaying world.[10]

Rational beings operate through emanation, which is comparable to a water source pouring out in all directions.

The effectiveness is everlasting. The world came into being through an emanation from God, and everything that occurs in the world is wrought by Him through emanation.[11] The workings of the lower world, our world of growth and decay, thus occur through forces that emanate from the spheres. "Down here, there is no plant and no herb that does not have a star in Heaven, a star that touches it and says to it: Grow!" Thus goes a Talmudic parable. In Maimonides's opinion, everything is ruled by God through the forces that the Bible calls angels. The philosophers speak of nonmaterial rational beings, which the Bible calls angels. These rational beings are intermediary between God and Being. Through them, the spheres move, and this motion is the cause of all growth and decay.

The view that natural occurrences are an uninterrupted emanation from God, that the cosmic movements are determined by an incessant striving toward the higher, a yearning to become like the higher, corresponded to Maimonides's own character. It is a *pathos*—in the Greek sense: a great passion—that rules the world. And the *pathetic* idea of the universe found its likeness and echo in Maimonides's *pathetic* character.

Several times, Maimonides had had to fight on two fronts: in Fez against the hatred of the Almohades and the fanaticism of a Jew, and in the letter to Yemen against Mohammedan pressure and Jewish zealotry. And now, once again, in his philosophical struggle, Maimonides had a battle on two sides. Gaining a view of the world from philosophical sources and from Jewish tradition constituted a prologue rather than an epilogue to his thinking. On the other hand, the Jews in their naïve faith rejected this conception; on the other hand, there were passages in the Aristotelian teachings that aroused the most vehement protests from Maimonides.

"If you tell a man who is counted among the learned of Israel that God sends his angel to penetrate into a woman's womb and shape the budding life, then this image will appeal to him. He will accept it and see in it the infinite omnipotence and wisdom of God, even though he believes that the angel is a body of flaming fire one-third the size of the entire world. All this will strike him as possible. But if you tell him that God has inserted a shaping force into the seed, a force that gives the organs their shape and determines their abilities; if you tell him this force is the angel, and that all forms derive from the activity of the 'active intellect'— the angel and ruler of the world of which our sages always speak—then this man will refuse to listen, because he does not understand the true conditions of omnipotence and all-powerfulness, which express themselves in the creation of forces that are not perceivable by the senses and that operate in things."

Judaism teaches that God summoned the world from total nothingness into existence, and that He alone existed and nothing outside of Him, that He then brought all Being into existence by dint of His will and approval. Maimonides did not include this precept in the table of dogmas that he set up in his youthful work; but in riper years he realized that the belief in the creation of the world "is the second main doctrine next to that of God's oneness."[12] Aristotle, however, in his view of the world, taught that the universe, heaven and earth, time and motion are eternal and ever-lasting, do not grow and do not decay. He taught that the forms enter things one after another by shedding one form and assuming another. This order of the higher and the lower world, he said, will never stop. Nor does anything come into being in this order without its genesis being founded in its nature. And it is impossible for God's will to change, or for Him suddenly to desire to create the world

at any given point in time. Instead, God called the cosmos
into existence through His will, but did not create it from
a state in which nothing previously existed.

Maimonides realized that Aristotle's arguments are not
any sort of proof. Aristotle, "who taught men how to
reason or to invalidate a proof and what the prerequisites of
a valid proof are," could not have regarded these inadequate
arguments as proof. In making this judgment on Aristotle,
Maimonides seems to have stood alone in his time. The
contemporary schoolmen felt that Aristotle had already
proved the everlastingness of the world. Very many "who
styled   themselves   philosophers"   accepted   Aristotle's
opinions on this matter and believed that everything he had
said about it was definitively and indubitably proven. They
said it was impossible to polemicize against him or conjecture that anything had eluded him or that he had made any
kind of mistake.[13] Maimonides was now forced to take a
position against those who misunderstood Aristotle.

To his mind, Aristotle himself did not claim to have
offered any proof in this matter. "But alas, passions have
taken the upper hand in many parties, even in philosophers,
and they therefore want to insist that Aristotle resolved this
question through proof. This may be their opinion, but it
never even entered his mind that he had proved anything.
Only his followers have dared to make this claim."
Maimonides himself was of the opinion that the question
whether the world was created or exists eternally cannot be
resolved by reasoning. "Many who regard themselves as
thinkers, albeit not understanding anything of the sciences,
pass a decisive verdict on the everlastingness of the world,
because this has come down to them from recognized
scholars, who say the world is everlasting, and they reject
the words of all prophets, because they are framed as a
proclamation in God's name rather than by the way of
didactic method."

The actual contradiction with Jewish doctrine, as Maimonides saw it, was not in the claim that the world is eternal, and not in the blurring of the "point in time," but rather in the connected view that the world necessarily follows from God, that the world is as determined by God's existence "as the effect by its cause. For it follows from the view of the everlastingness of the world that Being *necessarily* proceeded from God. The relationship between the Creator and the creature is, supposedly, based on necessity. It is therefore unthinkable that any of the existing things can be altered in their nature."[14]

Whatever ultimately rules the universe, free will or necessity; whether God is to be conceived of as the sovereign lord who rules the world according to His will or whether He is inalterably bound to the eternal order of nature—Maimonides realized that this alternative is the cardinal question, which has to derive from the alternative of the creation of the world or the everlastingness of the world.

Confronted with this dilemma, Maimonides would not be swayed by any religious prejudice. In regard to the Mu'tazilites, the Arab philosophers who sought to prove the createdness of the world at any price, he said: "I do not want to so delude myself as to call sophistical methods proof."[15] His refusal to believe in the eternity of the world was not founded on the Biblical explanation that the world was created:

"For the passages in Scriptures that indicate the createdness of the world are no more numerous than those depicting God as a physical being. Nor are the gates of exegesis in any way closed or inaccessible to us in respect to the createdness of the world. On the contrary, it would have been just as possible for us to interpret these Biblical verses as we did in regard to God's nonphysicality; nay, it would have been a great deal easier, and our interpretation of the Scriptural passages in terms of the everlastingness of the world would have been superior to our interpretation that excludes the notion of God's incorporeity." However, the incorporeity of God is proven, "and it follows necessarily that all passages whose literal understanding is refuted by that proof must be interpreted differently . . . on the other hand, the everlastingness of the world has not been proved, and there is no need to strip the Biblical verses of their literal meaning and reinterpret them in order to tip the scales in favor of an opinion which might possibly be decided in an opposite way by some other kind of argumentation." Maimonides therefore undertook to grapple with this unproven Aristotelian assertion, which "topples religion from its very foundation and denies all the miracles of Scriptures."[16]

A chief argument of Aristotle's is that motion cannot be conceived of as having come into being. For the genesis of motion is, as a transition from possibility to reality, itself a motion; hence, the allegedly first motion would have to precede another, and so on, ad infinitum. The frailty of this argument, which constitutes the transferal of a law operative in inner-worldly events to the problem of the genesis of the world, was demonstrated by Maimonides as follows:

"Everything that is created exists after previously not existing." For example, the female seed, so long as it is still blood and exists in the seed vessels, is not the same as at the time of conception, when it meets with the male seed and begins to move. Likewise, at this point it does not have the same nature as when it is a living thing after its birth. Hence there is no possibility of drawing an argument from the nature of a thing after its genesis for the condition it was in when it moved toward becoming; nor can one draw an argument at the time of its movement for the condition it was in before it started to move. Let us take a man who is born on an isolated island. His mother dies after nursing him for a few months. The father alone rears the child until he has grown up and attained reason and knowledge. This man has never seen a woman, and now he asks: 'How did we come to exist? In what way have we come into being?'

"He is told: 'Every individual among us comes into being in the body of another individual of our species and similar to him. This is a female and she has such and such qualities. Every individual among us is a small body in the mother's womb, a body that lives, moves, feeds, and gradually grows until it has reached a certain size. Then a gate is opened for him in the mother's body, and he emerges from it. But, even afterwards, he does not stop growing, until he has become as you see us.'

"The boy will have to ask: 'Does this individual of our species also take food and drink while living and moving and growing in the mother's body? Does it breathe through a mouth and a nose? And can it excrete its excrements?'

"The answer will be: 'No.' But he will no doubt try to deny this and offer proof that all these true things are impossible by drawing his arguments from the state of the person who has already come into being. He will say: 'Every individual, if he is prevented from breathing for even part of an hour, must die, and then all his movements become impossible. How then can one imagine that a human being could remain living and moving for months on end in a strong vessel surrounding it inside a body? And if one of us swallowed a live bird, would this bird not have to die immediately upon reaching the stomach or the abdomen? Any individual not taking in food and drinking water through his mouth would be bound to die within a few days; how then can the live individual remain without food and drink for months? Any individual taking in nourishment, but not excreting, is bound to die within a very few days amid great pains; and how can this individual survive without excreting for months? If one were to bore through a human being's body, he would have to die; how then can one imagine that this budding life can have an open navel? How does it happen that the eyes do not open, the hands do not spread, and the feet do not stretch, since all these organs are perfect and not struck by any illness?'

"And he will follow this line of reasoning until he concludes that it is absolutely impossible for a man to come into being in this way."[17]

While this critical reflection indicates a methodological error in Aristotle, Maimonides brings up an original question in a different argument. The insight that the creature is unable to know creation, the genesis of Being, was deeply rooted in the mind of Maimonides, who had sensed the limits of the intellect since his youth. At that time, he had described the problem of individual existence as a boundary-stone on the border of the possibility of philosophical solution. Now he introduced that problem in a different form, in order to shatter the rationalism of the "doctrine of eternity" and to substantiate the words of the prophets. In accordance with the situation of the problem, the problem itself becomes a question about genesis.

"What is the cause for the variety of species and of individuals within these species?" Maimonides asks Aristotle, in an imaginary dialogue. He demonstrates that the emanation theory, which tries to explain the world according to necessary laws, is incapable of accounting for the presence of the diversity of existent beings. Why are there "countless stars in the eighth sphere, which are all spherical, some large, some small, here one star, there another which appears to be one cubit away from the first, there ten, clustering thick and close together, and then a very large stretch in which there is nothing? Just what is the cause determining that one part must have ten stars, but the other part none whatsoever? Furthermore, the body of the entire sphere is a simple one, having no diversity. For what reason is one portion of the sphere more suitable for the star existing in it than another? All this and all similar things are truly quite improbable; nay, it is well-nigh impossible to believe that all this, as Aristotle thinks, derives from God under the aspect of necessity."[18]

However, if one believes that this is so through the will of a willing being, but that we are ignorant of the reasons that induced His wisdom to bring this forth, then all these problems vanish. Once one believes in the creation of the world, then the miracle is conceivable; but as soon as someone says that the world *must* be thus, then as a result questions will arise whose answers will include the denial and negation of the Biblical words. "That is why prestigious men have spent, and will spend, their days meditating upon these questions. The reason is that everything the philosophers have said in contradiction to our faith would have to collapse into nothingness if the creation of the world were proved. Likewise, if they were to confirm Aristotle's opinion with proof, then our Scripture would have to collapse in its entirety, and the matter would be settled in favor of other doctrines."[19] That is why Maimonides suspends knowledge, in order to make room for miracle.

Despite the insight into the importance of this decision, he considered his theses merely refutations of the opposing arguments, and not positive proofs. Since it had become clear to him that the question was unanswered by philosophy, he decided upon the teaching of prophecy, "which makes clear those things that investigation lacks the strength to know."[20]

When Maimonides was done with this contemplation, he declared with assurance that he had erected a tremendous rampart all around the Torah, making it impossible for anybody to cast a stone at it.[21] The path of thinking led Maimonides from the problem of purposefulness to that of creation. The question of concrete individual existence still haunted him and it was this that he marked the limits of reason. The criterion of purposefulness was now joined to that of genesis. Even though philosophy had managed, he said, to explain the genesis of individual existence in the earthly world, it is nevertheless unable to explain the variety of the astral world. Maimonides therefore felt that everything Aristotle says about the things "underneath the sphere of the moon . . . is true beyond any doubt." On the other hand, no man knows anything about what is in Heaven, aside from the little that the mathematical axioms offer. "However, burdening the mind with something that one cannot grasp and about which one does not have the means to attain knowledge indicates a lack of judgment or a kind of madness. What is more, we must stop short at the limit of our ability. Anything that cannot be understood through reasoning must be left to him who receives sublime inspiration from God."[22] Thus, prophecy alone is capable of solving the riddle of concrete individual existence.

15

Meditation on God

THE urge to know God had early on seized hold of young Maimonides. Thought, reflection, and the concentration of his soul on this highest of all problems had determined his spiritual and intellectual attitude through all periods of his life. His passion for reason, his almost naïve yearning, his probing and wooing of insight into the mystery never stopped. But in his mind, which was never free of this profound emotion, the longing to know God came not only from the uncertainty of vague feelings but also from the necessity of thinking: the desire of thought led him to fathom the possibilities of metaphysical knowledge.

"Man should not plunge into this sublime and venerable subject in a hasty and superficial manner without first familiarizing himself with the other sciences and with genuine knowledge. He must purify his character thoroughly and carefully, and subdue his desires and the passions springing from his imagination. However, if he knows the true premises, if he masters the methods of reasoning and deduction, if he knows how to guard against the sophisms of thinking, then he may be permitted to begin an exploration of this subject. But he must not, at the very outset of understanding, make a decisive judgment, or give full rein to his ideas by attributing to his thoughts the power to understand God. Instead, he must exercise hesitancy and restraint and wait until the truths little by little disclose themselves to him. It is in the light of such behavior that we must understand the verse: 'And Moses hid his face, for he was afraid to look upon God' (Exodus 3:6)."[1]

Which technique of meditation did he utilize? Maimonides kept asking his reason: How does one know God? What characteristics and qualities of God can be stated? "Our minds are simply too feeble to know even the essence of Heaven, which is, after all, merely a moving body. We have measured it in spans and cubits and, as for its parts, we are familiar with their size and most of their movements. We know that Heaven necessarily has matter and form, but this matter is not the same as that which we possess. Thus, we cannot describe it with positive affirmations, but only with expressions which are not affirmative, such as: Heaven is neither light nor heavy, it is not impressionable or subject to any influence and therefore does not take any influence, it has neither taste nor smell—and other such negative terms, all of which are necessary because we do not know the nature of this matter. How then shall the state of our knowledge be when it aims at understanding something that is immaterial, absolutely simple, and necessarily existent?"[2]

He took the following as an example: "A man has recognized as true that a 'ship' exists, yet he does not know to what this term is to be applied, whether it is an independent being or an accident. Another man subsequently comes to realize that the ship is not an accident. Still another man learns that it is not an animal, another man that it is not a mineral, another that it is not a plant attached to the earth. Then to another man it is revealed that it is not a single body whose parts cohere in a natural manner. Another man comes to the conviction that it does not have a flat form, like boards or doors; the next man finds that it does not have a spherical shape; another that it is not pointed; another that it is neither round nor equilateral; and finally another man that it is not a solid mass. It is now clear that this last man, through all these negative statements, has almost come to the correct notion of the ship as it really is, and to a certain extent he is on a par with the man who conceives of the ship as a long body of hollowed wood, made with many pieces of wood, but who has reached this notion by means of affirmative statements. As for the others, every man judging the ship is farther from the correct conception than his successor, so that the first man knows nothing but the name 'ship.' "[3] In the same way, Maimonides hoped to use negative statements to approach the knowledge and conception of God.

In his meditation upon God, Maimonides takes as his point of departure that, aside from perceivable and conceived things, a necessarily existing being is present. He says of this being that his non-Being is unthinkable. Then he acknowledges that this being does not exist in the same way as, for instance, the four elements, which are bodies without life, and he concludes: God's mode of Being is not similar to the mode of Being of bodies without life. He then realizes that this being does not exist in the same manner as Heaven, which is a living body. And he tells himself: God is not a body. Furthermore, he realizes that this being does not exist in the same way as one of the beings of reason, which are incorporeal and not dead, but are caused. He therefore tells himself: There is no cause that has produced God. Then he realizes that for this being it is not enough to exist to itself alone but rather that from it emanate the countless existent things of this world, not in the way that heat emanates from fire or light from the sun, but in such a way that its agency gives to existing things permanence, continuity, and order. He also realizes that this being is not powerless, not ignorant, not thoughtless, and not negligent. Furthermore, it has nothing similar to it; and thus he concludes: It is impossible for it to have plurality, it is one.

The denial of imperfections is the only intellectual means that Maimonides allowed himself to apply in the act of learning to know God. He thus realizes that God has no qualities, that He is not a being subject to an impression. God cannot suffer any influence, nor can He have any affect. He possesses no faculties, so that He has no inherent strength. Nor does He have a soul, so that shame and the like, health and illness, and so on, are alien to him.

There is no relationship between God and time, between God and space, between God and a thing created by Him. "For no man will doubt that there is no relationship between one hundred cubits and the sharpness of the pepper, between wisdom and sweetness, or between modesty and bitterness. How then could there be any relationship between God and a thing He has created, given the vast distance between their modes of being?"

Maimonides has the feeling that these things "almost elude thinking." He senses the inadequacy of "customary words, which are the chief source of our errors." For example, he complains about applying the word "eternal" to God: "For a thing can be spoken of as 'eternal' only if it is subject to time. But that to which the determination of time is not applicable cannot truly be called 'eternal' or 'come into being,' just as one cannot call a sweet thing crooked or straight, a sound salty or tasteless."[4]

This technique of meditation gave Maimonides the possibility of sifting through thousands of everyday occasions, through innumerable encounters with his environment, and wresting from negative knowledge the secret that is knowledge itself. In his meditation, he employed methodical thinking as an instrument for attaining to a knowledge of God. His passion to know something of God was fulfilled—not in intoxication, in emotional exuberance, but in disciplined circumspection.

One remark of his sounds like a self-avowal: "And that is why such a man strains for many years to understand science and metaphysics . . . but it is all in vain if the result of all this science consists in denying some notion of God . . ."⁵ His interior joy and his gratitude when this knowledge is attained is expressed like a hymn: "Praised be God, whose essence is such that our thinking is noncomprehension when we reflect upon Him, our wisdom folly when it contemplates how His works necessarily proceed from His will, and our excess of words stuttering and impotence when all tongues wish to glorify the attributes of God!"⁶

Maimonides, although otherwise denying any positive statement about God, does attribute thinking to Him. This theoretically inconsistent notion, akin to an error of logic, is justified by his experience. He senses that even if one concludes that one cannot speak of thinking in regard to God, this conclusion flows from God, the source of all thinking.⁷

The meditational technique of negation is a logical method. Maimonides, who from his youth aspired to prophetical as well as philosophical knowledge, builds up his meditation with the elements of prophecy. The individual's own existence, the individual's own reality are the starting points from which Maimonides wishes to arrive at a knowledge and understanding of God. When the prophets speak of God and attribute wrath, love, and mercy to Him, they are referring, says Maimonides, to God's effect in the world. "For example, one realizes the extremely meticulous care of His workings in the genesis of an embryo within the womb of a living creature, the way He produces powers in this living creature and in those who are to rear the child after birth, powers meant to protect them against death and destruction, to shield them against any harm and assist them in all that is required [for development]. Since such action occurs among us because of the intense feeling and emotion of mercy, God is therefore called 'merciful' . . . Likewise, in the workings of God that affect men, we find huge and powerful calamities that come upon certain individuals and kill them, or general disasters that destroy whole nations or regions and annihilate fathers, children, and grandchildren without leaving even the possibility of offspring or posterity, like the sinking of landscapes, earthquakes, deadly gusts of heat, or aggressions of nations against other nations to exterminate them with the sword and wipe out their property. There are many like deeds which one human being inflicts upon another, only because of violent anger, enormous jealousy, or passionate blood-revenge; as a consequence of these workings, God is called 'jealous,' 'vengeful,' 'angry and furious.' "[8]

Maimonides ultimately teaches "that things are all connected with one another, that there is nothing but God and His works—meaning by the latter, that is, everything in existence except Him. There is thus no way of knowing God but through His works, and these prove His Being or existence."[9]

PART TWO

Renunciation and Fulfillment

16

The Pilgrim to Maimonides

IN Ceuta, from which Maimonides had embarked for Palestine in 1165 when fleeing the Almohades, there lived at this time a young man named Joseph ben Judah ibn Aknin, a scholar, poet, physician, philosopher, and Talmudist. The Almohadean suppression was raging as wildly as ever; forced converts still lived under the Damoclean sword of suspicious authorities, and they were well aware of having desecrated God's name. In order to comfort these downtrodden souls, Ibn Aknin emulated what Rabbi Maimon and young Maimonides had done a few decades earlier: he composed a piece "on the healing of suffering souls and the medicine for sincere hearts." Among his points were that sufferings from religious persecution could be the means of leading Jews to salvation by making them aware of their sins, that all signs for the arrival of the Messiah had already appeared, and that all that was required was the nation's penitence and repentance, which are necessary for redemption:[1]

"The number of scholars is very small, they are almost entirely lacking, our sufferings are doubled, we have witnessed all these things personally. The prophets' threats of punishment have come true for us; we have plunged into suffering, we find no refuge from the destruction caused by those sufferings. The great synagogue, where pious men once gathered, is now a house of lewdness, learning and truth have vanished and evil has increased. The young despise the old, the daughter does not honor the mother, and the son is not ashamed of his deeds in the presence of the father. The insolence of this Almohadean government is well known, the denouncers are many, students grow fewer, and the food supply is diminishing. It is obvious that no age has endured such sufferings as the present age, so that it is appropriate to think that this is the time of the Messiah. This age is surely sinful through and through, and we can blame the delay in the arrival of the Messiah only on our utter lack of penitence and repentance, but we can in no wise maintain that the proper time has not yet come."

Even in this period, when many suffered martyrdom rather than accept Islam, the Jews continued with their Jewish and general studies. Ibn Aknin, raised as a pseudo-Mohammedan and suffering greatly because of his double religion, still had, despite everything, an ardent enthusiasm for the Torah, for mathematics and medicine, for philosophy and poetry. He was the first in Hebrew literature to write *makamas,** which later were highly praised. Al-Harizi called him the one true poet of Maghreb and apostrophized him: "The Holy Tongue dwells in thy heart, and the Arab also camps in it." But Ibn Aknin was moved most strongly by philosophical and theological problems. He was particularly interested in the question of how to interpret the Scriptures, especially the Song of Songs. The great Jewish commentators explicated the Biblical text according to its literal meaning, but this method did not suffice for a profound young man who lived in a Messianic mood. Beyond the "obvious," he sought the "inwardly concealed." He

---

* *Makamas*, a literary genre developed by Arab poets, consisted of tales in rhymed prose.

penned a commentary on the Song of Songs entitled *The Uncovering of Secrets and the Revelation of Lights*. Aside from the literal and Talmudic-allegorical methods, he applied a deeper, speculative exegesis, which read the contents of the Song of Songs as alluding to man's relationship with the "active intellect." He interpreted the male beloved as a metaphor for the "active intellect," and the female beloved as a metaphor for the rational soul. In such terms, he elucidated the entire Song of Songs. Without ignoring the simple literal meaning, he tried to grasp the "inner sense" of the Scriptures in accordance with the "science of inwardness." "I am the first to explain in this fashion; nothing whatsoever has been published in this manner," he remarked not without pride; and he believed he had ferreted out "hidden pearls" and secrets which are meant only for the select few who have reached the level of perfection and which would merely harm anyone else.

Maimonides's Codex, making its triumphal procession through the world, arrived in Morocco. Ever since his stay in Fez, where he had vindicated the honor of the pseudo-converts to Islam, Maimonides's name had been haloed. Neither time nor distance could dim the glory of his name. After leaving Fez, Maimonides had stayed in touch with the Moroccan Jews through letters and official missives.[2] Among his admirers was an outsider who was drawn to him by deep inner feelings, a fated sympathy whose source was not alone his wonder and astonishment at his work. Ibn Aknin, who aspired to the height of the spiritual, saw in Maimonides's personality a model and guide to glorious sublimity; and it was by Maimonides that he measured the steps of his own rise and the ideal of his life. Despite his proud bias for the new allegorical and speculative interpretation of Holy Writ, he wondered how Maimonides would judge this method. His uncertainty reached a level of concern when the Codex, the "magnificent work," came into his hands. "The man who dares to abandon the literal sense of the commandments is a liar, scoundrel, and heretic," Ibn Aknin read therein. This condemnation hit the proudest spot of his self-assurance. Did Maimonides, with this decision, wish to turn against the speculative method of exegesis, such as was first practiced by him, Ibn Aknin?

However, "careful examination" convinced him "that there is no difference between our words and those of Maimonides." The latter, said Ibn Aknin, was rejecting the allegorical method of exegesis because its effect is that "the commandment disappears altogether." For example, the consequence of interpreting the commandment of the sinew of the thigh-vein (Genesis 32:26–33) as referring to sensuality, and the commandment to maintain correct scales, weights, and measures (Deuteronomy 25:13–15) as referring to the rules of logic, would be that the former (i.e., to abstain from eating the sinew of the thigh-vein) would be cancelled and the latter would permit the use of differing sets of weights and measures. Such explanations would merely lead to neglecting the commandments and resorting to sophistries. That would be counter to the purpose in our writings, in which we have given deeper explanations. For we too believe in the literal sense, except that we also assume that a more profound meaning may lie at the bottom. Holding fast to the former and neglecting the latter merely demonstrates ignorance, such as is normal in the sect of the Karaites; the reverse procedure is customary among the Christians, and it is to these sects that Maimonides's words quite rightfully apply. I, however, am in full agreement with him, for we both start out from one and the same viewpoint."

Among the Moroccan Jews, Maimonides's unprecedented reputation aroused a deep feeling for him as the "wonder of the age." For them, plagued outwardly and inwardly by the scorn of the agitated fanatics around them and by their own contrition and despair, the tidings from this "light," a distant star in the free land of Saladin, were an inner aid. Ibn Aknin thought of that verse in the Song of Songs (7:13)—"The mandrakes give a smell, and at our gates are all manner of pleasant fruits, new and old, which I have laid up for thee, O my beloved"—as an allusion to the times of persecution, "when we practice the Law under threats of the sword, and especially in the current persecution, when we constantly busy ourselves with the study of the Law; one proof of this is the appearance of the great Maimonides, whose higher knowledge is known to all and who has composed a commentary on the Mishnah, the Mishneh Torah, and a book of commandments, aside from what he has already produced earlier in the most diverse branches of scholarship; he alone would suffice for this period of persecution."

But Ibn Aknin was moved by personal as well as national concern. The reverse side of his self-assurance was an inner irresoluteness, since he felt a contradiction between the notions of religion and the views of philosophy. At one time he believed he had accomplished as much for the understanding of the Song of Songs as the renowned commentators Alfarabi and Galen had for Aristotle and Hippocrates. In his book, which interprets the Biblical verses clothed in Aristotelian ideas, he had used the method of disclosing an "inner sense" in order to find a supposed balance between the Bible and philosophy. If the intention of wise King Solomon (to whom the Song of Songs is traditionally ascribed) had been the one that Ibn Aknin inferred, "then the greatest of the philosophers [Aristotle] achieved more by a shorter path," said a later critic.

At any rate, even though such criticism remained unknown to him, Ibn Aknin also felt that his method was inadequate, inappropriate, and questionable. The contradiction between the Biblical and the Aristotelian view now struck him in all its insolubility. Since he refused to forgo either truth, he could not do without the speculative method of exegesis, in which he saw the only possibility of reconciliation. However, he wavered between the literal understanding of the Scriptural words and a universal interpretation, and remained as perplexed as ever. Sometimes he followed his reason and rejected what the plain verbal sense of the Bible yielded; at other times he felt he had thus "abandoned the fundamental teachings of religion," and he despaired. Now he resolved to hold to naïve understanding, refrain from thinking, and make no use of reason. But soon he noticed that his decision "meant a loss for himself and a detriment for the Holy Writ." He lived "in fear and depression, feeling sorrow of the heart and wretched confusion incessantly."

It seems that even at the time when his own method could not lead him to the "science of inwardness," his desire grew to attain the highest knowledge. He held Maimonides to be the possessor of "higher learning," and he longed to move to Fostat and study with him. He obviously believed he had all the prerequisites for initiation into the mysteries of "higher learning." Just as the fragrance of a flower is harmful to a certain species of insect, so too the mysteries are dangerous for most people, he felt. They are meant only for those who are deemed to be on the level of perfection. Even though he tried to still his craving for the "mysteries" and was boldly confident of achieving fulfillment, there can be no doubt as to the extent of his self-assurance.

Ibn Aknin, a fiery man who felt a certain congeniality with Maimonides, made up his mind to leave his paternal city and move to Egypt; but at first he evidently met with insuperable odds and had to restrain himself in patience. Meanwhile, his yearning for Maimonides was strengthened by a further motive. He felt that so long as he resided in the "unclean land" and was sullied by the lie of pseudo-conversion, he would be denied the attainment of a higher level of knowledge. His conscience urged him to migrate: "If we failed to sacrifice our lives, we were in any case coerced and were by no means willing criminals; but this was only so long as the war raged and we had no other haven. Considering that we could now easily find a place in far-off countries, where we could escape compulsory religion, we have beyond doubt desecrated the name of God deliberately, while others have saved their souls, seen with the eyes of understanding, been shone upon by truth, and escaped this religious coercion."

Conditions in Morocco grew ever more dismal, ever more dishonoring. Abd-el-Mumin had promised Jewish converts to Islam all the rights and privileges that native Mohammedans enjoyed. But his successors ignored his promise and heavily afflicted the pseudo-converts. Al Mansur, ruler since 1184, decreed that all converts in Morocco must wear special garments: a black cloak with extremely wide sleeves hanging down to the feet, and a veil of an ugly yellow color instead of the customary turban. This attire exposed them to the fomented hatred of the mob. Proud Ibn Aknin, who had his own medical practice in Ceuta, felt bitterly injured by the "scorn and shame" of this humiliation. But the general deterioration had a positive effect on him, apparently encouraging him to carry out his plan. With fortified courage, he prepared for his departure. "Let us hope for God's kindly assistance," he prayed, "so that we can cleanse ourselves of the uncleanlinesses caused by the persecutions, and may soon fulfill our hope of leaving this cursed and sullied land."

17

"Back Home in Andalusia"

I N 1185, Ibn Aknin landed in Alexandria. After his
exodus from the land of spiritual bondage, he could
breathe free in Egypt. But his anxiety was at first stronger
than his courage. Ibn Aknin did not dare to visit Maimonides
immediately. He evidently felt he could present his request
more effectively in writing, from a distance. He sent a
letter to Fostat, describing how the desire to study under
Maimonides had brought him to Egypt from the "end of
the world." He added poems expressing his "powerful
yearning for truth and knowledge." The verses were also
meant to show his poetic gift and facilitate the introduction.

Maimonides was not very greatly taken with the form
and artistic value of the poems; however, he was struck by
their content, the "keen longing for speculative knowledge."
What could appeal to his sympathy more directly than
such a desire? In Egypt, the number of people thirsting for
knowledge and interested in philosophy was extremely
small. From faraway Ceuta, near Andalusia, a cry of
nostalgia came by way of Alexandria and found a response.
The critical Maimonides wondered, however, whether in
this scholarly pilgrim "desire did not exceed ability, and
the thirst for knowledge his intellectual talent." Nevertheless, he invited him to come to Fostat.

The dream of the man impelled by a "passionate urge," the yearning of an ardent heart which had glowed within him for many years, now found its fulfillment. Ibn Aknin soon stood before the man who possessed the "science of inwardness." For Maimonides, the arrival of the passionate disciple also meant a gain in human terms. Egypt was no center of learning as Andalusia had once been and Babylon still was. The existing academies could boast of neither a high-level tradition nor more recent accomplishments. The general standard of education was far below that of the countries Maimonides had come from. Hosts of men hungry for knowledge, as in France and Babylon at that time, could not be found here. There was a thin stratum of educated Jews, but Maimonides's great ideas had neither a response nor a following there. Even after many years, Maimonides still referred to his life in Egypt as a life "in a foreign place."[1] He mournfully longed for his Andalusian homeland. Evidently, the sensual, fatalistic, and phlegmatic mentality which prevailed in the land of the Nile was repugnant to him. The poor level of education, and the manner in which the Jewish way of life was permeated with Arabic and Karaite customs and superstitions, increased his repulsion. He even thought less of the physicians in this country than of his colleagues from Andalusia and Morocco. Nostalgia for the land of his childhood never left him, even in the final days of his life. Over and over again, the words slipped out of him: "Back home in Andalusia . . ."

Ibn Aknin came to Fostat not to pay tribute to Maimonides but to find answers to questions that tormented him, to attain the "higher knowledge," which attracted his imaginative mind. The timid admirer soon came forward with demands; the strange contrast between the teacher and the pupil generated a passionate tension. The path of gradual study was too long for the young man, and he nagged Maimonides for a speedy answer. He would have much preferred draining the "beaker of wisdom" at one draft. Maimonides, who had attained coolness and forbearance in the shadow of his ramified knowledge, remained controlled and composed. He incessantly tried to mellow "the overzealousness of the pupil, who was tortured by noble disquiet"; over and over again, he recommended slow and methodical study, for he wanted his pupil to have the truth revealed to him in a methodical and not a "random way."

Maimonides gave him an example: "When men investigate, they soon bristle with countless doubts, and objections soon cross their minds . . . for this is like tearing down a building. But the confirmation of doctrine and the quelling of doubts come only through many prerequisites, which are gained from these preparatory sciences. Now the man who studies without preparation is like a man who goes by foot to reach a place, but tumbles into a deep pit on the way and has no means of climbing out, so that he has to perish. Had he not bothered with his trip and remained in his place, it would have been more useful to him . . ."[2] Relentlessly, he instructed Joseph, who kept trying to push forward: "Very many scholars, namely those who are renowned for learning, are plagued by this disease, namely striving toward the goal and talking about it without first doing the basic preliminary studies. Some of them, however, are led astray by ignorance and lust for power to denigrate this preliminary learning, which they have learned only fleetingly and sought carelessly. They even attempt to show that it is harmful or useless."[3]

Plato had put the following inscription over the entrance to his academy: "Whoever has not studied mathematics, do not enter!" Maimonides similarly esteemed the propaedeutic importance of this science for attaining true knowledge; and since he so greatly desired to train Ibn Aknin, he began with mathematics, first having him study geometry and astronomy, especially since the pupil had the necessary prerequisite knowledge. Under Maimonides's guidance, Ibn Aknin read works of astronomy, including the *Almagest*. Maimonides then called upon his assistance in a major scientific task: the correction of Ibn Aphla's astronomical tables and Ibn Hud's mathematical *Istikmal*.[4] During this joint labor, Maimonides delighted in Ibn Aknin's swift grasp and correct conclusions. The mentor was astonished at the way his pupil, who had thirsted for metaphysics, now fully devoted himself to mathematics. He knew, however, where Ibn Aknin would ultimately land and how important such a preparation is. When the study of logic followed, Maimonides pinned his "hope" on Ibn Aknin. From then on, Maimonides regarded him as worthy of learning the "secrets of prophecy" in such a way as to "see in them what the perfect should see in them."

At first, Maimonides granted him mere hints. But Ibn Aknin demanded complex discussions and insisted on being initiated into the teachings of Maimonides. In dealing with the pupil, Maimonides never sidestepped "the task of explaining the words of the Bible or the sayings of the Talmudic sages, which were mentioned and referred to inside these doctrines." But he still hesitated to allow the young disciple, whom he had only been instructing a short while, to penetrate the final mysteries. And Ibn Aknin, as Maimonides remarked, was in the throes of "noble disquiet."

Maimonides was certainly willing to instruct anyone who asked him to do so in general matters of the Torah and science, but he was highly reticent when it came to metaphysical problems. The esoteric stance that had characterized him since his youth permitted him to instruct only one man and initiate him into the mysteries. But so far he had not encountered this one man.

No less powerful than his hesitance and reluctance was

his urge to teach and impart. This urge, which was a blazing compulsion, was for him the original force of the spirit: The divine effect, through which we think and which makes one man's reason superior to another's, is such "that perhaps one personality receives only a little of it, but the measure suffices to make him—though not another man—perfect. Yet it may also be that one personality receives too much and may have enough left over beyond his own perfection to make another man perfect. The impact on a scholar may be so strong as to move him to investigate, to contemplate, to acquire knowledge and understanding; but it may not induce him to teach or compose a work. Indeed, he may not even wish or be able to do these things; then again, the effect may be so powerful that it drives him to compose a work or teach. Likewise, a prophet can receive just enough of the gift of prophecy so that it makes him alone perfect, and no one else. But he can also receive so much that it forces him to address people, to teach them publicly, and to let some of his perfection flow over to them. It is clear that, without this excess of perfection, science and scholarship could never be described in books, and that the prophets could never have talked men into knowing the truth. For no scholar writes in order to instruct himself. Rather, the nature of the divine effect is such that it has to pour out to the general public and continue from one receiver to another. Its final destination is within a receiver to whom this outpouring is not in excess but serves toward his own perfection. However, this effect forces the man who has received it in excess to appeal to the people whether or not they accept him—nay, even if he is harmed in the act —so that we find prophets who kept appealing to the people until they were killed. That was why when Jeremiah was spurned by the rebels and deniers of God, he kept his prophecies a secret; he did not want to call his scorners to the truth. But he could not hold out (Jeremiah 20:8, 9): "For the word of the Lord was unto me a reproach and a mocking all day, and I said, I will not mention it, nor will I again speak in His name; but it was in mine heart as a burning fire, enclosed in my bones, and I was wearied to keep it, and did not prevail."[5]

In 1185, the year Joseph ibn Aknin came to Fostat, Maimonides's wife bore a son. Through the coincidence of these two events, he developed a love for both his son, whom he named Abraham, and for Joseph, whom he called "my son."

Joseph, who was quick to wax enthusiastic and was gifted with a warm heart and bold mind, soon gained the affection of the people around Maimonides, and his relationship to his teacher was not just scholarly. Thus, he once traveled to Alexandria for Maimonides to announce publicly the mentor's verdict in a marital case.[6]

In 1187, throughout all the countries of his empire, in Egypt, Syria, and Mesopotamia, Saladin circulated a call to Holy War against the Crusaders, and he marched to Palestine at the head of a great army. In the battle of Chittim, he won a brilliant victory over the Christians. The subsequent conquest of Jerusalem, which had been under the control of the "infidels" for more than eighty years, was a historic turning point; Islam triumphed. The behavior of the victor of 1187 was in deliberate contrast to that of the conquerors of 1099: the new occupation brought no mass slaughter, but rather a generous and noble treatment of the defeated. Even Maimonides, who was deeply concerned about the fate of the Holy Land, was satisfied with the triumph of the noble sultan. Saladin, who had always been benevolent to his Jewish subjects, favored the settlement of Jews in Palestine; and the victory also had its effect in Egypt. The position of the Sunnite ruler was greatly solidified, and Jews could hope for a favorable turn in the development of their community life.

In the course of this memorable year Joseph departed from Fostat for Aleppo. He had spent not quite two years with Maimonides. This period did not even suffice for all his intended mathematical studies. Had Joseph, whose "noble mind drove him to achieve his desire," reached his goal? Maimonides was not his first teacher in philosophy;[7] Joseph identified himself as a pupil of Averroës, who resided at the caliph's court in Marrakesh, not far from Ceuta.[8] Maimonides considered Averroës one of the "assiduous in philosophy," who knew "true scholarship" and was thoroughly grounded in the works of the philosophers. The theories of the Mu'tazilites, being unknown to anyone in Morocco, not excluding Averroës, were the only area of general philosophy in which Joseph was dependent on instruction from Maimonides.[9] However, he saw Maimonides as the "mystagogue," who was to initiate him into the arcana of prophecy and transmit "higher knowledge" to him. But Maimonides was all too reticent, and Joseph never got beyond the "preliminary studies." The reason for Joseph's departure is not known. "Through God's dispensation, we had to separate and you had to go to your destination," Maimonides wrote. He assured the departing disciple that he would soon complete an opus that would answer the questions on Joseph's mind.

How does one reach the highest level of perfection possible to a human being? This question moved Ibn Aknin, but it occupied Maimonides himself even more.

Maimonides knew enough to tell himself that God lets anyone achieve prophecy if and when He wants him to, but only when he is a perfect man. Maimonides felt it was as impossible for a simple man to become a prophet as for a donkey or a frog to prophesize. No one can go to bed as a nonprophet and then get up as a prophet, for prophecy is unthinkable without the proper qualifications and preparation; even then, its possibility is dependent on divine power. It is not necessarily found even if someone has reached the utmost level of speculative knowledge and possesses the highest virtues of character: these prerequisites must be joined by the greatest possible perfection of the imagination. Although the achievement of spiritual and ethical perfection depends on man's free will, the perfection of the imagination is beyond man's power; it has to be inborn. Imagination is a physical power; its degree of perfection depends on organic qualities. An organ which is bad from birth cannot become perfect even through the best life style. These conditions are indispensable because prophetic illumination is an emanation that pours out from God through the agency of the "active intellect": first in the ability to think and then in the imagination. Every human being with an innate perfection of the imagination is capable of prophecy. He becomes a prophet only if his reason is perfected, his character pure and steady, his thoughts always aiming at sublime things, and his goal the knowledge of God and the contemplation of His works. This man must also be one of those whose thinking and yearning about animal and material things have been overcome—namely, the desire for and enjoyment of food, drink, and sex.

There are three kinds of perfection that Maimonides sees as prerequisites for receiving prophetic illumination: perfection of the mind, character, and imagination. He himself obviously feels that he has already attained the first two kinds. His extraordinary appreciation of his own scholarly achievements, to which he frequently gives voice, and his utterances about the qualities of his character show that he does not by any means feel remote from the level of spiritual and ethical perfection. Similarly, his statement about his memory suggests that he considers his imagination perfect, for he teaches that memory is a function of the imagination. Only the reserve that has stamped his behavior induces him to keep silent about this secret of his life. All he does in this respect is once to compare the process of inspiration with the flashing of lightning in thick nocturnal darkness. There are people, he says, whose lives have shorter or longer intervals between one stroke of lightning and the next, and there are also those whose darkness is never lit up. There are people for whom the lightning flashes only once in their entire night, and there are those for whom the lightning bursts out over and over again, with little interruption, so that they dwell almost in a steady light and their night becomes day.[10]

Maimonides regards enlightenment as a natural phenomenon. The miracle, for him, is when illumination is not forthcoming, since only preventive interference by God can deprive man of the emanation of the "active intellect." But there can be "no doubt" that the emanation of the "active intellect" will pour out on the man who possesses the prerequisites.[11]

18

The Supreme Head of the Jews

UNDER Saladin, who pursued a large-scale policy of reconstruction, Egypt went through an economic and intellectual boom. Poets, grammarians, physicians, dogmatists, and Koran exegetes were working in Cairo. The Ayyubites, Saladin and his successors, were unusually magnanimous in cultivating intellectual, spiritual, and especially religious life. A religious renaissance determined the character of the era. Theological academies were founded. Saladin himself established madrasahs* for the three chief rites of Islam. And in the great madrasahs, the study of Fikh, Sufism, and Asharite dogmatism flourished.[1]

The Jews also took part in the general intellectual upswing. The final redaction of the tales of *The Thousand and One Nights*, many of which are of Jewish origin, was accomplished by a Jew in Cairo.[2]

The medical practice that Maimonides had been pursuing since David's death brought him in contact with one of the most interesting figures of the age—Saladin's vizier, Al Fadil. The latter, "an unbelievably enterprising, dried-up little mannikin," who could write a letter "and simultaneously dictate two others during an audience,"[3] was

---

* Madrasah, a Mohammedan mosque-school or college.

greatly respected by his contemporaries. It was supposedly known outside the borders of Egypt "that he has made it the task of his life to spread among all people the good things that God had blessed him with, to keep the people out of harm's way, and constantly bring them useful things with his wealth, his rank, his tongue, and his intelligence. His wealth he has spent for the satisfaction of the needy and poor, the education of orphans, the ransoming of prisoners, the construction of academies and the increase of scholars and researchers . . . It is well known that God has favored him with elegance of expression and wondrous speech; that he has saved many communities from destruction, not only individuals, but whole towns and provinces. He has also saved men's property from being looted by soldiers, and wives from being carried off by warriors. The many flames of hatred among the believers were dampened and extinguished by him," writes Maimonides.[4]

Al Fadil, who enjoyed Saladin's unlimited trust, had performed the most difficult feats in advising and guiding several rulers, and in so doing he taught them the principles of fairness and justice. Al Fadil helped Saladin with necessary reforms in taxation and the military. He was as orthodox as his master, and like him, he built a theological school in Cairo. Saladin knew his adviser's love of rare and beautiful books; in 1171, when the caliph's property was distributed, the ruler gave Al Fadil the famous book collection of the Fatimites, and in 1183 he rewarded him with a huge library that had fallen into his hands during a conquest. Al Fadil, vizier and head of the "ministry of correspondence," is still regarded in the Orient today as the epitome of the perfect stylist. The ornamental diction of his accounts, the artistic phrases and "elegant conclusions" of his letters are renowned.

The vizier normally accompanied his ruler on the campaigns in Syria. In 1187, Al Fadil was struck by an illness that prevented him from performing his official duties.[5] It was around this time that he appointed Maimonides court physician, entering him in the "register of physicians" and ordering an annual stipend for him. The position as royal doctor and especially the favor of Al Fadil, who showered him with demonstrations of his affection, established Maimonides' medical fame. He was a much desired and much sought-after physician, consulted particularly by the nobility of the capital, the officials and emirs.

Shortly thereafter, because of his position and prestige at court, he was awarded the title of nagid.[6] This was more than a personal distinction. The restoration of the office, which had been vacant for years, ever since Sutta's final removal, signified a moral and political gain for Egyptian Jews. The office of nagid, which had been disgraced and imperiled by the usurper's despotism, was restored to honor by the appointment of Maimonides. The new nagidship brought to an end the dismal state of chaos and aroused universal joy among the Jews.

Joseph ibn Aknin had now settled in Aleppo as a physician, and also was a teacher.[7] Although awaiting all news from Fostat with utmost sympathy, he responded to the appointment with mixed feelings. He knew that for Maimonides this appointment, while generally viewed as an honor and distinction, was meaningless. It was an honor for the Jews of Egypt and for the office, but Joseph feared that it would become a burden for the philosopher. This political and judicial supremacy over all the Jewish communities in Egypt involved countless time-consuming functions. The official demands could be obstructive, if not deleterious to Maimonides's literary activity in general and to the completion of his planned philosophical work in particular. It was in such a confusion of feelings that Joseph wrote his congratulatory letter.

He begins with a Hebrew salutation that runs to nineteen extensive Hebrew titles and bursts with exuberant admiration and unbounded love; and then he goes on: "May God prolong the life span of the great teacher; may He always grant him honor, assistance, and benevolence and establish his solid fame. God, the Omnipotent, knows the strong yearning of your servant for your sublime person, as well as his pain at being absent from your company and not abiding in your presence and listening to your highly venerable person. When I heard that God, the Almighty, had granted to the Jewish nation the bliss and dignity of this supreme distinction by the appointment of your high person, our master, the great teacher—may his fame be grand and his honor sublime—my joy and jubilation were very great, and I said: For the Lord will not turn away His people or abandon His property. I thanked God, the Almighty, and I said: Praised be the Lord who has not denied a Redeemer to his nation Israel. And as for me, I congratulate the Jewish community and the office on the honor that God in His goodness has granted both, through the supremacy of your high person . . . I do know that nothing new has been added to your high person but the diversion of your attention from the works and writings that are so profitable to the Jewish community and that your high person has already resolved to compose, and I am extremely afflicted by this." The letter closed with Joseph's wish that Maimonides might find favor at court and the request that he may not "take offense" at Joseph's frankness in judging the dubious consequences of the appointment.

"Know, my child," Maimonides writes in reply to Joseph some time later, "that the dignities and honorable offices of Jews in our times are things that I regard as neither happiness nor desirable goods nor minor ills, but—by God!—as utterly strenuous, arduous, and burdensome. The perfect man, who strives for true happiness, concerns himself with the problems of religion and the performance of his duties, and he stays aloof from the opinions of most people, the base actions and vicious qualities. If a man exercises power, his griefs and worries will accumulate."[8]

Maimonides had so often been made to feel the brutality of government power in his life. Now his appointment as supreme head of the Jews and as court physician filled him with apprehension. His experiences in Cordova, in Fez, and especially in the Sutta affair were still fresh in his mind: how easy it was to be calumniated! His conscience also made him uneasy. If he were to observe misdeeds and not take anyone to task, then people would accuse him of favoritism, of being misled by flattery. His heart burned with the warning not to spare the rebellious and the recalcitrant—the warning spoken by the divine man and prophet to Eli the high priest: He honors my sons more than me.[9] However, Maimonides realized that the exercise of power without constant circumspection is impossible. How gladly he would have forgone honorable offices! He may even have been repelled by the nagidship because he had worked toward the deposition of his predecessor Sutta. It was probably due to Maimonides's express wish that Jews never attached the title of nagid to his name in either documents or letters. Only the Arab chroniclers were an exception in this respect.[10]

One of his first edicts: in 1187, citing Torah scrolls and threatening excommunication, he decided that in Egyptian villages marriages and divorces could be performed only by expressly appointed judges. The purpose of this decree was to avoid having these ceremonies performed by unqualified men and to provide a central supervision of these matters.[11] The measure was probably related to another edict. The land of the Nile, because of its prosperity, was drawing many foreigners and the new immigrants often took local women as wives. Now, there were certain unprincipled men who would marry in Egypt even though they already had a spouse abroad. In order to protect women, Maimonides, together with three other rabbis, decreed that a foreign Jew could wed in Egypt only if he offered proof or swore on a Pentateuch that he was not already married. It also happened that some foreigners who wed in Egypt left the country and never returned. Maimonides therefore ordained that the court must prevent an immigrant who had married locally from traveling abroad, even if his wife agreed to the journey, unless the man filled out a bill of divorcement, which became valid if he remained away beyond a certain deadline, not to exceed three years.[12]

19

Arabesques

His expanding medical practice, the nagidship, his activity as a judge, and his own studies (especially in the art of healing, which he considered indispensable) consumed all of his time. Furthermore, he had countless inquiries from many countries to deal with. Scholars, rabbis, and judges, heads of academies and students appealed to Maimonides; the Jewish courts of Law in Egypt and in the Eastern countries submitted questions to him. The Arab judges, the kadis, relied on his decisions. His replies were tailored to the inquirer's station. For scholars, he presented his reasons in abstract arguments; for ordinary people, he communicated his decisions tersely and without explication. Sometimes, a responsum consisted of a single word. He demanded that careful heed be paid to every word in his responsum, and the recipients treasured his replies, the letters being preserved and gathered in collections. Maimonides's disciples made copies of many of these and circulated them; the verdicts were often read out in synagogues to congregations on the sabbath.[1]

In Yemen and poor neighboring countries, most Jewish communities could not afford to pay for the expensive copying of the vast and lengthy Codex. However, prosperous Jews offered to make the purchase. They dispatched messengers to Egypt to buy several copies, sending each country one copy, which then proliferated. In this manner, the Codex spread all the way to the borders of India. People sent copies to Maimonides so that he could check its accuracy and verify it with his signature.

During this period, when he was asked to make most complicated verdicts in civil law and clarify most subtle problems in ritual law, someone requested instruction on the three basic questions of metaphysics at that time: the existence of God; the relationship of the world in its origin to God; and the issue of whether the universe is everlasting or was created. The inquirer wanted a sort of compromise between the diametrically opposed views of the Aristotelian philosophers and the Mu'tazilite dogmatists. Maimonides readily composed a treatise on these topics. As a special favor to Joseph, he sent him a copy of the manuscript.[2]

Joseph's character was an odd blend of enthusiasm and criticism, a combination of poetic insight and speculative acumen. Joseph knew that Maimonides was gifted with "the most perfect judgment, the most excellent knowledge, correct thinking, the surest insight, the worthiest qualities, the noblest senses, the most penetrating perspicacity."[3] But Joseph did not exercise restraint if Maimonides's answers left him dissatisfied. Despite his total respect for the "head of the teaching," he decided to deal with these tasks himself. He attempted to prove the creation of the world on the basis of the purposeful functionality of the world. He rejected the emanation doctrine, with which the Arabic philosophers thought they could explain the genesis of the world and its variety as deriving from the oneness of God. He characterized the so-called "sphere spirits," the intermediary beings between God and the world, as products of the imagination and inventions of allegory. This assumption, he said, could not be demonstrated in the Bible. "If Your —— had replied exhaustively, then my words about this matter would be superfluous or even foolish, as Alfarabi puts it in the introduction to his book on music: 'To speak about something that has already been spoken about, and exhaustively at that, is superfluous or foolish, and both are bad.' But precisely because Your —— has not exhausted the subject, I felt induced to reply, to step before our master, the head of the Law, with what had been imparted to me from Your wealth, and the correct understanding, to which I have been guided by Your light. I am not laying claim to any merit, or to shine in scholarship—my aim is far more in keeping with what the poet sings about the ocean: the cloud pours out over the sea, which has no profit from this, for it is, after all, its own water."[4] Thus writes Joseph in his treatise, which he sent to Fostat.

One can easily guess the effect of this treatise on Maimonides. In one central point, it contradicted the spirit of Maimonides. The main thing in his philosophical stance was to practice restraint and not overlook the impotence of reason in dealing with the ultimate questions of metaphysics. Joseph's zealous attempt to solve these problems at any cost must have been as repellent to Maimonides as was the tendentious thinking of the Mu'tazilites. Maimonides's reluctance to transmit "secrets" was probably strengthened when he read this treatise.

Ibn Aknin, who had been promised initiation into the arcana of prophecy, waited. But the response was not forthcoming. Joseph suffered. Patience was not one of his virtues. He also sensed that there was a deeper reason behind this silence. Had Maimonides decided not to keep his promise? An intense sorrow took hold of Joseph. Was not such a change of mind a breach of faith? In the depression resulting from his fear of betrayal, Joseph's self-assurance grew all the greater. He, the first man to attempt an esoteric interpretation of the Holy Writ, evidently believed he had already reached the level of prophecy. The temperamental poet, whose verses had once elicited Maimonides's esteem and an invitation to his home, decided to employ the same tried-and-true device in this predicament. He composed a letter in rhyming prose, using all his artistic devices—humor, word plays, alliteration, and onomatopoeia:[5]

Joseph ibn Aknin to Maimonides

Behold, we are of one tongue and one mind, and no one else has come between us, and yet you start to act this way toward the friend who came to rest in your love's shade, who poured himself out unhesitatingly to your intellect and opened up his mind to your faith and loyalty. I, it is I who speak; and you must speak too, for I want you to be justified; if you have words, refute me. Recently, Kima,[6] your favorite daughter, captured my heart; the lovely, gracious maiden was a sweet delight to my eyes, and I wooed her according to the law of faith and the Halakha of Mount Sinai with the following trio: I gave her friendship money as the price of courtship; I wrote her a love letter; and I presented myself as her bridegroom. So she became mine, and I invited her into the tent of joy. I did not force her, nor did I press her with urging; it was purely my love that won me her love, and my soul embraced her soul. All this took place in front of two reliable witnesses: Ibn Obed-Allah [Maimonides] and Ibn Roshd [Averroës], the companions. But under a marital sky she became an adulteress, she turned her affections to other friends. Ancient poets once wrote: *Impudent the bride who breaks her troth under the canopy.* She found no failing in me, yet she left me, she stole out of my tent and withdrew her face, her lovely face, from me, and her voice full of lovely tones. And you did not rebuke your daughter's insolence, nor reproach her for her dereliction of duty; and you even spurred her on—that was not right. Now that you may restore the wife to the man who is, or will be, a prophet—he will pray for you, for your

long life,[7] and for her too will he plead, that she may stand
on her feet without reeling. And if you do not restore her,
you will get entangled in the end of the verse. So hunt for
peace and hold out your hands for reconciliation. So that
you may be well and so that your days may increase, listen
to the words of the sages. *Blessed is the man who restores
lost goods.* And what if the lost good is a beautiful woman,
the husband's crown? Thus I stand here, awaiting her return.
I ask every nation and every kingdom all around for her;
because of her, no day passes without the outpourings of
my soul. She will never find any rest among those nations.
Happy the man who hopes and achieves his hope!

The truest of your devoted servants; his desire is to look
upon your honor's countenance and to embrace your feet in
the dust:

JOSEPH BEN JUDAH BEN SHIMEON

Maimonides, who had a sense of humor, did not misunderstand the jocular earnestness of the bold correspond-
ent. He knew Joseph's temperament and fully realized that
a keen imagination might conceive the suspicion of a broken
promise. But the text also included some gaffes. Joseph was
asserting his qualification for attaining prophetic knowledge
through his studies with Averroës and Maimonides. The
latter was quite put off by this simultaneous mention of
their names with no distinction between the profane teachings of the one and the sacred thinking of the other.
Maimonides greatly respected the works of Averroës but
evaluating them as an initiation into prophecy was blasphemous in his eyes. The earnestness, the emphasis in the
letter was upon the claim to prophecy. Joseph, who claimed
that he "is, or will be, a prophet," was exhibiting a presumption that Maimonides did not want to leave unreprimanded.
Like Saul, a simple man who came to the prophet Samuel,
mingled with the prophets, and then imagined himself a

prophet, Joseph now dared to equate himself with his teacher.

Maimonides denied that the gift of prophecy was possessed not only by his disciple but also by his own mentor Aristotle.[8] Why had the great and intellectually perfect philosophers not attained the gift of prophecy, if it is something natural? Maimonides once asked himself this question. In the middle of presenting the ethical prerequisites of prophecy, he quoted Aristotle's statement that the sense of touch is a disgrace, which Maimonides glossed as follows: "It is truly a disgrace, for we possess it like the other animals, insofar as we are animals and nothing else; it has nothing of the essence of the human, whereas among the enjoyment of the other senses, like those of smelling, hearing, seeing, although they are physical, nevertheless certain pleasures occur that are pleasures for man insofar as he is man." Suddenly he noticed that this discussion was leading into an area outside the subject, and he apologized for the digression: "This too is vital to the discussion, for usually, the thoughts of well-known scholars are preoccupied with the pleasures of the sense in question and by the desire for them. But, nevertheless, they are surprised that they do not possess any gift for prophecy, as if prophecy is something lying in the nature of men."[9]

Maimonides did not appear, however, to disallow Joseph's claim. He esteemed him like no other man of his time and had a high opinion of his qualities. He left him with one hope—the year 1216. It was not that the road to prophecy was too steep for Joseph; but, rather, the time had not yet come.

Nor was Maimonides at a loss in a humorous battle of words. When he had to utilize the technique of forming a mosaic of Biblical and Talmudic phrases, he proved no less skilled than the most elegant stylist of the period. He did not even hesitate to use Biblical expressions glorifying God and to reconstrue them humorously:

MAIMONIDES TO IBN AKNIN

Hear ye, O sages, my words, bend your ears, and step forward. Settle a dispute between me and my opponent, and if I have erred, then bear witness against me. I married Kima, my child, to K'sil.[10] But he, who was not favorably inclined toward her, regarded the maiden, reared in the sphere of faith, as tainted with sin because she covered her face. Ever since she fell into his clutches and, to his disgrace, stood before him in her nakedness, the spirit of jealousy came over him, and hatred of his wife flared up. He deprived her of food, clothing, and a dwelling, and lied about her, bringing her ill fame. After tying the knot of his traps for her, he treacherously impugned her honor, and to her bridal gifts he added the fires of jealousy. His witnesses were bastards, which the law forbids, and thus he increased the number of his sins. His goal was to make her disreputable in my eyes, and thus the husband said to me: "Your daughter became adulterous under the marital sky. Oh, look upon her shame and avenge her sin and adultery, and compel her to return to her husband, for he is a prophet and will pray to God for you and her. He promotes her welfare, he makes her steps solid, and he will pardon her sin, for he does not desire her death; and God too forgives her, for the father's plea defended her."

Now you know the man and the way he speaks, the way he reveals all his thoughts, the way he builds up his mind, and shows the Halakha in the teacher's presence.[11] And he, the inventor of frivolous chitchat, imagines he is a prophet among prophets, like a blind man holding on to the door-post; he thinks only of the right occasion for grand phrases to undermine a reputation. He is known to be a man of impure lips, but she is immaculate, and no hands have ever touched her. It is impossible for her to break her troth to the lord of her marriage, or for Israel to suffer any shame from her, or for her to follow any path save that of Saul and Samuel.

Now form a circle so that I may inflict a penalty on him; but do not wax wroth and do not be saddened. Like a loving father taking his son to task, I will speak to him chidingly. "Because you fought me and spoke to me harshly and yelled your din into my ears; because you confronted me about your wife; because you boastfully offered two witnesses, a Jew and an Arab, and did not distinguish between the holy and the profane; because you associated yourself with the prophets, and among men of pride took first place—for all these reasons, if I did not care for my honor and that of dear faithful Kima, I would tame your arrogance and shame you with one word."

O my son, your thoughts are a perplexed people, none of which shows reflection. God has sown them in a soil that bears no fruits. You are the master of your people, so listen and learn: You are ill-advised to cast suspicion of immorality on any wife, especially your own. A skillful poet could wield his allegory against you: "His lips bring his mouth to the brink of ruin." And: "He has horns by his own hand."

But listen, my son, here is your wife, take her and go. Trust in God, whatever may happen to you. Know that He is present in all your actions, while we walk along separate paths. He will see to it that your roads and thoughts are straight and do not waver. Listen to your teacher's warning, do not let your tongue lead your flesh to sinful ways. My lips announce only truth; you may seek and sift, you will find nothing false or twisted. And do not be proud and elevate yourself to the level of prophets. It was not that their way towers high above yours, but that their hour had come.[12] And do not say: "Because Samuel prophesied correctly, I, a giant of wisdom, will do the same." If you are wise, then you are so for yourself, to understand and to teach; you do not have to worry about hidden things; and do not cite the Talmud by way of proof that a sage is more than a prophet. After all, not every man who wears a sword has to kill, just as not every man who is eager for glory has glory. Even though Samuel prophesied and worked wonders, does Samuel necessarily have to be a prophet? So do not boast about wisdom. Banish haughtiness and turn your mind to the modesty of our fathers, for those who are called prophets today in the past were known as seers. Forgo all pride; do as I counsel you. I will lead you to the path of wisdom. Do not nourish any arrogance until your end; honor intelligence as a father and wisdom as a sister. Meanwhile, may men like you increase in Israel.

We do not know how Joseph reacted to this reprimand. But a later account discloses a bit of the secret. The famous poet al-Harizi visited Aleppo around 1218—that is, after 1216; and in the following verses he celebrated Joseph, who lived there and had a high rank:[13]

> *You were mighty, you were a rabbi in the West,*
> *And in the East God anointed you a prophet.*

20

The Opposition

JUST as quickly as reports of Maimonides's renown spread through the world, seeds of suspicion and misunderstanding also sprouted. His opponents used their imaginations to spawn all kinds of reasons for rejecting and condemning the Codex. They accused Maimonides of poor scholarship in presenting legal guidelines without indicating their sources and naming their authors, without citations or proofs. This was seen as a presumption of sovereignty, which not only made verification difficult but in general tended to impede free research. The greatest astonishment, however, was aroused by the fact that Maimonides offered an extremely large number of his own decisions without explanation, as though they were established laws. The indisputable solidity of the verdicts, all of which were verified, did not lessen the distrust. Critics were also offended by countless individual items: in Baghdad, for instance, they misunderstood the Halakhic notion of Mosaic Law—in contrast to the post-Mosaic—and objected that the Codex regarded the sign of the covenant between God and Israel as a Mosaic law and not, in accordance with the Talmud, as stemming from Abraham.[1]

Doubts were cast on Maimonides's competence as a legislator for all Jews. Until then, only the decisions of the geonim, the heads of the great academies in Babylon, were acknowledged as universally binding. Their validity was not based on personal qualities but on the authority of the academy; it was the institution and not the person that was recognized by the Jews. People generally felt that only the rector of the Baghdad academy had the right to legislate. Maimonides, however, who had not studied at this academy nor possessed its ordination diploma, lacked any formal basis for the authority to which he laid claim. How could he, neither a rector nor a professor, arrogate the right to publish a book of law for all Jews?

The lack of source references and his plain diction were not such as to win the respect of scholars. Some even viewed the general enthusiasm for this work as delusion. After all, anyone fairly knowledgeable in the Talmud could write such a book, which did not even contain source references or scholarliness.[2] In Cairo itself, a few savants preferred not to touch the book, so that no one would think they had learned anything from it . . .[3] At the same time, the position of the critics was made precarious by the lack of references. They could demonstrate that several regulations did not coincide with Talmudic discussions, but such evidence was far from a refutal, since Maimonides might have based his decision on a Talmudic passage that had slipped the critic's mind or was formulated differently in the manuscript that Maimonides had employed.

More dangerous than the reproach for scholarly inadequacy was a further "annoyance" caused by the author. In his introduction, Maimonides had explicitly written that the Codex would make the study of post-Biblical literature dispensable. This was construed as a tendency to drive the Talmud out of the house of study, which was felt to be not only a desecration but an outright peril. If the Codex were allowed to establish itself, then that would mean abandoning all post-Biblical writing.[4] This rejection, grounded in religious devotion to Talmudic literature, truly shook the position of the Codex.

Maimonides, who had unambiguously admonished Ibn Aknin's slight faux pas, failed to condemn a horrible misinterpretation of his own doctrine in time. Some of his readers were freethinkers, who construed as freethinking his spiritualization of religious beliefs and his rejection of superstition according to their own mode of thinking. By an irony of fate, the man who created a systematic dogmatics of Judaism was accused of heresy. The charge arose when an orator in Damascus expressed the view that physical resurrection, a return of the soul to the body after death had separated them, would never take place.[5] There were protests, and the orator's rejoinder was to cite evidence from Maimonides's Codex, which said that the ultimate purpose of man was life in the future world but that such life would be noncorporeal. The auditors then offered popular opinions and the words of the sages as evidence for the resurrection of the body. The orator called these words allegories that were not to be taken literally. And thus the discussion went on. When Maimonides heard about this misinterpretation of his teaching, it struck him as a foolish issue that did not deserve refutal. But it was a mistake to disregard it; later on, the twisted interpretation of his teachings was to echo far more seriously from another source.

Maimonides's works were extremely popular among the Yemenite Jews, whose cause he had espoused years earlier and who, in grateful veneration, had inserted his name in the daily kaddish ("May God establish His kingdom in your lifetimes and in your days and in the lifetime of our teacher Moses ben Maimon").[6] Soon the Yemenites began not only reading but also interpreting his writings, and his dogmatics became the first victim of the misled exegetes. Maimonides had presented the purely spiritual character of the immortality of the soul quite thoroughly, but treated the resurrection of the body only peripherally. People therefore inferred that Maimonides was not very serious about the doctrine of resurrection, and they spread the opinion that the body is doomed to disintegrate after death, especially since Maimonides had written: "If one of us is found worthy of living after death, he will most likely not be able to feel the sensory pleasures, nor will he wish to have them; just as a powerful king is unwilling to give up his kingdom and play ball in the street, even though there must have been a time when he preferred playing ball to his kingdom."[7] The misinterpreters, however, confused resurrection with the nature of afterlife. Maimonides's authority was so great that one could cite him merely to give popular credence to a view openly contradicting a traditional belief. The orthodox sniffed the danger; and in 1188 one of them finally asked Maimonides to take a precise stand on the issue of resurrection.

In his response, Maimonides explained that a belief in resurrection is the "cornerstone of the Torah" and must be considered the "soul's return to the body," as he expressly pointed out in his commentary to the Mishnah. Maimonides assumed that this reply would put an end to the "public offense."[8] But such was not the case.

For at the same time the Yemenites had sent a letter to the gaon in Baghdad, complaining that Maimonides's work denied the resurrection of the dead in the popular sense, and that he interpreted the Biblical mention of resurrection as an allegory, promising reward or punishment in the afterlife only for the soul as detached from the body.[9] This work, they said, had "injured the faith of many Jews" and propagated much error. Many had abandoned their belief in redemption and begun reading "heretical writings." There was no leader to guide the people to the road of truth. The gaon of Baghdad ought therefore to intercede and enlighten, for the "teachings of the sages, prophets, and geonim" had been vilified. The Yemenite zealot depicted this danger in dark colors in order to get the powerful rector to speak out publicly against Maimonides.

For many centuries, Babylon had had the princely office of the exilarch, which was hereditary in a certain dynasty going back to the royal house of David. The exilarch headed the Jewish self-administration, and this position made him the supreme secular leader of the Jews of Babylon. The spiritual chief was the gaon, the rector of the Talmudic academy. Even though their powers and privileges were traditionally spelled out, conflicts were frequent between the exilarch and the gaon. In the second half of the twelfth century, when the exilarch died, leaving no sons, the gaon, Samuel ben Ali, managed to fuse the two offices in his own person: the gaonship and the princely office of exilarch.

The upswing of Jewish settlements in Europe and North Africa had led to new centers of education, and for a long time now these centers had been greatly weakening the influence and prestige of the Babylonian gaonship. But Samuel was an active and learned man, and he succeeded in generating a kind of renascence of this lofty institution. "Nowhere in all Syria, in Damascus, in the cities of Persia, Media, or Babylon," writes the traveler Pethahiah of Regensburg, "is there a single Jewish judge who was not appointed by the rector Samuel. In every town, the right to judge and to teach goes back to him; diplomas bearing his seal are valid in all countries, even Palestine, and he is feared by everyone. He has sixty servants at his beck and call, and they chastise the disobedient with floggings. Like the king, he wears gold-brocaded garments, and his apartments are lined with silk stuffs like those of the royal palace. He has a deep knowledge of the written and oral tradition, as well as of secular science, so that there is nothing that is concealed from him." For his lectures, which he gave while enthroned on a high cathedra, only thoroughly trained students were admitted, and yet his audience never numbered fewer than five hundred.

The opponents of Maimonides managed to get this high dignitary to agree to an attack. Samuel ben Ali wrote a polemical work that, while feigning to take Maimonides under his protection, presented his views as either heresies or forgivable errors.

21

The Guide for the Perplexed

MAIMONIDES was forced to realize how easily his philosophical discussions of religious beliefs could be misconstrued and even harm the naïve faith of the common people. If casual reflection could have such an effect, what could be expected from a detailed presentation of his philosophical views? He was apparently haunted by such qualms when he began wondering whether to complete the work that he had promised Joseph. The future "guide for the perplexed" was himself perplexed. His time-consuming activities as physician and head of the Jews were preventing him from helping his disciple, who was "tormented by noble disquiet." The real impediment lay in the esoteric nature of the knowledge to be presented; the point was to do away with this exclusivity, which seemed invulnerable. According to a Talmudic precept, one could initiate a single disciple into these teachings only if he were a scholar who could grasp the problems with his own understanding. But, even in this case, only the main ideas could be imparted, and only in a very general way. Joseph was learned and worthy of instruction. But Maimonides knew that if these things were treated in a book, it would be like preaching them to thousands of people. "The Holy Writ expressly forbids any communication about them unless it be also yielded by reason." And he did not want to act unsuitably against God's intention, which had seen to it that the truths referring particularly to the knowledge of God are to remain unavailable to the greater mass.[1] "Furthermore, some things that I know about this can be made valid only as hypotheses, since no *prophecy from God* has come to me, enabling me to know what is meant, nor have I heard from any teacher what I should believe about this. On the other hand, the things written in the books of prophecy as well as the words of our teachers and my previous philosophical knowledge have taught me that this is undoubtedly the meaning. However, it is also possible that the situation is otherwise and that something else is meant."[2] "Were I to forgo the task of writing down my knowledge, so that it would absolutely be lost upon my inevitable decease, then this would, in my eyes, be an awful disadvantage to you [Joseph] and every thinker assailed by perplexity; it would be virtually a refusal of truth or a malevolence of the testator toward his heirs."[3] "God knows that I have always hesitated to discuss these subjects, because they are concealed things, about which no work by any of our brethren has been written in these times of exile. How then can I make bold to introduce such an innovation?"[4]

The issue was finally settled when Maimonides realized what our sages used to say in a case of this sort: "If one has to do something for God, then one can let the Law remain inoperative . . . For it is written: Everything that you do, do for the sake of God."

"After all, I am the man who—if the subject urges him, if the road is too narrow for him, and if he knows no other way to teach a proven truth except appealing to one chosen man even if failing to appeal to ten thousand fools—prefers imparting the truth to this one man. I do not heed the complaints of the greater crowd, and I wish to wrest the one chosen man from his irresoluteness and show him the way out of his perplexity so that he may become perfect and sound."[5]

The medical practice, the political and administrative functions of the nagidship, the demanding duties of the supreme judge, the answering of countless inquiries and the penning of medical reports and general medical treatises consumed all the hours of his day. In between, he composed the opus for Joseph.

His goal was to transmit the "main things" and to "deliver them not in an orderly manner and a logical sequence, but scattered and mixed with other themes, so that the truth might be visible through this elucidation, but beyond the general ken."[6] Maimonides employed various tricks to reconceal the exposed—if possible. Proper reflection and the assistance of God, he said, had led him, while presenting the hidden mysteries of Ezekiel's vision, to explain this vision in such a way that everyone would have to believe that the author had not added the slightest bit, but rather "translated the words from one tongue into another or briefly put forth the obvious meaning of the text. If, however, the man for whom this book is written focuses on it carefully, and contemplates all its chapters with perfect attention, then the entire subject will be as clear to him as it is to me, and the most secret thought will be obvious to him, so that nothing will remain concealed."[7]

His reluctance induced him to employ words with double meanings, "so that the greater mass, in line with the measure of their understanding and the weakness of their imaginative faculty, will grasp them in one sense, while the perfect and the capable readers will grasp the words in another sense." But despite these tricks, he had a difficult time wresting the ideas out of himself.[8]

Upon resolving to compose the work, he no longer had any intention of keeping it a secret. Still, he did not care to make his knowledge intelligible to beginners in philosophy or to those who study only the Talmud. He saw no reason "to be mindful of the greater mass." He was writing for Joseph and men of his ilk, "albeit there are very few of them."[9] He wanted to "offer guidance to the man who is knowledgeable in religion, familiar with the Torah, believes in the truth of the Torah and is flawless in faith and character, but who has also studied philosophy, knows its problems, and is attracted by human reason . . ."[10]

Nor did he plan to write a textbook of metaphysics or lay out general philosophical doctrines. For this, he felt, the existing books were enough. The thrust of his book was to be: "Enlightenment on the doubts of religion and the analysis of the real meaning of its hidden teachings, which are withheld from the understanding of the crowd."[11] By no means did he hope that his book would "banish the doubts" of all who understood it, but rather that it would "clear away most important doubts."

"The king is in his palace. His subjects are either urban or rustic people. Some of the urban subjects have turned their backs on the house of the king and wish to go somewhere else; some, however, wish to go to the house of the king. They set out for it and wish to ask the way to the palace and come before the king; but, so far, they have not gone far enough to descry even the outermost wall of the palace. Among those, however, who wish to enter the building, there are several who are still circling it, trying to find the entrance gate. Others have already passed through the gate and are standing in the forecourt; still others have come far enough and have entered the interior of the building, and thus they are in the same place as the king; namely, in the king's home. But even when reaching the interior of the palace, one can see the king or speak to him only after making various efforts . . .

"The people outside the city are actually all those who have no religion, whether it be achieved through investigation or through tradition . . . These people are to be viewed as irrational animals and, in my opinion, they are not on the level of human beings, their rank is lower than that of men and higher than that of apes, since, after all, they do look like men and possess higher understanding than apes. The city dwellers, however, who have turned their backs on the house of the king are those people who have attained untrue opinions about faith, either because of a serious error or because they have been led astray by other people. And these people are far worse than the ones mentioned first. Those, however, who wish to reach the king but have not yet laid eyes on the house of the king are the great majority of those who believe in the Law; namely, the ignorant who practice the commandments. Now, those who have arrived at the royal palace but are wandering around it are the men knowledgeable in the Talmud, who, by way of tradition, have accepted the true dogmas and mastered the practical worship of God, but are not familiar with the study of the tenets of the Law and do not even ask whether the truth of a dogma can be proved. Those, however, who have gone so far as to think about the dogmas of the faith are those who have already entered the forecourt. They, without any doubt, occupy different hierarchical rungs. However, the man who has reached the point of knowing the proofs for all that can be proved, and understanding all that can be understood about Godly matters, has already arrived in the interior of the royal palace . . .

"But know, my son, that so long as you occupy your mind with the mathematical sciences and logic, you will be one of those men who circle the building to find the entrance. However, if you comprehend natural science, you have already entered the forecourt of the building, and when you have completed natural science and are studying metaphysics, then you have entered the house of the king and are passing through the covered walks of the forecourt. But this is the level of the sages. They too reach different degrees of perfection. The man who focuses all his thinking on the Godly is entirely devoted to God, turns his mind away from everything else, and puts all his reason to deriving the knowledge of God from the existing things—that man is one of those who have come into the house of the king. And this is the level of the prophets."[12]

This typology, which Maimonides announced frankly and bluntly, caused a stir and a scandal, and it might have thrown the intellectual order of Jewish life out of joint. The author was claiming that the study of Talmudic literature, which went back to the tradition of Mount Sinai and was sacred to all Jews, did not grant admission into the "palace," while philosophy, which was generally regarded as profane and un-Jewish, was the route to God, the admission into the "palace." This was an assertion of unprecedented boldness. The new hierarchy of the spiritual and intellectual powers, undertaken by a man who had devoted the better part of his life to investigating the Talmudic traditions, could be legitimate and comprehensible only if it sprang from a desire for a new order. Indeed, the new hierarchy was the crowning achievement of Maimonides's lifework.

Maimonides appeared with a mission: he wanted to guide Jews to metaphysics. For him, metaphysical knowledge was a primordial property of Judaism, but had gotten lost in the Exile. This loss, he felt, was the tragedy of exile. The rebirth of higher knowledge, he said, would usher in the Messianic age; the regaining of philosophy was the redeeming action, which he himself, the first in the period of Exile, believed he was starting.

The will to lead people into the "palace" with speeches of admonition and conversion was foreign to his esoteric attitude. His philosophical magnum opus, *The Guide for the Perplexed*, was written for individuals. But the goal, to which he pointed unequivocally, was the same for every man who wants to take the road to God. Averroës considered it reprehensible and damaging to deprive the common folk of their anthropomorphic notion of God, which corresponds to the external message of the Scripture. Maimonides, passionately striving throughout his life for a purer knowledge of God, saw his task as bringing every man to the idea of the incomparability of God.

This enterprise had not only recourse to the past (the pre-Exilic period) in common with the codification: the philosophical mission was actually carried by the "reformation of education." Maimonides himself, as he admits in his Mishnah commentary,[13] never enjoyed teaching any subject so much as the "dogmas of religion," "the philosophy of faith." He wanted to make this good the common property of the people. The indispensability of thinking is the keynote of his life. At an early time, he had already deemed a minimum of philosophical knowledge the prerequisite for partaking of eternal life. This awakening of thought may have been one of the motives for the codification; in any event, the codification cleared the way toward it. In the Codex, Maimonides had offered, in readily understandable language, the instructions necessary for the practice of religious life. Maimonides believed that anyone could, with little trouble, acquire the requisite knowledge. This made possible a restructuring of education, which could, in turn, prepare for philosophy's entry into Judaism. Since the age of the Tannaites, the intellectually demanding study of the Talmud had been the chief means of educating the people. A receptivity to logical and dialectical doctrines was not a rare quality. The formal ability to think, the dispositional prerequisite, was widespread. In the academies, thousands and thousands of students mulled over the logical constructions of the Talmudic texts and commentaries. Instead of the great strain of dialectical study, the codification made simple reading sufficient. The students thereby gained time and opportunity for philosophical studies. Thus, the spread of philosophy would be a further result of the educational restructuring intended by the Codex. All that was needed was to inspire students with philosophical problems in order to funnel energy of thought into metaphysics. That was Maimonides's desire. For just as he put contemplation higher than action, so too he put the study of metaphysics, the "roots of the Teaching," higher than the dialectical study of the Talmud, the "branches of the Law," even though the Halakhic portions of the Talmud were unconditionally binding and even though he esteemed the Haggadic portions as treasure troves of philosophical wisdom.

Much later, a sixteenth-century thinker said that one "could not stop praising this work," which so rapidly attained an authoritative place in world literature, making Maimonides the teacher of Christian scholasticism. Alexander of Hales, Albertus Magnus, Thomas Aquinas took up his doctrines as bricks for their own systems. And for Meister Eckhart, Rabbi Moses ben Maimon was an authority "second at most to St. Augustine." However, Maimonides's system was also important for the thinking of Nicholas of Cusa, Leibniz, and Spinoza.

This detour in his work was an inevitable consequence for Maimonides. He approves only of faith through thinking. When philosophical certainty is tied to faith, "so that the opposite of the belief is not possible in any way, when thinking has no room for the refutal of this belief . . . then it is true faith."[14] Knowledge is the *conditio sine qua non* for the immortality of the soul and the participation in God's providence. Thus, as the apostle of intellectuality, he could not help proclaiming this ideal of education.

Maimonides's intense reformism owes its impetus to his reevaluation of both the Talmud and Aristotle. The Talmud teaches that "action and not investigation is the important thing." But Maimonides felt that knowing is more valuable than doing, for the love of God corresponds to one's knowledge. His key idea is the superiority of contemplation to the ritual and the ethical. The germ of this idea lay in a centuries-old development and had sprouted in the minds of several of his predecessors. But the full development first took place in Maimonides.

The conquest of the intellect for religiosity had already gone forward in the Tannaite period. The religious value of Talmudic study had long since become part of the national awareness. But subordinating the value of ethics to that of theory, making contemplation the purpose of all commandments and actions, the very goal of life—those were Maimonides's achievements.

Maimonides canonized philosophy. His Mishnah commentary and his Codex presented philosophical teachings in the form of religious commandments. *The Guide for the Perplexed* consummated the "marriage" of the Bible and Aristotelianism. This philosophical success, the compromise between revelation and philosophy, was construed as a "mixed marriage" and rejected. Nevertheless, these ideas exerted incomparable influence: Maimonides is the only medieval thinker to have a lasting effect on the theology of other religions, on Christians, Arabs, Karaites, and Jews.

The development of Jewish writing has always orbited around a midpoint. For centuries, *The Guide for the Perplexed* was for Jewish philosophy what the Talmud was for the Halakha and the Zohar for the Cabala.

The secret of this impact lies not in the subtle conceptual distinctions or artful intellectual constructions but in the philosophical and religious experience forming the kernel of knowledge presented in the work. The doctrines, articulating with extraordinary descriptive powers the art of philosophical learning, are creations of a tremendous metaphysical life.

Maimonides is not aiming for the solution, the answer. The basic features of his reason are discipline and passion. Thinking and the act of knowing are no less important for him than that which is thought; thinking is holy. He emphasizes over and over again that he does not want to erect a system of philosophy, he merely wants to pave the way to the knowledge of God. He does not focus on inventing original elements of thought. He lives in the intoxicating wealth of the universal sciences, he is filled with experiencing and understanding this magic.

If logic fails in the face of religion, Maimonides considers it lazy to settle down comfortably in faith, in tradition. He is aware of the limits on reason. But to *live* in the kingdom of reason is an imperative for him. He does not care to build his home on the narrow borderstone of ignorance. Reason, for him, is not a hiding place to store away all doubts; it is located in the kingdom of God, albeit not at the center but on the border.

His philosophy, *The Guide for the Perplexed*, is not a goal, it is a lodestar whose path leads to God. How different the existence and accomplishment of Judaism would be if Maimonides's idea had gained wide acceptance. But its sphere of influence was confined to individual periods or communities. It was not the codifier and "guide" Maimonides but the commentator Rashi who became the shaper, teacher, and educator of his people; it was not the metaphysics of Maimonides but the Cabala and Hasidism that molded the future. Maimonides's influence on the people was only indirect and altogether heterogeneous. Later, offshoots of the Codex determined Jewish life; the contemplation of the Cabala and the ardor of Hasidism guided Jewish minds to the "roots of the Law," to his goal, but in a way different from what Maimonides had dreamed.

Maimonides proudly named his Codex the *Mishneh Torah*, but the title did not catch on; Maimonides fought against magic practices, but legend foisted miraculous deeds upon him; Maimonides called himself Moses ben Maimon the Spaniard, but literature referred to him as Moses the Egyptian; Maimonides rejected dialectics, but his Codex promoted pilpul; Maimonides disapproved of poetic phrase-mongering, but his thirteen articles of faith, *The Guide for the Perplexed*, and even the Codex were eventually versi-fied; Maimonides, who would always employ his *ratio* to demarcate the limits of reason, was later styled the "classicist of rationalism." A true acceptance of his idea, peaking in the unification goal of the *Mishneh Torah* and *More Nevukhim*, has not come about in these past eight centuries. It remains a prospect for the future.

22

Renunciation

In the years between 1187 and 1190, while Maimonides struggled with the inhibitions of his esoteric nature and the infirmities of esoteric language in order to complete the work that Joseph was awaiting, he also worked on a compendium of medicine.

In the Codex, he had known how to extract a clear, terse tenet out of intricate Talmudic discussion; and in this new work, which was aimed at his medical colleagues, he likewise educed the fundamental ideas from Galen's verbose analyses and paraphrases. The fanatic of brevity revealed himself here too. For the form of presentation, he picked the aphorism, after the model of Hippocrates. This new work, which was widely respected in the Middle Ages, expounded on the physiological, anatomical, therapeutical, and hygienic teachings of medicine; it was known in Cairo by 1191.

"For the skeptic and researcher, and for caution's sake," Maimonides, enlightened by the objections to the Codex, indicates his source at the end of each aphorism.

Contemporary medicine was dominated by Galen. And Maimonides's work was mainly a refresher course in Galen's theory. But while following Galen in most issues, Maimonides nevertheless dared to voice criticisms. He pointed out over forty gross contradictions in Galen. Notwithstanding his recognition of Galen's medical authority, he denied the Greek's capacity for judgment in the area of philosophy. Galen had boasted of prophetic illumination and had cast doubt upon the notion that the world was created. Maimonides, who was working on the presentation of his philosophical system (in which he gave a central position to the idea of the creation of the world) and who emphasized the high human prerequisites for attaining prophetic inspiration, mounted an unusually sharp attack against Galen.[1]

The hallowing of life, above all the control of sexuality, is Maimonides's constant demand. Although repeating himself is repugnant to his sense of form,[2] he constantly quotes Aristotle's statement: "The sense of touch is our disgrace!" He cannot laud this idea highly enough. In *The Guide for the Perplexed*, he says: "It is a disgrace for us to speak about anything regarding sexual intercourse, even about something permitted in this respect; it is proper to hold our tongues about it and keep it secret."[3] However, his position as court doctor brought him into a ticklish predicament.

The sultans, who consulted their viziers about diplomatic and military issues, would turn to their royal physicians in matters regarding the harem.

In 1186, Saladin had enfeoffed his nephew al-Malik-al-Muzaffar with the Biblical Hamat, which lay on the bank of the Orontes, on the road from Aleppo to Damascus. "The very wise, just sultan, King al-Muzaffar, the lord of well-protected Hamat, glorious be his victory," now asked "Doctor Moses of Cordova, the Jew, who deals with medicine—praise God for His favor and His peace upon His saints"—for "a presentation of the tested devices of the deepest mysteries of medical art."

The Book of Secrets, Memorandum for Noblemen and Tested Remedies for the Well-Born, which Maimonides

penned with his usual scholarly earnestness and objective
learning, contains a list of numerous remedies, not only
from professional medical literature but also from the
Talmud. Several prescriptions came from his own research.
It is remarkable that Maimonides was entering a richly
worked field and yet managed to surpass the traditional
wisdom of his forerunners in theory and practice.[4] With
unadorned realism and the terseness of prescriptions, the
language of this treatise is delicate, but seldom euphemistic.

A few times, he concluded his observations by saying:
"And God knows this." The multivocal significance of this
phrase is obscure. Is one supposed to add: "And God knows
the effect of the prescribed medicine"? Or: "God knows
how I feel when prescribing an aphrodisiac"? In any event,
this almost prayer-like mention of God is lacking in the
other medical writings, where Maimonides discusses asthma,
hemorrhoids, poisoning, and melancholy.

A second treatise on medicine was written for a sultan
who—perhaps deliberately—is not named by Maimonides.
"And the servant depicted in his heart what the master had
drawn for him. And the servant saw to it that he selected
medicaments and foodstuffs that are useful for health . . .
and the servant made sure of placing a fundamental dis-
sertation into the hands [of his master]."

Aside from the numerous remedies that Maimonides
attributes to his medical predecessors, he also lists a few
new cures, to which he always remarks: "And this is a great
secret, which no one has mentioned before me," or
"Nothing of the sort has ever been compounded before."

As luck would have it, the first treatise was written in
the same year as *The Guide for the Perplexed:* "The immediate essential reason why prophecy has ceased in the
times of the Exile is the dejection or grief afflicting a man in
some matter, and even worse, when he is a servant, at the
beck and call of ignorant and wicked people, in whom the

lack of true knowledge is combined with the predominance of all animal lusts, and he can do nothing against that. This is why the prophet foretold disaster for us: 'They run to and fro to seek the word of God, but do not find it . . . Her king and her princes live among the nations, there is no more instruction, even her prophets find no visions from the Lord.' "[5]

Around 1190, a vehement polemic blazed out between the gaon (and prince) of Baghdad and Maimonides.[6] In Baghdad, where legal inquiries would reach Samuel ben Ali from the most remote countries, a certain Abraham Kohen sent a question to Maimonides, "the light of the West, the wonder of the world." He asked him whether a Jew is allowed to travel on deep rivers like the Euphrates, the Tigris, and the Nile on a Sabbath. In his responsum, Maimonides wrote that it *is* permitted; but, probably for the sake of tact, he urged the addressee to show the answer to the gaon and obtain the latter's decision.

Maimonides's opinion went against the tradition of the Babylonian Jews, who, following an ordinance of the most important geonim, regarded traveling on rivers as breaking the Sabbath rest. But Samuel ben Ali, in restoring the past glory of the gaonship, wanted to keep foreign authorities out of the Babylonian sphere of influence. And he most likely viewed Maimonides's decision as interference with the competencies of the gaonship from a man who was sometimes called "the last of the geonim of the time, the first in importance."

Nevertheless, Samuel ben Ali used the opportunity to establish contact with Maimonides, whose works were also circulating in the empire of the Abassites. In his piece dedicated to "the sages of the era," the gaon, justifying his opinion in detail, informed Maimonides that he had not failed to praise his works. When the Yemenite communities were grumbling against Maimonides because of his doctrine of resurrection, the gaon, as everyone knew had protected Maimonides and lauded his virtue, nobility, and humility. But, out of fidelity to truth, he was forced to contradict the responsum about traveling on rivers on the Sabbath. After all, he, the gaon, knew that Maimonides also wished to have his errors pointed out to him; even the prophets and the greatest sages had not always escaped error. Now he wanted to show Maimonides that the latter's decision was based on a false assumption that the permissible distance for traveling on the Sabbath was a rabbinic regulation rather than a Mosaic Law.

This was typical of the way people attacked Maimonides. The opposition resorted to such tactics in order to expose the allegedly defective knowledge of the codifier. And because Maimonides was supposed to be above any objection, the opponents praised his pure character, his "virtue, nobility, and humility" and, as it were, they excused his alleged errors.

First, Maimonides pointed out that Samuel ben Ali, like other opponents who "excused" him, had not read his (Maimonides's) words carefully. But he was more deeply offended by the dishonest tone. "You seem to be of the opinion," he replied to the gaon, "that we are among those who cannot endure any criticism or a refutal of their opinion. But God has preserved us from this weakness. The Creator of the world knows that we gratefully accept instruction from anybody, even the least pupil, be he friend or adversary. If the objection is valid, then we are delighted at the correction. If it is invalid, then we do not despise the man who raised it . . .

"We are acquainted with your good reputation and high rank; your Talmudic learning is said to be great. You no doubt have an important activity as a teacher. But we do not wish to reprimand you for the errors in your piece, since they do not stem from defective understanding or inadequate memory, but rather from an insufficient perusal of our words. You probably glanced at our response only casually; that is why you have made mistakes . . . The legal regulations which, in your opinion, we have overlooked are expressly included in our Codex, after all. Had you checked this work, which, as we have heard, is widely circulated in your region, especially since it serves as the basis for legal decisions in most academies, then you could not possibly have misunderstood me . . . We see that you have a great deal of sympathy and compassion for us. We ask and beg you to forgo this compassion and, instead, to heed carefully every single word in our response. Only then will a debate promote scholarship. If you then still find errors, please let us know. 'Even a father and a son, a teacher and a pupil become adversaries when they battle one another in the Law, yet they will not budge from their spots until they become friends again.' "[7]

This was a fight over principles. Just as Maimonides always disregarded custom when dealing with synagogal issues, here too he ignored usage and emphasized the Law. "In legal questions, one should decide as permissively as possible and not burden people. One should make things hard only for oneself."

His position as court doctor forced Maimonides to spend the entire day in Cairo. Upon returning to Fostat, he was far too tired to read medical books the rest of the day, much less at night. "The art of medicine is an endless field. And it is especially hard for the man who fears God, loves truth, and does not wish to make any dubious, unfounded utterance," he wrote to Joseph. Nor could he find a free hour for study. He devoted the Sabbath to the Torah, but he could not study the other sciences at all.[8]

The king of England, Richard the Lionhearted, who in 1191 entered into close friendly relations with Saladin's brother, Al Adil, at Askalon, made an effort to get Maimonides as his personal physician. But Maimonides, who had known life in five empires, refused to migrate to the barely civilized North.

His high reputation and noble practice did not bring him any joy. He was ill-humored, depressed. The princes he treated were not on his level. Among the scholars in Egypt, none gained his intellectual confidence. The only person he felt close to was Joseph. But Joseph now lived in Aleppo: "Do not withhold your letters, they are my only solace."[9]

For the suffering man, prematurely aged, the profession he had to follow was too strenuous. The hatred of his opponents, the envy of the many, were not conducive to raising his spirits. Around this time, the little daughter his wife had borne a few years earlier died.[10]

His son, Abraham, who was to inherit the offices of nagid and court physician, but also the "amiability and modesty" of his father, felt very close to him. And perhaps he was, outwardly; Ibn Abi Usaibia depicted him as a sheik "with a tall and slender body." Maimonides entrusted him with exegeses on the Bible that he did not impart to others. Abraham asked his father about various knotty passages in the Codex and had "a privileged position in the nagid's cabinet."

"Only two things in my life give me pleasure: my studies and the realization that my son Abraham possesses the grace and fine qualities of our forefathers. He is utterly modest and humble, with a sensitive mind and a noble character. He will, I hope, make a name for himself among the great. I pray to God to protect him and grant him His grace,"[11] Maimonides wrote to Joseph. But because his patients were so demanding, study was only a rare delight for him. He felt this to be very harmful. Around this time, Averroës's commentaries on Aristotle arrived, excluding the one on

De sensu et sensitu. Maimonides read a bit of it, noticing, to his joy, that Averroës "interprets Aristotle in the true and correct method."[12] But, much as he yearned to go through all the writings, he could not find the time.

Maimonides's fame also extended to the non-Jewish world. The educated circles in Baghdad esteemed him as one of the most outstanding men of the age. His name exerted such an attraction that the young scholar Abdallatif, who lived in Baghdad, decided to visit Egypt in order to meet Maimonides. Having attended lectures by all the great teachers in Baghdad and having studied grammar, theology, jurisprudence, and medicine, he was convinced by 1189 that there was nothing more for him to learn in the city in which he lived. In 1191, he arrived in Cairo, hoping to make the acquaintance of Maimonides and two other scholars.[13]

Abdallatif, who entered Saladin's service, was not charmed by Fostat. He felt that the Greeks had chosen Alexandria for their residence, deliberately avoiding the area where Fostat was later built, because it was too close to the mountains, which stand in the path of the "refreshing and beneficial morning wind."[14] Just as he was disappointed by the "lack of the . . . morning wind" in Fostat, so too he was annoyed about his acquaintanceships; Maimonides evidently had no time for him. In fact, several contemporaries frivolously accused Maimonides of arrogance the moment the man, who was busy night and day, did not answer letters instantly and thoroughly or jotted his reply on the same page as the inquiry.

Maimonides's position at court was of utmost importance for the Jews of Egypt. He drove out the influence of the Karaites, and his defensive action, which had been launched decades earlier, now ended with success.

His urbane attitude stood him in good stead. He possessed the unsurpassable courtesy that the Arabic language and mentality had raised to a luxurious elegance of manners at that time. The princes must have felt very flattered by his acts of respect. The faultfinder Abdallatif even noted that Maimonides "liked to pay court to the great." It is a sign of Maimonides's skill that his politeness could induce such a judgment. The praises he showered on the rulers must have been truly remarkable. Thus, once, in a medical report on the sultan's illness, he wrote that "the servant is familiar with the *perfection* of our lord in the knowledge of his own ailment . . ."[15]

Despite all the demands upon him, Maimonides could not turn away the common people. His reputation grew precisely because of his rank as court doctor. The sick poured in from near and far. Ibn Abi Usaibia, the Arabic historian who later functioned as head doctor at the grand hospital of Cairo, recalls in his *History of Arabic Physicians* that Maimonides (whom he must have known personally) "occupied the first place among the physicians of his time both in theoretical and in practical medicine."[16] The Arabic poet and kadi Sa'id ibn Sana' al-Muk, "an old man of great prestige and extraordinary merits," glorified Maimonides in this poem:[17]

> Galen's art heals only the body,
> Maimon's the flesh and spirit both.
> Just as his knowledge has made him the physician of
>   the century,
> So too he heals the disease of ignorance with wisdom.
> The moon entrusts itself to his art,
> He heals it of the infirmities that sometimes afflict it,
> The spots in the time of the full moon
> And the pain of the moon's waning.

The Guide for the Perplexed quickly became renowned. Jewish, Christian, and Islamic theologians familiarized themselves with his ideas. While the philosophers and peripatetic observants reproached Maimonides for "deliberately falling away from Aristotle,"[18] pious and antiphilosophical Jews and Moslems accused the *Guide* of "misleading" people to impiety, a charge which could have serious effects in this area of reactionary religion. It was about this time that Averroës was charged with heresy and banished because of the objections that theologians had raised against his writings. His philosophical works were publicly burned circa 1195 at the command of Al Mansur, the caliph of the Almohades. By ignoring the dogma of resurrection when going through his reasons for the idea of immortality, Maimonides reinforced suspicions against himself. More and more doubts were voiced against his orthodoxy, threatening to undermine the influence of the Codex as well.

Meanwhile, Maimonides heard about the letter that the Yemenites had sent to Samuel ben Ali at the same time as the inquiry to Maimonides. The philosopher also got to see the epistle that the gaon had composed on that occasion, and he felt insulted by both its form and its content. Samuel ben Ali, by listing the absurd opinions of the Mu'tazilites, whom he obviously considered authoritative philosophers, convinced Maimonides even more strongly that the gaon was incompetent in philosophical matters.

Now the news spread through the Jewish world that the gaon, as the legitimate representative of the Jewish tradition, had sided against Maimonides, exposing him and his denial of resurrection. Even Joseph, the loyal disciple, then went so far as to rebuke Maimonides for reinterpreting the Biblical verses that deal with resurrection.

A new intrigue was being spun in secret. Samuel ben Ali took up contact with a Jewish dignitary named Zechariah, who then began charging alleged infractions in Maimonides's Mishnah commentary. Thus the least controversial of his works was drawn into a public battle.

Maimonides would never have dreamed of paying attention
to such a "wretched man, whose ignorance is comparable
to that of a newborn baby." When Zechariah received no
answer to his letter of objections, he dispatched a second
letter to Maimonides, apologizing very humbly and extolling
Samuel ben Ali as "a man unique in his time." Thereupon,
Samuel wrote to Maimonides, praising the sublime talent
and great knowledge of Zechariah, "who is thoroughly
familiar with four orders of the Talmud." This cheap trick
was repulsive to Maimonides.[19] But so as not to seem
evasive, he composed an *Epistle on Resurrection:* "When I
tried to elucidate a precept on this matter, the same thing
happened to me as to God, especially since the basic
doctrine of God's oneness has been misunderstood and a
trinity has been made of the unity. If this can happen to
God's words, then how much more so to a man's words. I
composed the Codex not to attain fame and glory, but for
the sake of God and to serve the mass of our people, whom
I wanted to help toward a better understanding of the Law.
However, I deemed it wrong to occupy myself only with
the branches of the Law while ignoring its roots. That is
why I decided to discuss the precepts of the faith. After
all, I myself have seen a man who considered himself a
Jewish scholar and had studied the branches of the law
since his youth, and yet felt doubts as to whether God is
corporeal and possesses eyes, hands, feet, and internal
organs. I have also known scholars who looked upon anyone denying the corporeity of God as a heretic. But because
comprehending the evidence of these basic teachings requires intimacy with many sciences, I have solely presented
them but not adduced the evidence. And that was how I
treated the doctrine of resurrection. I presented the view
that one must conceive of the future world without any
connection to resurrection; but I expressly emphasized that
the reanimation of the dead is a cornerstone of religion.

What should I add to what I have said in my works? If I have expressed the view that no bodies can exist in the future world, then I stand up for this view, and if even *one* rational man agrees with me, then a thousand ignoramuses can turn away from it. But to claim that I said the soul never returns to the body is calumny, since denying this would also mean denying miracles; but that would be tantamount to spurning religion."[20]

Now a man turned up in Baghdad who took a stand against the powerful gaon and penned an *Apologia for Maimonides*.[21] He demonstrated that Maimonides had been misquoted, that statements cited in his name did not exist in any of his works, and that he actually was unequivocal about teaching resurrection. The writer criticized the gaon: for quoting the assertions of the Mu'tazilites as opinions of true philosophers, for citing theories on the soul whose authors were physicians and not philosophers; and for including further unnecessary things against Maimonides in his epistle merely to increase the size of the piece. Maimonides, said this writer, had never negated the resurrection. Anyone doubting Maimonides's orthodoxy had little knowledge, and his notions could not grasp the truth; for, in reality, God's words could be applied to Maimonides: "My servant Moses—he is faithful."

And now Maimonides's honor began to be defended by poets and thinkers in hymns and apologies: "His wisdom is like the garden of God, his lips preserve knowledge, one seeks instruction from his mouth. The sacred oracle rests upon his breast, he does priestly service before God. He felt the suffering of the people and took pity on the poor. He constructed a shrine to reconcile the fathers with the sons and the sons with the fathers and to wipe out the spirit of superstition."[22]

23

"I Seek No Victory"

How did Maimonides react to the opposition that was mustered against the Codex as the years went by?

"I knew, when writing it, that this work would come into the hands of wicked and envious men who would defile its beauty and denigrate its value, interpreting it with their own inferiority and narrowness. The uneducated fool will not see the achievement and will consider the work useless; the rash and misguided beginner will deem many passages difficult, since either he will find no source or his mind will not suffice to grasp the meaning of my thoughts. The people who regard themselves as thinkers will be offended by the presentation of the dogmas.

"However, the work will also come into the hands of the few subtle and understanding men who will recognize the measure of my effort. You are one of these," he writes to Joseph, "and if I had no one else but you during my lifetime, it would be enough. Now letters have come from France and other countries; people admire the accomplishment. The work is already distributed in one portion of the inhabited world, and people long for it in places it has not reached. That is how things stand in my lifetime. But I know for sure that in the coming times, when envy and power lusts will cease, all Jews will yearn for the work and doubtless forgo all other books except to pass the time.

"If somebody said that I was neither pious nor religious, it would not anger me; even if I had to hear it with my own ears, I would not resent it—on the contrary, I would speak good, gentle words to him or hold my tongue, depending on the circumstances. I seek no victory for the honor of my soul; character consists in deviating from the paths of fools, but not in conquering them. If a man wanted to wax wroth about the ignorance of men, he would never stop being angry and he would have to lead a life of grief and affliction. One cannot blame you, my child, for being wrought up by the matter and being unable to endure the shame, for I am your father and your teacher. But my heart aches for your injury and sorrow."

Joseph ibn Aknin, in Baghdad, noticed the hostile feeling against Maimonides and was furious. He wanted to plunge into the fray, remain in Baghdad, and found an academy, in order to conquer this venerable stronghold of scholarship —which did have a few admirers of Maimonides—for the teachings of his master. He asked Maimonides to authorize his plans.

"I have nothing against your opening an academy in Baghdad and teaching my Codex there; but I fear that you will expose yourself to constant insults from them and never reach your goal. Furthermore, if you switch to teaching, then you will neglect your profession, and I advise you not to take anything from them for that. I would rather earn a drachma through weaving, tailoring, or carpentry than have an office under the exilarch . . . In my opinion, you should limit yourself to your calling and the practice of medicine, while studying the Torah. But you should only peruse Alfasi's work and compare it with the Codex. If you spend your time commenting on the Talmud and interpreting obscure passages, you will only be wasting your time and have little use from it." Joseph gave up his plan.

A rebellion against Maimonides broke out in Alexandria: the Jewish masses rose up against the Codex. "The entire people, big and little, old and young, formed a mob, which gathered outside the home of Rabbi Pinchas ben Meshullam and declared: 'We can no longer obey you, for you permit what you like and prohibit what you do not like. It has been handed down to us that a sullied man is not to pray before immersing himself in a bath. But you have allowed men to pray, attend your synagogue, and read the Torah without prior cleansing.'" The indignant people threatened to indict the rabbi, who had founded his decision on the Codex, and complained to the authorities that those who decided on the basis of the Codex were trying to bring innovations into religion. Under this pressure, the rabbi not only revoked his decision but also gave a sermon on the importance of the old custom. Pinchas sent a report to Maimonides—with whom he had been on friendly terms for years—delivering the speeches of the indignant as his own and agreeing with them "as if they were words of great sages."

When this account reached Maimonides, he was sick and felt that he was dying. Pinchas also made the most diverse reproaches against the Codex in general, particularly attacking Maimonides's alleged plan of having the Codex supersede the Talmud; the rabbi also pointed out the corruptive effects of the work and especially the lack of source references.

Most of Pinchas's criticisms did not faze Maimonides. The elements that were generally offensive had developed logically from his conception. He stood unshakably by the overall work and the details. However, the reprimand about the want of sources struck him deeply, for he found it justified. After all, it would have been possible to list sources without damaging the unity of the work.

A judge called upon Maimonides with the Codex volume containing the book *On the Injuries*. He opened to a passage in the chapter on murder and asked Maimonides to read it. Maimonides read and asked what objection the judge had.

"Where does this decision come from?" the judge asked.

"Probably from the tractate dealing with murder, *Makkot* or *Sanhedrin*."

"I have looked everywhere, I have hunted through the Talmud and *Tosefta*, and I could not find the source anywhere," said the judge.

These words left Maimonides stunned for quite a while; but he finally said: "It just occurred to me that the source of this decision is the tractate *Gittin*."

He took the tractate *Gittin* and leafed through it; but, to his astonishment and bewilderment, he could find nothing. He was forced to ask the judge to give him time to recollect the source. No sooner had the judge left than Maimonides remembered the Talmudic passage on which his decision was based. He quickly sent a messenger to catch up with the man. The judge could see for himself that the basis was an unexpected passage in the tractate on the law concerning a man's duty to marry his widowed sister-in-law.

Had Maimonides grown old? Had his memory suffered? "I am profoundly embarrassed," Maimonides admitted. He now resolved to do all he could to make up for the mistake and to save the work by indicating all the sources in a special book.

24

The Sages of Lunel

IN Provence, where Talmudic scholarship and philosophical speculation were flourishing, the works of Maimonides created a stir that was unprecedented in the history of the Jews. The most outstanding scholars looked up to the faraway Maimonides as to the greatest master since the completion of the Talmud. But by no means did they blindly submit to his authority. With sober criticism, they studied every precept of the Codex, trying to justify every single word. Since a few of the decisions did not make sense to them, they turned to the author himself.

Lunel had a Jewish community which, although numbering only a few hundred, had an extraordinarily vast sphere of influence. Both Talmudic learning, which was having a great upswing in France and Germany, and the versatile Jewish culture of Spain equally enriched the spiritual and intellectual life of the Jews in Lunel. Owing to the intermediary role of this community, the scientific literature of Jews and Arabs in the Pyrenean peninsula became a component part of medieval Christian learning.[1]

In 1195, an address in the Hebrew language from the "sages of Lunel" arrived in Fostat. Like a solemn procession, a host of glorifying words preceded the name of Moses ben Maimon. In a diction whose fantastic élan could only be attained by the splendor of Biblical language, there followed an avowal of devotion and love.

In the Christian countries, where there was no exilarch, no gaon, nor any similar dignitaries, where the prestige of the academies was scant in contrast to the nimbus of the old and venerable academy in Baghdad, there was nevertheless the prospect not only of a brilliant scholarly future but of true research. In Baghdad, the frantic and superficial efforts to restore the decaying institution of the gaonship endangered any unbiased and selfless cultivation of learning. While the letters from Baghdad contained untenable and hairsplitting notions, the questions and objections offered by Jonathan Cohen, the spokesman of the "sages of Lunel," in his accompanying letter were imbued with a true scholarly spirit. "Praised be God, who lets my writings come into the hands of such men, who penetrate deep into the substance and grasp my words. That is a comfort for my soul and a support for my old age,"[2] said Maimonides when reading the critique from the "sages of Lunel."

The strains of medical practice, the self-sacrificing activity that Maimonides had been pursuing uninterruptedly for about seven years, wreaked their vengeance. A serious illness chained him to his bed for a whole year. "The yoke of the sick weighs heavily on my neck. By seeking cures from me, they ground up my strength. They left me no free hour, either day or night."[3]

Nor was his health restored, even after a year. The danger was no longer mortal, but his organism, which had been assailed by illness for decades, was weakened and undermined by his long sufferings. "Even now, I still pass most of each day sitting on my bed. It is no longer as in my youth. My strength is shaken, my heart ill, my tongue heavy, my senses are dimmed and my hands tremble in weakness. I even find it difficult to write a brief letter."[4]

His condition did, however, allow him to dictate a reply to the scholarly portion of the correspondence; in his own hand, he answered the personal address from Lunel. He spoke to the group with the Biblical verse: "Moses said: I will surely go there and see this great phenomenon." He then continued: "Only great scholars raise such objections." The rectors of the Babylonian academy had also raised objections, he said, but only minor and trivial ones, "which would never even cross your minds." Maimonides apologized for being unable to take care of correspondence personally because of his physical and spiritual fatigue and because of his patients, "who burdened [him] incessantly." He asked the sages to read his work with unsparing criticism and to test the individual decisions. No one, he said, was immune to errors, nor was forgetfulness rare, least of all among older people.

Aside from his practical activity, he also had to put his theoretical knowledge at the service of medicine. Abulridha, a nephew and medical student, acted as his secretary in the composition of countless medical writings[5] which he had to set down at this time.

For climatic reasons, the study of poisons was greatly cultivated by Arabic medicine. In Egypt, where poisonings were frequent and sudden, the treatment of this condition was especially important. Al Fadil had ordered physicians to take the precaution of preparing large quantities of "great treacle" and "mithridate." However, compounding these remedies was extremely difficult, since the necessary plants did not grow domestically. At the vizier's orders, the ingredients were brought from the far East and West, and the two specifics were manufactured and distributed among the patients. But all these measures proved inadequate.

In July 1198, Al Fadil said to Maimonides: "It dawned on me yesterday that someone might be bitten by a venomous animal, and before he could come to us and take treacle, the venom could spread through his body, and he would die, especially if he had been bitten at night and only came to us in the morning. Furthermore, both these electuaries, which are hard to prepare, are used on minor occasions—e.g., for a scorpion's or a spider's bite—for which the treacle of forty-two species or the like is enough." He therefore commissioned Maimonides to write a treatise of "small dimension" and in a terse style, offering popular instruction on first aid, in the absence of a physician, for poisonings.

Maimonides knew the countless and extensive writings on this topic, and his aim was not, as he said, to propose new theories. He merely wanted to gather a number of do's and don'ts "of great use," and name "the most effective remedies found most easily in this region"; he also wanted to describe how to prepare them, so that a patient could dispense with a doctor's help. The piece, which he himself called "the Fadil treatise," found wide acceptance in professional circles and was frequently quoted by medieval surgeons.[6]

Saladin had seventeen sons, and when he closed his eyes in death in 1193, fighting broke out among them. However, in his will he had divided the empire: his eldest son Al Afdal inherited Damascus and Syria and was to rule supreme over his brothers. Scarcely a year after Saladin's death, the conflicts resumed, and the warfare would not end. Saladin's empire disintegrated into tiny, powerless states. Al Aziz, who had become governor of Egypt at fifteen and sultan of Egypt upon his father's death, was a kindly but weak ruler. He had the best intentions to govern the country justly, but he was unable to regulate the difficult economic situation of Egypt. Yet he was loved by his subjects. In November 1198, Al Aziz died, and his older brother Al Afdal was appointed atabeg, or regent, of the deceased's minor son by the Egyptian emirs. This educated prince had been instructed in the Islamic sciences by the finest teachers in Cairo and Alexandria; poems of his are extant. At the age of twenty-three, he had inherited supremacy over the other princes. But he soon proved inadequate for his task; on being granted supreme power, the once pious and ascetic man plunged into all kinds of debauchery. Soon the emirs turned away from him, and his throne began to totter.

The friendly relationship between Al Afdal and Maimonides apparently stemmed from the time when the former was still a prince; the acquaintanceship had probably been mediated by Maimonides's brother-in-law, the "privy scribe" to Al Afdal's mother. The sultan made Maimonides his personal physician. Maimonides warned him that his dissipations had undermined his health, and never ceased recommending temperance to him.

Al Afdal then asked Maimonides to write a treatise on health for him. The sultan complained of poor digestion and "occasional gloom, bad thoughts, nervous anxiety, and fear of death." "The lowly servant Moses Ibn Obed Allah, the Jew from Cordova," now explained the essence of the good life to the sultan of Cairo. He taught him that the emotions leave an impression only on "youths, women, and common ignoramuses," who have no knowledge of ethics. Such people are fearful and feeble because of their "softness of soul." When struck by misfortune or disaster, they wail and weep. When they receive something good, their joy is great and, given the defective education of their souls, they imagine they have received an uncommonly great good and their pride and arrogance grow. But for those who decide in favor of philosophical maxims or ethics, "their souls gain strength, they are truly heroes, so that their souls are only very slightly influenced and altered. The more spiritual training a man has, the smaller is his change in both situations, that of happiness and that of unhappiness, so that, when receiving a great good—what the philosophers call imaginary good—he is not excited by it. Likewise, when struck by a great unhappiness—which the philosophers call imaginary ills—he is not unsettled or saddened, and he bears it bravely." A precise diet, a detailed list of recommended foods and specifics, and other directives constitute the bulk of *The Guide to Good Health for Al Afdal*.[7]

The sultan left the royal residence and made his home in the provinces. Many court physicians followed the sick ruler. Maimonides, the chief personal doctor, did not join the sultan. Letters kept him informed of the prince's condition, and he gave his medical advice from afar. But the sultan seemed to miss Maimonides, the only person in whom he had full confidence. A note of apology that Maimonides once sent to the ruler goes as follows:

"And God, the sublime, is witness, and He suffices as witness! He has strengthened the hope of the lowly servant that he may devote himself to serving our master in our own person and with personal discourse, not with paper and quill. However, his own nature is bad and his bodily constitution weak. Even more so than in his youth, this has been an obstacle for many pleasures in his old age—I do not mean simply pleasures—but noble accomplishments, whose greatest and highest is the devotion to serving our master. But God be thanked for all conditions, whose universality is to be found in the universe of existences and whose specificity is to be found in every single individual, by dint of His will, His wisdom, whose depth no human being fathoms. May the praise for every single condition be constant, no matter what the situation may be!"[8]

The sultan's state of health had not improved in two years. "The best thing he had was slumber." In the autumn of 1200, Maimonides received a "discreet" letter personally dictated by the sultan and depicting in detail all the symptoms of the illness, especially the complaints of the heart, head, and digestion. Maimonides, as the great medical authority, was then asked for his verdict on the medical prescriptions of his colleagues who were treating the sultan. Maimonides knew the patient's ailment and said that "the best physicians of our time lack the necessary knowledge to diagnose this ailment." He approved of most of his colleagues' prescriptions, while rejecting some soberly and calmly and some ironically. Together with his opinion, he sent precise instructions on what the patient should do and eat. There were specific instructions for every hour of the day and night, summer and winter. Maimonides hoped that careful observance of his advice would improve the sultan's condition within a short time; he desired this improvement with all his heart and he even inserted the following words into the dry prescription style of this treatise, which was probably his final medical work: "God make his sufferings pass, and prolong his days!"[9] Al Afdal lived for another twenty-five years.

The scholars of Lunel, with Jonathan Cohen at their head, penned a letter to Maimonides, asking for a copy of *The Guide for the Perplexed*, if possible in a Hebrew translation or in the original. Maimonides complied with their request. When an Arabic copy arrived, this philosophical group asked Samuel ibn Tibbon, the son of the famous translator, to render it into Hebrew. Admirers and opponents, as well as Samuel ibn Tibbon, asked the author to elucidate various points in his system. But Maimonides was bedridden with a serious illness. Meanwhile, Samuel ibn Tibbon was working on his version with an awe that is usual only for translating sacred writings.

"You holy man, our teacher and master, you light of exile, please hear the request of your servants, who wish to

draw from your wellspring; and let us find sustenance and
satisfaction in the book *The Guide for the Perplexed*, of
whose reputation we have heard and which has appeared in
Egypt." Enthusiastic tributes arrived from Marseilles,
Lunel, and other Provençal towns. From al-Harizi, who
was working on Hebrew translations of the Mishnah commentary and *The Guide for the Perplexed*, Maimonides
received these verses:

> *From thee, O prince, comes our glory;*
> *From thee, in thee is our salvation.*
> *Thou art a messenger of God, art created*
> *In His image, and if we do resemble thee—*
> *Then it was for thy sake that God spoke:*
> *I want to create man in Mine own image.*

Samuel ibn Tibbon, "who yearned to join one of
Maimonides's disciples," was shaken upon learning of his
protracted illness, "which he was forced to suffer because
of our sins." In this mood, he wrote to Fostat: "May we be
the atonement for him and his sickness."

The task he had to cope with was extremely difficult.
Aside from the linguistic problems, the contents of several
passages were unintelligible to him. He had no choice but
to appeal to the author himself about the dubious places.
When he then discovered mistakes in his copy, "his heart
could not rest" until he had corrected the work. He sent it
back to Fostat, requesting that "the holy philosopher" have
one of his pupils go through this copy once or twice very
attentively, until they could be certain that no mistake was
left. The places in which Samuel suspected errors he
marked with ink, or with his fingernail on the margin of the
questionable line, and hoped that the correctors would
write the corrections clearly in the margins, rather than
crossing out any letters. Maimonides was asked to sign the
copy after making sure the revisions were correct. Only

then would it be sent to Rabbi Abraham Cohen in Alexandria, who would seek a way of dispatching the book to Lunel with southern French Jews, who frequently traveled there. This scholar immediately did everything that Samuel asked him to do; and how much more of an effort would he make to carry out a request from Maimonides.

The impact this letter had on Maimonides could be likened only to the feeling aroused in him some fourteen years earlier by Joseph ibn Aknin's letter from Alexandria. Maimonides had known Judah ibn Tibbon by reputation for years; prominent and learned men from Granada had told him about Judah's learning and his fine Hebrew and Arabic style. A prestigious scholar from Toledo who had come to Egypt, a disciple of Abraham ben David from Posquières and of Abraham ibn Ezra, had told him about Judah. But Maimonides did not realize that this man had a son. When he received Samuel ibn Tibbon's letter in Hebrew and Arabic, and came to know his ideas and his art of presentation, when he saw that Samuel had detected the erroneous passages and raised cogent objections, Maimonides thought of the words of the "old poet" (Judah Halevi): "If one had known his parents, one would have said that the merits of the father had gone over to the son. Praised be the Lord who rewarded this wise father and granted him such a worthy son. And not to him alone but to all scholars has this blessing been granted, for this dear child was born to all of us, this beloved son was given to all of us!" It was with such enthusiasm that the world-famous man hailed the young and unknown Samuel.

In his letter, Maimonides answered all the questions, offering instructions on the art of translating and directions on reading philosophical works. He expressed his amazement that an inhabitant of the South of France possessed such skill in Arabic.

Like Joseph ibn Aknin before him, the modest and sedate Samuel ibn Tibbon wished to visit Maimonides, but he had less luck. The circumstances of Maimonides's life had changed. "You mention that you want to visit me—then come, blessed man of the Lord, and be the most blessed of all visitors. I am looking forward to it, I long for your presence, and I yearn more to see you than you to see me, even though I am distressed that you have to expose yourself to the perils of a sea voyage. I also want to tell you my opinion and advise you not to expose yourself to any danger, since your only purpose in visiting me is to see and receive tributes in the measure of my strength. But you can never expect to gain any scholarly benefit or to converse with me alone, even for one hour during the day or the night."

He then describes his daily schedule: "The sultan lives in Cairo and I live in Fostat; the two towns are two Sabbath leagues apart. I have a difficult time with the sultan; I must visit him every morning. If he himself or one of his children or harem members is sick, then I may not leave Cairo. I spend most of the day in the sultan's palace. Usually, I also have to treat some dignitary. In a word: I go to Cairo every morning at the crack of dawn, and if nothing keeps me there and nothing unforeseen occurs, I can come home only in the afternoon, but by no means any earlier. Here, starving as I am, I find the antechamber full of people: Jews and non-Jews, nobles and lowly people, judges and officials, friends and foes, a motley company awaiting me with impatience. I dismount from my horse, wash, and enter the waiting room with the plea that they may not feel offended if I have to make them wait a bit longer while I partake of a hasty light meal, which normally happens only once every twenty-four hours. Then I go out to them again, treat them, and prescribe medicaments on notes. Thus the people go in and out of my home until late in the evening. Sometimes, I swear it on the Torah, it is 2 a.m. or even later before I manage to consume anything. I am then so worn out that I collapse on my bed; I have to say good night, I am totally exhausted and incapable of speaking. Only on the Sabbath can anyone speak to me alone, or can I be alone with myself for even an instant. Then all or most of the members of the community gather in my home after the morning prayer. I indicate what is to be done in the community during the coming week; then they listen to a short lecture until noon, go home, and return in a smaller number. Now a second lecture takes place, between the minkhah and the maariv prayer.

"Thus do my days go by. But I have depicted only a portion of what you will see for yourself if you come here, with God's help . . . When you have completed the explanation and translation for our brethren, then come to me in joy . . . The Lord of the universe knows in what condition I write these lines. I have withdrawn from people and sought peace and quiet in order to remain undisturbed. At times, I lean against the wall; at times, I continue my writing; I am so feeble that I mostly have to lie down; a weak body has joined forces with my age."

Around 1201, letters from the South of France arrived, signed by many people and filled with lively praises, requesting that Maimonides himself translate *The Guide for the Perplexed* into Hebrew.

"It would be a great delight for me to give the stolen goods back to its owners," wrote Maimonides, who had the feeling that by writing the work in Arabic he had robbed Hebrew of something that belonged to it by right. But where was he to find the time for this if he did not even have time to jot down a few lines? He was not even able to look through the commentaries and other writings begun in his youth in order to publish them, much less translate an entire book. The letter from Lunel touched him deeply, but he did not

find time for an immediate response. Other questions and
letters were usually answered by his pupils. But feeling
great veneration for this community, he wished to reply
personally.

"My friends and colleagues," he wrote to Lunel around
1202, "be strong and of courageous hearts. In this difficult
period, you and those who live in your vicinity are the only
ones who carry high the banner of Moses. You study the
Talmud and cultivate the other sciences as well. But here
in the East the men of wisdom are decreasing and dying
out. Palestine still has three or four places where intellectual
life prevails. In all of Syria there is only Aleppo, where a
tiny few cultivate the study of the Torah, but they are not
very ardent about it. In Babylon there are two or three
places of learning; in Yemen and the other Arabic countries
there is little study of the Talmud, and there is no interest
whatsoever in theoretical research. The Jews in India are
not even familiar with the Holy Writ, and all they know of
the Law is the Sabbath and circumcision. In the Turkish
provinces they have only the Bible, and they stick to its
literal meaning. In Maghreb, as we know, a heavy doom
weighs upon the Jews. Thus, salvation can reach us only
from you. Be therefore strong and courageous and stand
by the Law. You cannot rely on my labors. I can no longer
come and go. I am old and weary, not with the burden of
years, but because of my suffering body. The Lord grant
you assistance and preserve you for blessing and glory in
this world!"

25

Imitatio Dei

MAIMONIDES as nagid possessed full power. Nevertheless, he did not bother to carry out synagogal reforms, which would have been very easy for him now. The synagogues of the Palestinians survived next to those of the Babylonians through the following century. Maimonides's action was crowned only in legend: "Maimonides constructed a house of prayer, which he completed in one night with the help of God. It was a splendid building. In it, the Babylonians prayed according to their customs."

In a piece written in those years, Maimonides distinguished between two kinds of pious men. Some devote themselves exclusively to their own destiny, avoiding the affairs of the world and the consequent distractions; they perform their duties quietly and are therefore beloved by God and men. The others are involved in the affairs of men, they are drawn into conflicts, collide with unruliness, and cannot avoid anger, complaints and unsuitable speech. The great sages, perceiving this, chose to withdraw and devote themselves purely to study.[1]

The high political position he had attained as nagid and the prestige he had achieved through his personality enabled him to act on behalf of his brethren in the lands of the empire. Thus, he freed the Yemenite Jews "from the harsh

measures and heavy taxes ordained against them," and the
Jews could recover a bit "from the burden imposed on
them by the rulers."[2] "Throughout his life, he was helpful
to many lands and places; with his letters and notes of consolation, he solidified many communities of Israel in the
faith. His wisdom was joined by great piety and generosity;
his house was open to everyone."

As supreme head of the Jews, Maimonides had a lofty
political position; he was considered the premier physician
of his age, the most important Talmudist of the millennium,
an epoch-making philosopher, an outstanding mathema-
tician, scientist, and jurist; he was admired by the masses,
honored by princes, celebrated by scholars; he corresponded
with famous rectors and insignificant judges; the complaints
of the simple fellahs, the diseases and whims of the rulers,
the spiritual and physical sufferings in the harem took up
his attention; he maintained the most cultivated forms of
court etiquette as well as plain helpfulness and cordiality
toward the most common of men. In all this, he asserted
his retiring, self-willed personality. The sick and heavily
suffering man did not rest; the impulses that had been
forcing him to do scholarly work all his life drove him now
to the patients. In his ethics, he fought against negation of
life, asceticism, and he taught the middle path, balance;
however, his self-sacrifice went far beyond equilibrium. He
was a man of willpower, resolution, and freedom. He
devoted the last fifteen years of his life purely to medicine
with more energy than he had sacrificed in the ten years of
the codification. The passion for scholarly labor, dominating him since his youth, was replaced by a different motive.
After the final chapter of *The Guide for the Perplexed*, he
wrote nothing but responsa and one epistle. His plan to
write a book on the Haggada, demonstrating philosophy
from Judaism and thus legitimizing his own philosophy; his
wish to translate his Arabic writings into Hebrew; the

necessity of completing the Talmudic commentary he had started once before; his work on the Jerusalem Talmud; his desire to compile the promised book of sources on which the future of the Codex, his life's work, depended— all these things were given up, and he now only treated the ill. At the height of his life, he turned from metaphysics to medicine, from contemplation to practice.

That was Maimonides's last transformation: from contemplation to practice, from knowledge to the imitation of God. God was not only the object of knowledge. He was the Model one should follow. His works, the creatures of the world which He guides in Providence, replaced abstract conceptions which constitute a spiritual act through intellectual knowledge of God. The observation of and absorption in concrete events replaced abstract viewing. Now the thinker no longer made any effort to deny any characteristic of God; instead, he strove to "become similar to God in his actions."[3] The most vehement enemy of all anthropomorphisms, which try to make God similar to man, found that the ultimate conclusion of wisdom was to become similar to God; just as the cosmic motion of the spheres and all the events of the world take place in order to become similar to God. The trend of waning antiquity toward gnosis, toward contemplation as the goal of man— often by way of flight from the world and the negation of life—coincided in Maimonides with a trend toward ethos, toward action, as the aim and primacy, the most consistently developed tendency in Biblical–Talmudic Judaism. The purpose of the last fourteen years of his life was conquering the antinomy that had thus come about. During his youth, the ideal of life had been human perfection. This was now replaced by the imitation of God. The private self, which was determined not by the self but by God, vanished from his stance.

He had arduously labored to attain the knowledge that

God, for all the sublimity of His essence, has immediate knowledge of individual things, and not just of the species.[4] The imitation of God now meant service for individuals. Maimonides renounced the postulate of withdrawal, the maxim that "one should join other people only in an emergency."[5] He could now "speak to other people and at the same time think incessantly about God and stand incessantly before God in his heart even though he was with people physically, just as it is written in the Song of Songs: 'I sleep, but my heart is awake.' "[6]

The love of thinking was the fundamental motif of his life. He related to thinking as to something personified. Every act of thinking was the reception of a revelation for him. The uninterrupted effluence of the divine entered thinking, but it also entered every event in the world, wherever matter gained form. This idea too was a spoor on Maimonides's path to the concrete.

The mystery of thinking was the most penetrating experience of his life. God is sublime; any definition of His being is impossible; the knowledge of His person lies beyond the limits of reason. God is remote; the pull, the urge, the need for God drove Maimonides to the "active intellect." Thinking was personified; he was imbued with the myth of the "active intellect": "The thinking that pours out from God upon us is the link between Him and us, and it is up to you to solidify this link and make it more intimate or to gradually loosen it until you dissolve it altogether."[7] Nor did he have to think of holy things in order to be close to the holy; thinking per se is holiness. "If a man is at home alone, he does not sit and move and act as though he were in front of a mighty king. Nor will he speak and make a great number of words at will in front of the king as when he is with his relatives and the members of his household. And thus the man who wishes to become a man of God must wake up and realize that the mighty king, who always protects him and is linked to him, is more powerful than all kings of flesh and blood, even David and Solomon. This protecting king, who is connected with us, is the 'active intellect,' the bond between God and us. And just as we know God by the light that He has streaming out to us, thus does He look through us by means of this light and for the sake of this light."[8] Nevertheless, his sense of the limitations of reason did not vanish from his awareness. The preeminence of prophecy over philosophy became more distinct than ever. "Know that there is a level that is higher than all philosophy: this is prophecy. It is a different world. Arguing and investigating are out of place here; no evidence can reach prophecy; any attempt to examine it in a scholarly manner is doomed to fail. It would be like trying to gather all the water on earth in a small cup,"[9] he wrote in his final years.

"But I say that there is a limit to human knowledge, and so long as the soul is in the body, it cannot grasp the supernatural."[10] No matter how greatly the mind may strive to know God, it will find a barrier; matter is a powerful dividing wall.[11] Maimonides was one of those "who are saddened if the needs of matter carry them to defilement and obvious disgrace; they are ashamed and they scorn themselves for being thus afflicted, and they attempt to lessen the disgrace and to control themselves. They behave like a man the king is angry at and whom, to expose to scorn, he orders to sweep away garbage; and the man strives to hide in this time of disgrace and only touches a little so as not to sully his hands and clothes or be seen by anyone."[12]

Immortality, for Maimonides, is the eternal life of the spirit in the process of knowing. The soul surviving after death is not the soul that comes into being with man; the original soul is only a capacity, a sheer faculty; in contrast, the soul that leaves man after death is real and acquired reason.[13] The measure of immortality thus depends on the amount of acquired knowledge.

It was not hard for Maimonides to depart from time, from the agitations of life. Time was not eternal for him, it was creatural, an "accidental quality" of movement, of happening. Motion itself is only an "accidental quality" of substance; time is thus an "accidental quality" of an "accidental quality."[14]

"When the perfect man has gotten on in years, his happiness over what he knows increases and his yearning for the known increases until the soul in the time of such enjoyment separates from the body. Knowledge becomes stronger at the time of death, and always remains with its object, for then the obstacle which at times separates the known from the to-be-known is cleared away, and man remains with this sublime enjoyment. Moses, Aaron, and Miriam died that way when God kissed them. For the knowledge of God is like a kiss."[15]

On the night of the 20th of Tebet 4965 (December 13, 1204), "the glorious column of clouds arose to the heavens: Moses ben Maimon, God's servant in Fostat." The Jews and the Arabs mourned him for three days.[16] When the news reached Alexandria, the grief was enormous. A fast was ordained, the cantor read from Leviticus 26:2 until the end of the threats of punishment, and the last man to be summoned to the Torah read from the first book of Samuel, chapter four, until the words: "For the Ark of the Lord is taken away."

Years later, when the corpse was being brought to Palestine, pirates attacked the caravan. They wanted to hurl the coffin into the sea, but they were unable to lift it even though there were more than thirty of them. Upon seeing this, they said: "This was a godly man." They sent for the Jews and provided an escort for them.

At his own wish, Maimonides was buried in Tiberias, in

the place where Rabbi Judah ha-Nasi had so often tarried. An unknown hand wrote the following inscription on his gravestone:

Here lies a man and yet not a man;
If thou wert a man, then heavenly creatures created thee.

Later this inscription was wiped away and replaced by another:

Here lies Moses Maimuni, the banished heretic.

The people erected a monument for their teacher with the words:

From Moses to Moses, there was no one like Moses.

On November 30, 1204, two weeks before the death of Maimonides, Samuel ibn Tibbon finished his Hebrew translation of *The Guide for the Perplexed*. He boarded ship immediately and journeyed to Fostat to meet his master. It was too late.

Notes and Sources

ABBREVIATIONS

EDI   *Enzyklopädie des Islam*
EJ   *Encyclopaedia Judaica*
JQR   *The Jewish Quarterly Review*
K   Kobez, ed. Lichtenberg
MGWJ   *Monatsschrift für Geschichte und Wissenschaft des Judentums*
MN   *More Nevukhim* (Warsaw, 1872)
MT   *Mishneh Torah*
P   *Commentary on the Mishnah*
R   *Responsa*, ed. Freidmann (Jerusalem, 1934)
REJ   *Revue des Etudes Juives*
SB   *Sammelbuch Moses ben Maimon*
SP   Introduction by Abot (eight chapters)
ZDMG   *Zeitschrift der Deutschen Morgenländischen Gesellschaft*
ZFHB   *Zeitschrift für Hebräische Bibliographie*

In the original (1935) German edition, the translations by
A. Weiss (Leipzig, 1923); M. Wolff, (Leiden, 1903); and
M. Rawicz (Offenburg, 1910) were frequently used.

1 Life in Exile

1. A. Müller, *Der Islam im Morgen und Abendland*, II, 640ff; EDI I, 330ff.
2. Goldzieher, "Materialien zur Kenntnis der Almohadenbewegung in Nordafrika," ZDMG 41, 67ff.
3. This is evident from Maimon's epistle (*Chemda Genusa*, Lebanon, 8, and JQR II) and Maimonides (K II, 12ff.).
4. EJ 6, 965.
5. Goldzieher, ZDMG 41, 67ff.
6. Juchassin, ed. Philippowski, p. 219.
7. 14th of Nissan = 30th of March, after 1 p.m., 1135, in Cordova.

2 In Fez

1. Eppenstein, *Abraham Maimuni*, p. 59.
2. Dozy, *Geschichte der Mauren in Spanien*, II, 394.
3. MN III, 24.
4. MN III, 49.
5. K II, 37d.
6. Toledano, *Ner Hamaarab*, p. 34; *Misrach umaarab*, IV, 266.
7. Kremer, *Kulturgeschichte des Orients*, II, 447ff.
8. E. Mittwoch, "Ein Geniza-Fragment," ZDMG 57, 61ff.
9. A. Müller, *Der Islam*, p. 651.
10. See *Chemda Genusa*, p. LXXIX.
11. See Schreiner, "Samau'al b. Jahjâ al-Magribi und seine Schrift *Ifhâ al-Jahûd*, MGWJ 42, 123ff.
12. SP 5.

13. MN I, 33.
14. MN I, 34.
15. MN II, 9. 24; see MT Kiddush, Hachodesh XVII, 25.
16. SP 5.
17. SP 5; MN III, 19.
18. K II, 25.
19. Kremer, *Kulturgeschichte*, II, 461.
20. P on Chelek, ed. Holzer, p. 20.
21. P on Abot V, 21.
22. K II, 12c.
23. E. Mittwoch, ZDMG 57, 61ff.
24. SP I.

3 Prophecy

1. Rosin, *Ethik des Maimonides*, pp. 10ff.
2. K II, 28d. The authenticity of this passage is no longer debated; see Eppenstein in SB, II, 49.
4. The speculation about prophecy occupied a major position in Islamic thought. However, the central position of the epistemological reflection upon prophecy in Maimonides's philosophy can be explained neither by its polemical, its apologetic, nor its Jewish-dogmatic significance.
5. Introduction to P, ed. Hamburger, p. 11; P to Chelek, ed. Holzer, p. 24; SP i and 5.
6. Foreword to MN.
7. SP 7; introduction to P, ed. Hamburger, p. 7.
8. Introduction to P, ed. Hamburger, pp. 45ff.
9. Source for the following: introduction to P, pp. 50ff.
10. MN I, 73, tenth thesis. For the following *cf.* C. Diesendruck, *The Teleologie bei Maimonides* (Cincinnati, 1928), p. 426, A. 28.
11. Introduction to P, p. 49.
12. P on Abot V, 12.
13. K II, s. 29d, after Rosin: *Ethik des Maimonides*, p. 127; Munk, *Notice sur Joseph ben Jehouda*, p. 46; and Toledano, *Ner Hamaarab*, p. 225. Maimonides assumed that Ibn Aknin, who lived in Ceuta, knew about these discussions.
14. SP 4.
15. P to Abot IV, 23.

16. Millot, *Hahiggajon,* XIV.
17. K II, 13b, and so on.
18. SP 4.
19. SP 4.
20. Introduction to P, ed. Hamburger, p. 53.

4   *The Model*

1. K I, p. 12c.
2. P on *Shabbat* XXIII, 2; *cf.* MT *Shabbath* XXIII, 19, and Karo.
3. Introduction to P.
4. Introduction to P, ed. Hamburger, p. 60.
5. P to Mikvaot IV, 4.

5   *Respect for Israel*

1. P to Berachot IX; source for the following: K II, 12ff.

6   *Journey to Palestine*

1. K II, 15a.
2. *Chemda Genusa,* p. 30; REJ, IV, 174.
3. Kremer, *Kulturgeschichte,* II, 437.
4. REJ IV, 174.
5. Mez, *Die Renaissance des Islams,* p. 473.
6. K I, 34a.
7. Concluding remark on P, ed. Derenbourg.
8. SP 4.
9. SB I, 111.
10. SP 4.
11. P on Abot IV, 4.
12. P on Abot IV, 4; K II, 24a; see Josef ben Jehuda, *Sepher Musar,* ed. Bacher, on Abot IV, 4.
13. K II, v.
14. Röhricht, *Geschichte des Königreichs Jerusalem,* p. 314.
15. Prutz, *Kulturgeschichte der Kreuzzüge,* p. 104.
16. Henne am Rhyn, *Kulturgeschichte der Kreuzzüge,* pp. 187ff.
17. Prutz, *Kulturgeschichte der Kreuzzüge,* p. 323.
18. K I, 7c.
19. R, no. 99.

20. P on Sota II, 4.
21. P on Para III, 9.
22. P on Berachot II, 4; P on Erubin VII.
23. P on Tohorot.
24. K II, 23f.
25. K I, 14b; Geiger, *Moses ben Maimon*, p. 7a (Hebrew).
26. MN III, 45.
27. Graetz, *Geschichte der Juden*, VI, 134.
28. Prutz, *Kulturgeschichte der Kreuzzüge*, pp. 119 and 123.
29. MT Deot VI, 1.
30. MT Deot VI, 1.
31. J. Guttmann, "Über Abraham bar Chijjas *Buch der Enthüllung*," MGWJ 47, 450.
32. Prutz, *Kulturgeschichte*, p. 100.
33. Prutz, *Kulturgeschichte*, p. 316.
34. R, no. 159.
35. Prutz, *Kulturgeschichte*, p. 134.
36. Poznanski, *Babylonische Geonim*, p. 96.
37. K II, p. V.
38. Prutz, *Kulturgeschichte*, p. 48.
39. P to Kellim XV, 1, ed. Derenbourg.

7   Fight Against Assimilation

1. After Röhricht, *Geschichte des Königreichs Jerusalem*, p. 330, and Benjamin.
2. Al-Harizi, see Geiger, *Nachgelassene Schriften*, III, 240.
3. See also letter to Joseph in *Birkat Abraham*, ed. Goldberg.
4. P to Avot IV, 6.
5. Concluding remark to P.
6. D. Kaufmann, "Juda Halewi und seine ägyptischen Freunde," MGWJ 40, 420ff.
7. The term was coined by David Koigen.
8. Röhricht, *Geschichte des Königreichs Jerusalem*, pp. 328ff.
9. Mann, *The Jews in Egypt*, II, 288f.
10. R, no. 162 and 178.
11. K I, 35c ff.
12. K I, 17b.
13. P to Abot I, 3; see R, no. 46.
14. Asulai, *Schem Haggdolim*, see Maimonides.

8 *In Fostat*

1. Since the Mishnah commentary was apparently concluded in Fostat (see concluding remark to P), the removal probably took place before 1168.
2. D. Kaufmann, "Juda Halewi und seine ägyptischen Freunde," MGWJ 40, 420.
3. Source for the portrayal of the Sutta affair: "Scroll about Sutta," *Hashiloach*, XV, 175ff.
4. Concluding remark to P, ed. Derenbourg.
5. Introduction to Chelek, ed. Holzer, pp. 29ff.
6. P to Berachot IV.
7. K II, 10b.
8. Röhricht, *Geschichte des Königreichs Jerusalem*, p. 338.
9. EDI I, 855.
10. Goldzieher, *Vorlesungen über den Islam*, pp. 209, 211.
11. C. H. Becker, *Islamstudien*, I, 191ff.
12. Röhricht, *Geschichte des Königreichs Jerusalem*, pp. 350ff.
13. D. Kaufmann, MGWJ 41, 215ff.
14. K I, 51c.

9 *Educational Reform*

1. In Maimonides's time, Rashi's Talmud commentary was still unknown in the Islamic countries.
2. Introduction to *Mishneh Torah*.
3. K II, 30c.
4. Introduction to *Mishneh Torah*.
5. K I, 25c ff.
6. Introduction to *The Book of Commandments*.
7. Poetic compositions of the 613 commandments.
8. R, no. 76.
9. *Cf.* his etymologies in P.
10. MT Ishut XI, 13.
11. MT "Malve Melove," XV, 2.
12. Introduction to Tohorot, ed. Derenbourg, I, 30.
13. MT Kiddush, Hachodesh XIX, 16.
14. Foreword to *Mishneh Torah*.
16. K I, 25c.
17. A handwritten piece by Sheshet Benveniste about Maimuni's influence, MGWJ 25, 509ff.

10 Messianic Yearning

1. Source for the following: *Epistle to Yemen*, K II, 1ff.
2. MT Melachim XII, 4ff.
3. J. Guttmann, MGWJ 47, 446ff.
4. J. Friedländer, "Das arabische Original der antikaräischen Verordnung des Maimonides," MGWJ 53, 469ff; K I, 30.
5. Büchler, JQR 5, 421.
6. Mann, *Texts and Studies*, pp. 416ff.
7. D. Kaufmann, "Zur Biographie Maimunis," MGWJ 41, 460ff.

11 Epistle to Yemen

1. Graetz, *Geschichte der Juden*, VI, 281; but see Fritz Baer in MGWJ 70, 155ff.
2. See Schreiner in MGWJ 42, 123ff.
3. See Schreiner in MGWJ 42, 123ff.
4. See *Bustan al Ukul*, ed. Levine (New York, 1908).
5. P to Ab. Zara IV, 7.
6. SP 8.
7. See also P to Chelek, ed. Holzer, p. 28.
8. Mann, *Jews in Egypt*, I, 204ff; EJ I, 248.
9. Margulies, "Zwei autographische Urkunden von Moses und Abraham Maimuni," MGWJ 44, 8ff.
10. MT Sefer Torah, VIII, 4; IX, 10; see the account published by Gaster in *Dewir*, p. 33.
11. SP 8.
12. MN I, 71.
13. Goldzieher in ZDMG 41, 65.
14. Goldzieher, *Vorlesungen über den Islam*, p. 135; see MN I, 73.
15. MN I, 73, thesis 6.
16. MN I, 71.
17. MN I, 73, thesis 10.
18. K I, 30.
19. A. Marmorstein, "Spuren karäischen Einflusses in der gaonäischen Halacha," *Festschrift Schwarz*, pp. 455ff.
20. R, no. 209.
21. K II, 1b.

12 Sutta

1. Mann, *Jews in Egypt*, I, 231.
2. Röhricht, *Geschichte des Königreichs Jerusalem*, p. 343, 35g.

3. Huart, *Geschichte der Araber*, II, 23.
4. K II, 37d.
5. See Berdyczewski, *Der Born Judas*, V, 109.
6. REJ IV, 177f.

13 The Transformation

1. K II, 37d.
2. MN III, 41.
3. *Gesundheitsanleitung für Al Afdal*, ed. Kroner, p. 82.
4. MN II, 36.
5. Introduction to P, ed. Hamburger, pp. 54ff.
6. P to Berachot IX.
7. MN III, 22.
8. MN III, 23.
9. MN III, 22.
10. MT Awel XIII, 12, see Karon on this passage.
11. MN III, 12.
12. MN III, 12.
13. MN III, 12.
14. MN III, 30.
15. MN III, 8.
16. MN III, 10.
17. K II, 30c.
18. Munk, *Notice*, p. 68, and Goldberg, *Birkat Abraham*, and K II.
19. A. Maimonides, *High Ways to Perfection*, ed. Rosenblatt (New York, 1927).
20. Introduction to P, Hamburger 55.
21. Millot, *Hahiggajon* VIII, K II, 25a.
22. K II, 26cd; to p. 155, *cf.* R, no. 368; see also MN III, 8–end, K II, 27c, 22d–23a, and Goldzieher, *Studien über Tanchum Jeruschalmi*, p. 19, A. 2.

14 Maimonides and Aristotle

1. MN II, 11; see I, 71.
2. Introduction to MN.
3. MN I, 46.
4. MN I, 33.
5. MN, foreword.
6. MN I, 36.

7. MN I, 72.
8. MN II, 4.
9. MN II, 4.
10. MN II, 11.
11. MN II, 12.
12. MN II, 13.
13. MN II, 15.
14. MN II, 21, 25.
15. MN II, 16.
16. MN II, 25.
17. MN II, 17.
18. MN II, 19.
19. MN II, 25.
20. MN II, 16.
21. MN II, 17.
22. MN II, 24.

15　Meditation on God

We are attempting here to render the process of thinking instead of the crystallized thought, the act of contemplation instead of its results. This kind of rendering, which should generally be used for presenting medieval philosophy, strikes me as suitable for Maimonides's thinking in its origin, even though it disregards the conventions of intellectual activity and writing style in the Middle Ages.

1. MN I, 5.
2. MN I, 58.
3. MN I, 60.
4. MN I, 57.
5. MN I, 59.
6. MN I, 58.
7. J. Guttmann, *Philosophie des Judentums*, p. 186.
8. MN I, 54.
9. MN I, 34; see also MT *Yesode Hatorah* II, 2; IV, 12.

16　The Pilgrim to Maimonides

1. The following presentation and quotations are from M. Steinschneider, *Gesammelte Schriften*, I, 35ff.; Neubauer,

"Joseph ben Aknin," MGWJ 19; Munk, *Notice sur Joseph ben Jehouda,* and the introductions to MN.
2. REJ IV, 173ff, and above, pp. 128f.

17 "*Back Home in Andalusia*"

1. K II, 37d.
2. MN I, 34.
3. MN I, 34.
4. Steinschneider, *Gesammelte Schriften,* I, 35ff.
5. MN II, 37.
6. R, no. 157.
7. Introduction to MN, beginning.
8. See Joseph's letter in chap. 19.
9. Introduction to MN, beginning.
10. Introduction to MN.
11. MN II, 36.

18 *The Supreme Head of the Jews*

1. Becker, *Islamstudien,* I, 192.
2. EDI I, 266–68; *1001 Nacht,* ed. Littmann, VI, 697.
3. *Virchows Archiv,* 52.
4. A. H. Helbig, *Al-Qadi Al-Fadil, der Wesir Saladins* (Berlin, 1909).
5. Friedländer, "Ein Gratulationsbrief an Maimonides," *Cohen-Festschrift,* pp. 257ff.
6. K II, 30c.
7. Friedländer, op. cit.
8. K II, 31d.
9. K II, 31d.
10. See Chwolson, in *Literaturblatt des Orient,* 1846.
11. R, no. 156.
12. R, no. 155.

19 *Arabesques*

1. A. Freimann, *Responsa* (Jerusalem, 1934), foreword; R, no. 237.
2. M. Löwy, *Drei Abhandlungen von Josef ben Jehuda* (Berlin, 1879).

3. M. Löwy, op. cit., pp. 2ff.
4. M. Löwy, op. cit., pp. 37ff.
5. The German translation of the following correspondence comes from MGWJ 14, 25ff., 69ff.
6. Kima means Pleiades, the symbol of wisdom.
7. Cf. Gen. 20:7.
8. K II, 28d.
9. MN II, 36.
10. K'sil means Orion, the husband of Kima, but also a fool.
11. The Talmud prohibits making a decision in the presence of the teacher.
12. See above, p. 28.
13. K II, 31.

20   *The Opposition*

1. K II, 15d.
2. K II, 31a.
3. K II, 30d.
4. K I, 25c.
5. K II, 8c.
6. K III, 9a.
7. Introduction to Chelek, ed. Holzer, pp. 12f.
8. K II, 8d.
9. ZFHB 2, 125ff.

21   *The Guide for the Perplexed*

1–6. Introduction to MN.
7. Foreword to MN III.
8. MN III, 7.
9. Introduction to MN; K II, 30c.
10. Introduction to MN.
11. MN II, 3.
12. MN III, 51.
13. P to Berachot.
14. MN I, 50.

22   *Renunciation*

1. *Pirke Moshe*, chap. 25.
2. P, introduction to Tohorot.

3. MN III, 43.
4. Kroner, *Ein Beitrag zur Geschichte der Medizin des XII. Jahrhunderts* (Oberdorf, 1906), p. 17.
5. MN II, 36.
6. R, no. 67, 68, 69.
7. R, no. 69.
8. *Birkat Abraham.*
9. *Birkat Abraham.*
10. K II, 31d.
11. K II, 31c.
12. *Birkat Abraham.*
13. EDI I, 50.
14. Abdallatif, *Denkwürdigkeiten Egyptens* (Halle, 1790), pp. 16f.
15. *Instruction for Al Afdal.*
16. Chwolson in *Literaturblatt des Orients*, 1846.
17. Chwolson, op. cit.
18. MN II, 22.
19. *Birkat Abraham.*
20. K II, 7ff.
21. ZFHB II, 125ff.
22. MGWJ 51, 74; to p. 256, *cf.* Münz, *Moses ben Maimon*, p. 310; Eppenstein, *Abraham Maimuni*, p. 2; SB I, 413; and *Birkat Abraham*, p. 37.

23 "I Seek No Victory"

1. K II, 30ff; I, 25ff., and the letter to Joseph in *Birkat Abraham.*

24 The Sages of Lunel

1. EJ 10, 1190.
2. K I, 12b.
3. K I, 12c.
4. K I, 12c.
5. Pertsch, *Die arabischen Handschriften der Herzoglichen Bibliothek zu Gotha*, no. 1937.
6. Steinschneider, *Virchows Archiv*, 52, 66–120.
7. Kroner, *Janus*, Vol. 27–29.
8. Kroner, *Der medizinische Schwanengesang des Maimonides*, p. 84, *Janus*, B. 32.
9. Kroner, op. cit. Poem on p. 266, translated by J. Elbogen.

25 Imitatio Dei

1. *Maamar Hajichud*, p. 39 and xiv, ed. Steinschneider.
2. K II, 9a.
3. MN III, 54.
4. MN II, 20.
5. MN III, 51.
6. MN III, 51.
7. MN III, 51.
8. MN III, 52.
9. K II, 23c.
10. K II, 23b.
11. MN III, 9.
12. MN III, 8.
13. MN I, 70.
14. MN II, 13.
15. MN III, 51.
16. *Sheret Yehuda*, Lif.

Index